HOW BRANDS
BECOME ICONS

HOW BRANDS
BECOME ICONS

The Principles of
Cultural Branding

Douglas B. Holt

Harvard Business School Press
Boston, Massachusetts

978-1-57851-774-9 (ISBN 13)

Library of Congress Cataloging-in-Publication Data

Holt, Douglas B.
    How brands become icons: the principles of cultural branding / Douglas B. Holt.
        p.   cm.
    Includes bibliographical references and index.
    ISBN 1-57851-774-5
    1. Brand name products. 2. Business names. 3. Popular culture. I. Title.
HD69.B7H647 2003
658.8¢27—DC22

                                                                      2004002697

The paper used in this publication meets the requirements of the American National
Standard for Permanence of Paper for Publications and Documents in Libraries and
Archives Z39.48-1992.

For Tuba

Contents

Preface and Acknowledgments

I grew up in Rockford, Illinois, a small industrial city that boasted one of the nation's highest unemployment rates in the late 1970s, right up there with Flint, Michigan. While Rockford always seemed to end up around 297 on lists of the top 300 livable cities, for teens who didn't yet have to hustle up a job, the city could still be a good time.

Like most guys I knew, I was a rock-and-roll kid. I bought albums, played air guitar, attended dozens of concerts, made my own cassettes, and took hundreds of concert photos. When famous Chicago radio deejay Steve Dahl blew up a dumpster full of disco records at Comiskey Park before a baseball game, I cheered. As a high-schooler, I loved many bands—at first Boston and Kiss, and then Styx, Aerosmith, and Ted Nugent. But my heart belonged to the hometown heroes—Rockford's own Cheap Trick.

My hero was Cheap Trick's lead guitarist, Rick Nielsen. I even dressed like him for Halloween parties. Nielsen felled every stereotype in the rock handbook. At a time when rock guitarists had long hair, wore tight pants, showed chest hair, and played their guitars as if they were Freudian appendages, Nielsen dressed like a nerdy teenager. With his cardigan sweater, short hair, and baseball cap, he pranced around stage, kicking his legs in the air like a Las Vegas chorus girl, plying the crowd with strange, cartoonish expressions. Yet his guitar sound was even tougher and more inventive than those heavy metal heroes; he did them one better but without the testosterone. I thought this was very cool (but had no idea why).

Cheap Trick made four amazing records (as every rock fan knows), and then someone pulled the plug. The band started pumping out album after album of trite, melodramatic songs. I stopped listening to them over twenty years ago, and I was not alone. But for me, as for millions of American teens, Cheap Trick mattered a lot for those precious few years of the late 1970s.

Fast-forward twenty-five years. I'm seated in an office that could be a movie set for a corporate drama. The oversized room is overflowing with white furniture. The New York skyline beckons through the long row of windows. Two senior executives of PepsiCo's ad agency BBDO New York join me to discuss Mountain Dew. Before we begin, one of them pops in a video of a competitive ad that has just arrived. It's for Diet Coke. A new campaign had just launched; the spots were quirky, slice-of-life ads with celebrity voice-overs.

One of the ads centered on the song "I Want You to Want Me"—a number one hit by Cheap Trick in 1979. In a scene seemingly inspired by Hitchcock's *Rear Window,* an attractive young woman (with voice-over by Renee Zellweger) watches a less attractive young man in the apartment directly across from hers. "I watch this guy in his bathroom when he's getting ready for work," she says. We cut to the guy in his bathroom flossing his teeth and, with neither shame nor pitch, belting lyrics to the Cheap Trick hit. The slightly nerdy guy sways as he sings, totally involved. "He's really not my type," she says. "He flosses too much. But you can't rule out a guy who knows all the lyrics to one of the greatest songs of all time." We're left with the new tag line for Diet Coke, "That certain something."

The ad tugged at me. I identified with the guy. Not because this was some sort of consumer truth: I never sing unless I'm forced to! Nor was this an automatic, emotional triggering of a song I had once loved. In fact, I don't particularly like the song. I tolerate the extremely catchy tune only because it's by Cheap Trick. And I didn't respond because of nostalgia. I certainly don't yearn to be a teenager in Rockford again, for sure.

Rather, this ad touched me because Diet Coke had grabbed familiar cultural source material and used it to tell a story about manhood, a story I wanted to believe in. The story tells us that guys caught up in frivolous pop music, guys so immersed in their music that they find spiritual moments in the most mundane of tasks, are endearing, even cool in a way. His humanity, though quirky and off-tune, shined through, and the beautiful woman loved him for that. In casting judgment on what makes for an attractive man, Zellweger's voice rejects its opposite: guys who are wrapped up in making money rather than enjoying themselves, guys too instrumental to lose themselves in their morning flossing, guys who have so deeply internalized impression management skills that they'd be too embarrassed to sing out loud, even by themselves in front of a mirror.

When you're seventeen, you do these kinds of things. (Even air guitar!) When you're forty, you're not supposed to be so frivolous and expressive unless you work in the creative professions or have rejected the carefully measured life of middle-class work for a more bohemian existence. Like many of my professional peers, I'm caught between these two worlds: striving for professional success, yet trying to remain true to the creative humanist sensibilities that still lurk within. The Diet Coke ad provided me with a little ammunition to manage this contradiction, encouraging me not to lose track of the latter.

The Cheap Trick tune worked as source material for this myth because it's a shorthand way to bring me, and many others of my generation, into the story. Moreover, the song was an ideal choice because it dredged up images of Nielsen and the other band members. Not unlike our ad hero, these cartoonish rocksters defied rock's macho stereotypes. An Aerosmith song wouldn't have worked.

This kind of identification is forged by advertising that presents meaningful stories, myths that work as salves for contradictions in the nation's culture. Such ads are the most important means by which brands create identity value for their customers. Yet today's conventional branding principles, dominated by what I call the mind-share model, would find this ad incoherent. (The BBDO executive suggested as much, but then, his job was to belittle the competitor's work.) Diet Coke's approach isn't an anomaly. Rather, this kind of identity myth has been a central feature of branding for many decades. Conventional branding models, however, ensconced in psychological assumptions, have entirely ignored the role of identity myths in building brands.

Unearthing Cultural Branding Strategies

This book offers the first systematic, empirical research on some of the most powerful identity brands of the past half century, brands commonly called *iconic brands.* I analyze these brands historically to uncover the principles that account for their success—what I call cultural branding. This research combines the case research methodology typical of theory-building research in the social sciences and the cultural analysis techniques practiced in the humanities.

Cultural branding efforts, even the most successful ones, have not been guided by formal strategic initiatives. In my research, I've yet to find a cultural brand strategy articulated in formal documents like marketing plans, brand bibles, and creative briefs. The language of mind share dominates, especially among brand managers, account managers and planners at ad agencies, and conventional market researchers. Strategy documents are full of "onion" models that describe the brand in terms of rational benefits, emotional benefits, personality, and user associations. Junior managers with newly minted M.B.A.'s talk about mind share with gusto largely because we (professors at business schools) have taught them to speak this way. The idea of mind share holds such rhetorical strength that managers routinely reinterpret the most cultural of brands in mind-share terms.

Cultural branding strategies have lurked primarily in the gut feel of ad-agency creatives and other commercial artists hired by brand managers. Creatives developed powerful identity myths from the practical knowledge they gained after many years of searching for a cultural sweet spot for the brand. And despite their commitment to a cultural approach to branding, even creatives rely heavily on mind-share language to explain their own efforts. After many interactions with clients, creatives recognize that this language sells work and explains the work's effectiveness to the outside world.

It is surprising that cultural brand campaigns have been developed in this seemingly contradictory organizational environment. Iconic brands have delivered powerful myths guided by formal strategic documents that were supposed to push the branding in different directions. Managers try to guide their brands and interpret their own actions in mind-share terms, even while their branding activities routinely defy these principles. As a result of this contradiction, even the most successful iconic brands routinely move away from their effective mythmaking activities, sometimes for decades at a time.

Iconic brands are thus the hodgepodge result of the cultural intuition of commercial artists who have "sneaked" in cultural content to strategies that asked them simply to deliver on benefits in a creative, entertaining, and memorable manner. As part of this process, the clients are willing to go along for the ride and consequently give their artists wide latitude. Unfortunately, most creatives aren't usually focused on aligning the brand in culture. Instead, they race to be the most creative among their peers. Most attempts at cultural branding badly misfire. This book seeks to unearth the principles behind the best creative instincts—which are really cultural instincts rather than just random creativity—and using these principles to create a strategic language that can be used to build iconic brands.

Acknowledgments

The origins of this book stretch back to my days as a doctoral student at Northwestern University in the late 1980s. My initial curiosity about brand symbolism was sparked by my department chair, Sidney Levy, one of the pioneers in the field, and further provoked by my advisor, anthropologist John Sherry.

The cultural branding framework I develop in this book is informed by theories advanced in sociology, mass communications, history, anthropology, and cultural studies. My intellectual debts here are too numerous to list. But the authors who have had the most significant influence on my thinking are listed in the reference section at the end of the book.

In marketing, two people in particular pushed me in the right direction. Linda Scott's seminal articles outlining a cultural approach to the study of advertising changed how I looked at ads. Her work first got me thinking about the advantages of studying brands from an historical perspective. And I am particularly indebted to my friend and intellectual sparring partner Craig Thompson. Our ongoing conversations over the past decade have stimulated many of the ideas here. The discussion of how brands tap into ideals of American masculinity is a direct product of our collaboration.

My research assistant Michael Genett dug up valuable research material on both the ESPN and Harley-Davidson cases and also provided excellent editorial support throughout the book. I am also grateful to the many people who have given me useful feedback on my analyses, including Doug Cameron, Al Silk, and Tuba Ustuner, as well as the participants in a variety of seminars where I presented sections of the book. My editor Kirsten Sandberg pushed me to communicate sometimes complicated ideas in an accessible style, and patiently tolerated several lengthy delays.

The Harvard Business School generously provided the financial support for this project. I am also indebted to the many managers at Anheuser-Busch, PepsiCo, DDB–Chicago, Goodby Silverstein & Partners, Arnold Worldwide, BBDO New York, and Kirshenbaum & Bond for graciously opening up their advertising archives and discussing their past work. In particular, I owe special thanks to Dave Burwick, Jeff Goodby, Lance Jensen, Bob Lachky, Ron Lawner, Ted Sann, Bob Scarpelli, and Steve Wilhite, who were all extremely generous with their time, given busy schedules.

HOW BRANDS
BECOME ICONS

CHAPTER 1

What Is an Iconic Brand?

FROM NELSON MANDELA TO RONALD REAGAN, from Steve Jobs to Sam Walton, from Oprah Winfrey to Martha Stewart, from Michael Jordan to Muhammad Ali, from Andy Warhol to Bruce Springsteen, from John Wayne to Woody Allen, cultural icons dominate our world. These icons can be fictional characters as well as real people: Li'l Abner, Archie Bunker, Superman, and Rambo have all been American icons. Moreover, cultural icons needn't be human. Companies like Disney and Apple, non-governmental organizations (NGOs) like Greenpeace and Amnesty International, and universities like Harvard and Oxford have been cultural icons. Objects can also fit the bill. For example, the Jeep, the Zippo lighter, and Coke became cultural icons during World War II. Places often become cultural icons as well, consider Paris, Harlem, the Statue of Liberty, and Silicon Valley.

People identify strongly with cultural icons and often rely on these symbols in their everyday lives. Icons serve as society's foundational compass points—anchors of meaning continually referenced in entertainment, journalism, politics, and advertising.

The *Oxford English Dictionary* defines a cultural icon as "a person or thing regarded as a *representative symbol*, especially of a culture or a movement; a person or an institution considered worthy of admiration or respect [italics added]."[1] More generally, cultural icons are exemplary symbols that people accept as a shorthand to represent important ideas.

The crux of iconicity is that the person or the thing is widely regarded as the most compelling symbol of a set of ideas or values that a society deems important. James Dean was the quintessential 1950s American rebel. More than anyone else, he represented the idea that men should live an autonomous life, following their own whims rather than succumbing to the postwar nuclear plan of corporate work and suburban family.

The dictionary provides a useful definition but not an explanation. How do we come to accept cultural icons as symbols for valued ideals? To address this question, we must first acknowledge where icons originate and then isolate what these icons do exactly to earn their hallowed place in society.

Cultural icons are as old as civilization, but their mode of production has changed dramatically since the mid–nineteenth century. In premodern times, icons (mostly religious) gradually diffused through oral storytelling traditions and scarce written documents. With modern mass communications beginning with books, magazines, and newspapers in the nineteenth century, then films in the 1930s, and television in the 1950s, we increasingly inhabit a world in which the circulation of cultural icons has become a central economic activity. The market gravitates to produce what people value most. Today, the culture industries—such as film, music, television, journalism, magazines, sports, books, advertising, and public relations—are bent on cultivating and monetizing these icons.

What separates a cultural icon from the massive volumes of cultural content that these industries produce? Outside of the business school, the academic disciplines that study mass culture—anthropology, sociology, history, mass communications, and film criticism—have analyzed why cultural icons take on such intensive and pervasive meaning in society. These studies consistently indicate that icons come to represent a particular kind of story—an *identity myth*—that their consumers use to address identity desires and anxieties. Icons have extraordinary value because they carry a heavy symbolic load for their most enthusiastic consumers. Icons perform the particular myth society especially needs at a given historical moment, and they perform it charismatically. James Dean's film work, personal life, sense of style, and untimely death in a car crash all contributed to an enigmatic story about pushing against society's mores.

My research demonstrates that many of the world's most valuable brands have developed according to similar principles. Since not all brands can become icons, let me first circumscribe the kinds of brands that I'll cover in this book.

What Is a Brand?

Consider a new product that a company has just introduced.[2] Although the product has a name, a trademarked logo, unique packaging, and perhaps other unique design features—all aspects that we intuitively think of as the brand—the brand does not yet truly exist. Names, logos, and designs are the material markers of the brand. Because the product does not yet have a history, however, these markers are empty. They are devoid of meaning. Now, think of famous brands. They have markers, also: a name (McDonald's, IBM), a logo (the Nike swoosh, the Travelers umbrella), a distinctive product design feature (Harley's engine sound), or any other design element that is uniquely associated with the product. The difference is that these markers have been filled with customer experiences. Advertisements, films, and sporting events use the brand as a prop. Magazines and newspaper articles evaluate the brand, and people talk about the brand in conversation. Over time, ideas about the product accumulate and fill the brand markers with meaning. A brand is formed.

A brand emerges as various "authors" tell stories that involve the brand. Four primary types of authors are involved: companies, the culture industries, intermediaries (such as critics and retail salespeople), and customers (particularly when they form communities). The relative influence of these authors varies considerably across product categories.

Brand stories have plots and characters, and they rely heavily on metaphor to communicate and to spur our imaginations. As these stories collide in everyday social life, conventions eventually form. Sometimes a single common story emerges as a consensus view. Most often, though, several different stories circulate widely in society. A brand emerges when these collective understandings become firmly established.

Marketers often like to think of brands as a psychological phenomenon which stems from the perceptions of individual consumers. But what makes a brand powerful is the collective nature of these perceptions; the stories have become conventional and so are continually reinforced because they are treated as truths in everyday interactions.[3]

Identity Value and Iconic Brands

Customers value some products as much for what they symbolize as for what they do. For brands like Coke, Budweiser, Nike, and Jack Daniel's, customers value the brand's stories largely for their *identity value*. Acting as vessels of self-expression, the brands are imbued with stories that consumers find valuable in constructing their identities. Consumers flock to brands

FIGURE 1-1

Iconic Brands Are Brands That Have Become Cultural Icons

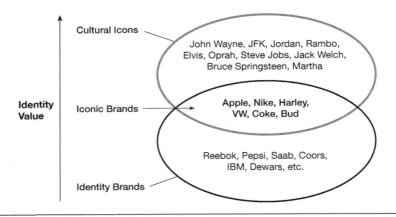

that embody the ideals they admire, brands that help them express who they want to be. The most successful of these brands become *iconic brands.* Joining the pantheon of cultural icons, they become consensus expressions of particular values held dear by some members of a society (figure 1-1).

Identity value usually matters less for brands in low-involvement, business-to-business, critical service delivery, and highly technical categories. But even in these cases, identity value can play a crucial role in the brand's success, as Ogilvy & Mather's global advertising campaign for IBM and Richard Branson's public relations efforts for Virgin Airways have demonstrated.

Conventional branding models largely ignore how brands buttress consumer identities. Managers typically view identity value superficially as *badging,* that is, the idea that consumers use brands as status symbols to earn the admiration of their peers. And consultants and academics routinely invoke one-size-fits-all models that lump together all types of brands into a single framework.[4] These analysts group brands like Levi's and Chanel, which are driven by identity value, with brands like Clorox and Southwest Airlines, which consumers value for entirely different reasons (such as perceived quality and reliability). This lack of specification is a mistake. Identity brands create customer value differently than do other types of brands, so they must be managed differently as well.

Which Products Need Cultural Branding?

In this book, I develop a new branding model—*cultural branding*—which I derive from the best-in-class identity brands, the brands that have spun such compelling myths that they have become cultural icons. We needn't limit these principles to the most obvious kinds of identity brands, however. Cultural branding applies particularly to categories in which people tend to value products as a means of self-expression, such as clothing, home decor, beauty, leisure, entertainment, automotive, food, and beverage. Marketers usually refer to these categories as lifestyle, image, badge, or ego-expressive products. In these groups, competition to create advantages derived from other bases of customer value (quality reputation, trust, distinctive benefits) is fierce and typically limited to incremental and often momentary gains. But competitors cannot easily replicate the brand's myth embedded in these products. The ability to build valued myths into the product often distinguishes success from mediocrity in these lifestyle categories.[5]

Cultural branding also applies to other marketed entities that people rely on to express their identity. The most obvious examples are other *culture industry products*, such as film and television stars, musicians, heroes in novels and on screen, and even cartoon characters. In addition, NGOs, tourist destinations, other places (nations, cities, neighborhoods), social movements, and politicians are all prime candidates for cultural branding.

Despite their distinguishing characteristics, no hard and fast line separates products susceptible to cultural branding. Generally, managers can apply the lessons of cultural branding to any market offering that people regularly use, or else idealize as a means to improve their lives.

While not all brands should mimic Nike or Budweiser, most consumer brands need a cultural strategy as part of their branding tool kits. Often enough, brands require hybrid strategies. For instance, in the auto industry, successful makes like BMW combine a conventional focus on benefits and quality reputation with cultural branding. For fashion industry brands, such as Polo, Levi's, and Diesel, the challenge is to combine cultural branding with the viral techniques typical of that industry. In this book, however, I set aside the question of hybrid branding models and focus on how cultural branding works.

This benign neglect of identity brands directly results from the dominating influence of psychology and economics, which have shaped our basic assumptions regarding how brands work. Models derived from these disciplines have helped managers understand important aspects of brands—how brands build reputations for quality and how brands come to own certain category benefits, for instance. But this disciplinary focus has also seriously handicapped managers' understanding of how brands work as symbols. Iconic brands become immensely valuable because they function much like the cultural icons noted at the beginning of this chapter. If managers want to build an iconic brand, then they must use a distinctive kind of strategy.

Axioms of Cultural Branding

To explain how iconic brands evolve and are sustained over time, I draw on my academic training in socio-cultural analysis. I conducted systematic historical research on six American iconic brands. From this research, I discovered that these brands have followed a set of tacit principles—the *cultural branding model*—that are entirely different from the principles found in conventional branding frameworks.

This model hinges on several key axioms, which I outline here and in chapter 2. In the rest of the book I build on these axioms to detail the strategic principles of cultural branding (figure 1-2).[6]

Iconic Brands Address Acute Contradictions in Society

Iconic brands provide extraordinary identity value because they address the collective anxieties and desires of a nation.[7] We experience our identities—our self-understanding and aspirations—as intensely personal quests. But when scholars examine consumer identities in the aggregate, they find that desires and anxieties linked to identity are widely shared across a large fraction of a nation's citizens. These similarities result because people are constructing their identities in response to the same historical changes that influence the entire nation.

For example, Budweiser became the most desirable beer in the 1980s because the brand addressed one of the most acute contradictions of the day. Working men were motivated by Ronald Reagan's battle cry as he invoked America's frontier myth to restore the country's economic might.

FIGURE 1-2

Cultural Branding Principles

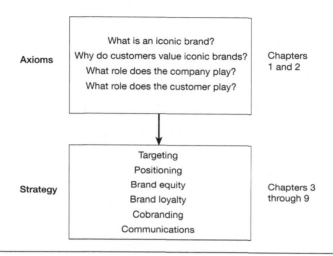

The country's economic and political meltdown in the 1970s, along with the increasing independence of women, had left them feeling emasculated. Reagan's call to arms gave these workers hope that they would soon regain their lost manhood. These same men, however, were beginning to realize that their vocations as skilled manual laborers, their primary source of masculine identity, were becoming obsolete as these jobs were replaced by technology and outsourced overseas. Budweiser targeted this acute tension between the revived American ideals of manhood and the economic realities that made these ideals nearly unattainable for many men.

Iconic Brands Perform Identity Myths That Address These Desires and Anxieties

Most iconic brands have been built through the mass media, usually with television advertising. For decades, managers have assumed that they can build identity brands by associating the brand with aspirational figures: the good-looking, wealthy, and charming guy who happens to drink Heineken, wear Tommy Bahama, or drive a Mercedes. While many so-so brands employ these sorts of straightforward status appeals, iconic brands do not.

Consider three iconic brands that I will discuss later in the book. One of Mountain Dew's breakthrough ads featured the Vegas crooner Mel Torme leaping off a casino. For Volkswagen, a seminal spot featured a hobbling old African American man breaking out of an old-folks home. Budweiser's comeback in the late 1990s was led by two mechanical lizards commiserating on a branch in a swamp. None of these ads could be considered aspirational in the conventional sense of that word.

Brands become iconic when they perform identity myths: simple fictions that address cultural anxieties from afar, from imaginary worlds rather than from the worlds that consumers regularly encounter in their everyday lives. The aspirations expressed in these myths are an imaginative, rather than literal, expression of the audience's aspired identity.

Identity myths are useful fabrications that stitch back together otherwise damaging tears in the cultural fabric of the nation. In their everyday lives, people experience these tears as personal anxieties. Myths smooth over these tensions, helping people create purpose in their lives and cement their desired identity in place when it is under stress.

Academic research has demonstrated that the extraordinary appeal of the most successful cultural products has been due to their mythic qualities—from Horatio Alger's rags-to-riches dime novels of the nineteenth century, to Shirley Temple's depression-era films, to John Wayne's postwar Westerns, to Harlequin romance novels, to the action-adventure films of Willis, Schwartzenegger, and Stallone.[8] Iconic brands work the same way.

Identity Myths Reside in the Brand, Which Consumers Experience and Share Via Ritual Action

Over time, as the brand performs its myth, the audience eventually perceives that the myth resides in the brand's markers (e.g., its name, logo, and design elements). The brand becomes a symbol, a material embodiment of the myth. So as customers drink, drive, or wear the product, they experience a bit of the myth. This is a modern secular example of the rituals that anthropologists have documented in every human society. But rather than religious myth, in modern societies the most influential myths address people's identities.

Customers use iconic brands as symbolic salves. They grab hold of the myth as they use the product as a means to lessen their identity burdens.

Great myths provide their consumers with little epiphanies—moments of recognition that put images, sounds, and feelings on barely perceptible desires. Customers who make use of the brand's myth for their identities forge tight emotional connections to the brand.

These Identity Myths Are Set in Populist Worlds

Identity myths are usually set in *populist worlds:* places separated not only from everyday life but also from the realms of commerce and elite control. The people living in populist worlds share a distinctive ethos that provides intrinsic motivation for their actions. Often populist worlds exist at the margins of society. But what unites people in a populist world is that they act the way they do because they want to, not because they are being paid or because they seek status or power.

Marlboro's populist world was the Western frontier, Corona beer relied on the Mexican beach, Harley drew from outlaw bikers, Nike borrowed from the African American ghetto, and Mountain Dew sifted from rural Appalachia. The myths performed by iconic brands draw from populist worlds as source materials to create credibility that the myth has authenticity, that it is grounded in the lives of real people whose lives are guided by these beliefs.

Iconic Brands Perform as Activists, Leading Culture

Iconic brands function like cultural activists, encouraging people to think differently about themselves. The most powerful iconic brands are prescient, addressing the leading edges of cultural change. These brands don't simply evoke benefits, personalities, or emotions. Rather, their myths prod people to reconsider accepted ideas about themselves. The value of a particular myth resides not in the myth itself, but in its alignment with society's incipient identity desires.

Easy Rider became an iconic film when it was released in 1969 because this "hippie-fied" Western provided young American men with a seductive new recipe for manhood at a time when the masculine models of the postwar era were in shambles. Five years earlier, the film would have been incomprehensible; five years later, it would have been redundant. Likewise, the identity value created by a brand's myth depends entirely on how well it fits a particular historical context.

Iconic Brands Rely on Breakthrough Performances, Rather Than Consistent Communications

Iconic brands become tremendously desirable as the result of a few masterful performances rather than a bevy of consistent communiqués. These brands typically use commercial media to weave their stories into the culture. In the main, most communications are forgettable. Even for companies with extraordinary track records, like Nike, the brand's performances usually work as filler, as incremental extensions of previous ideas.

What gels in the collective imagination of the country, what turns the brand into an icon, is a handful of great performances. When Coke took a hillside full of beautiful young people and taught the world to sing in 1971, Americans understood that they must come together to overcome the divisive war effort. And when a nagging beeper rattling on a beachside table got flung into the water like a skipping rock, Corona precisely captured people's exasperation with the nonstop stress of the dual-income, late-hours work life of the 1990s. People forget the vast majority of ads within weeks after they are broadcast. What lingers, years and even decades later, are the few great performances, those that get the myth just right.

Iconic Brands Enjoy a Cultural Halo Effect

When a brand delivers a powerful myth that customers find useful in cementing their identities, this identity value casts a halo on other aspects of the brand. Great myths enhance the brand's quality reputation, distinctive benefits, and status value. For example, when Budweiser's "Lizards" ad campaign embedded in Budweiser a captivating new myth, Bud drinkers reported that the beer tasted much better.

Organization of the Book

In chapter 2, I develop these axioms further by comparing them to the taken-for-granted assumptions that undergird today's three predominant models—what I call the mind-share, emotional, and viral branding models. Chapter 2 charts for the reader a path from today's entrenched conventions about how branding works to the unfamiliar world of cultural

Glossary of Key Terms

brand genealogy: a historical method for understanding how brands create identity value (see appendix)

cultural branding: the set of axioms and strategic principles that guide the building of brands into cultural icons

cultural halo effect: the positive impact of high levels of identity value on conventional brand metrics, such as perceived quality and association with key category benefits

cultural icon: a person or thing regarded as a symbol, especially of a culture or movement; a person, institution, and so forth, considered worthy of admiration or respect

genealogical mind-set: the managerial worldview necessary for the management of identity brands

iconic brand: an identity brand that approaches the identity value of a cultural icon

identity myth: a simple story that resolves cultural contradictions; a prerequisite for an icon

identity value: the aspect of a brand's value that derives from the brand's contributions to self-expression

identity brand: a brand whose value to consumers (and, thus, its brand equity) derives primarily from identity value

populist worlds: autonomous places where people's actions are perceived to be guided by intrinsic values, not by money or power; populist worlds serve as the cultural raw materials from which identity myths are constructed

ritual action: the process through which the consumers of an icon experience the identity myth that the icon contains

branding. Along the way, I also respond to the counterarguments that necessarily arise when one challenges the status quo. I use three short brand genealogies—of Coke, Corona, and Snapple—to make these comparisons.

The remainder of the book develops the implications for brand strategy that flow from these axioms (figure 1-2). To do so, I reverse-engineer the strategic principles that led to the successes of five brands: Mountain Dew, Volkswagen, Budweiser, ESPN, and Harley-Davidson. I relied on detective work because cultural branding has been until now a tacit practice. Working against brand strategies that told them to do something quite different, ad agency creatives have employed in-the-trenches gut feel, which has occasionally produced iconic brands. In this book, I analyze these subterranean practices and organize them into a systematic model of how iconic brands form.

In chapter 3, I tackle the first stage of any brand strategy: segmentation and targeting. I use a case study of Mountain Dew to demonstrate that iconic brands operate not in product markets, but in myth markets. In chapter 4, I use Volkswagen as a case to develop a cultural approach to the conventional positioning statement, what I call the cultural brief. I use Budweiser in chapter 5 to present a cultural view of brand equity, which arises from the brand's cultural and political authority.

Chapter 6 outlines an ethnographic study of ESPN consumers to describe the three constituencies of an iconic brand, and the distinctive network model of brand loyalty that holds such brands together. Chapter 7 uses Harley-Davidson to develop how the brand's coauthors—the culture industries and the populist world—can contribute to the brand's myth. Along the way, I demonstrate that the conventional explanations for Harley's success are incorrect. Chapter 8 revisits Mountain Dew and Budweiser to dig into the nitty-gritty of managing a brand's myth on an ongoing basis. Finally, chapter 9 lays out an agenda for firms that want to build successful iconic brands.

The overarching goal throughout is to socialize readers into the genealogical mind-set—a view of brands as historical entities whose meaning and value depends on how the brand's myth addresses a particular tension in society. Toward this end, the book consists of a series of detailed historical case studies, all of which rely on brand genealogies, a new method that I developed for this research and describe in the appendix.

CHAPTER 2

How Is Cultural Branding Different?

I CONIC BRANDS HAVE BEEN GUIDED by a set of tacit strategic principles that I call the *cultural branding model*. These principles differ entirely from those advanced by conventional branding schemes. In fact, cultural branding upends many verities by which managers have sworn for decades. To learn how cultural branding works requires setting aside conventional thinking and developing a new mind-set. To seed this mind-set, I begin with three short case studies in which I contrast cultural branding with the three branding models that dominate business practice today.

Since the 1970s, managers have overwhelmingly relied on a cognitive model of branding—what I call *mind-share branding*. In the 1990s, some experts expanded the mind-share model, which they believed ignored the emotional and relational aspects of branding. These writers pushed for what I call *emotional branding*. With the recent rise of the Internet, another challenger has become popular as well: *viral branding*.

Together, these three branding models account for virtually every consumer branding initiative today undertaken by brand owners, ad agencies, and brand consultancies. When managers seek to build the identity value of their brands, they draw on some combination of these three approaches. Table 2-1 compares the key characteristics of these three models with the cultural branding model.

My research indicates that, while these conventional models may work for other types of branding, they do not build iconic brands. In this chapter, I develop short genealogies of brands often used as exemplars of conventional strategies—Corona (mind share), Coke (emotional), and Snapple (viral)—to demonstrate that implicit cultural branding strategies have built each of these iconic brands.

TABLE 2-1

Comparison of Axioms Across Four Branding Models

	Cultural Branding	Mind-Share Branding	Emotional Branding	Viral Branding
Key Words	Cultural icons, iconic brands	DNA, brand essence, genetic code, USP benefits, onion model	Brand personality, experiential branding, brand religion, experience economy	Stealth marketing, coolhunt, meme, grass roots, infections, seeding, contagion, buzz
Brand Definition	Performer of, and container for, an identity myth	A set of abstract associations	A relationship partner	A communication unit
Branding Definition	Performing myths	Owning associations	Interacting with and building relationships with customers	Spreading viruses via lead customers
Required for a Successful Brand	Performing a myth that addresses an acute contradiction in society	Consistent expression of associations	Deep interpersonal connection	Broad circulation of the virus
Most Appropriate Applications	Identity categories	Functional categories, low-involvement categories, complicated products	Services, retailers, specialty goods	New fashion, new technology
Company's Role	Author	Steward: consistent expression of DNA in all activities over time	Good friend	Hidden puppetmaster: motivate the right consumers to advocate for the brand
Source of Customer Value	Buttressing identity	Simplifying decisions	Relationship with the brand	Being cool, fashionable
Consumers' Role	• Personalizing the brand's myth to fit individual biography • Ritual action to experience the myth when using product	• Ensuring that benefits become salient through repetition • Perceiving benefits when buying and using product	• Interaction with brand • Building a personal relationship	• "Discovering" brand as their own, DIY • Word of mouth

From Mind-Share Branding to Cultural Branding

We can trace the roots of mind share to the unique selling proposition—the principle, advocated by hard-sell advertisers in the 1950s, that each product must tirelessly communicate a single distinctive benefit to its consumers. The idea really took flight in the early 1970s, when Al Ries and Jack Trout published their famous exposition on positioning in the trade magazine *Ad Age*. They later expanded the idea in their best-selling book *Positioning: The Battle for Your Mind.*[1] Their argument was simple: For a brand to succeed in a society whose volume of mass communication far exceeds what consumers can manage, the brand must own a simple, focused position in the prospect's mind, usually a benefit associated with the product category.

Since the 1970s, this provocative image—of brands contesting for scarce mental real estate in consumers' minds—has been the most influential idea in branding.[2] Academics and consultants have taught an entire generation of marketers that all brands work according to these principles.

Everyone who's taken a marketing course has seen the ubiquitous onion model of the brand. The hard, durable, objective reality of the market offering—the product or service—resides in the nucleus. Attached to the core are various subjective associations that consumers attribute to the product: product benefits, user attributes, emotions, personality attributes, and the like. The power of the brand lies in these abstract associations that one finds when one "ladders" up from basic functional properties of the product to these softer values, thoughts, and feelings that consumers link to the brand. The mind-share view is today perpetuated by leading academics (such as in books by Kotler, Aaker, Zaltman, and Keller) as well by leading consultants such as Sergio Zyman.[3]

Mind share is familiar to anyone who has read famous stories about how Procter & Gamble used dentists' recommendations to convince Americans that Crest has distinctive cavity-fighting ingredients, or how Unilever built Dove soap into a premium mainstay by telling consumers time and again that Dove is gentle on sensitive skin because each bar contains one-quarter cleansing cream. Many successful and durable brands have been built by the compulsive reiteration of the distinctive benefit (cavity fighting, gentleness) supported with rational arguments (dentists' recommendation, one-quarter cleansing cream) and emotional appeals.

Some variation of mind share is today found in virtually every strategy document used for the world's most prominent brands. The terminology sometimes changes—other popular terms that reference virtually identical ideas include brand essence, DNA, brand identity, genetic code, and brand soul—but the idea has remained remarkably consistent since the 1970s.

Brand strategy, in the mind-share model, begins with identifying the brand's distinctive constellation of these abstract concepts in the consumer's mind. Managers must ensure that this brand essence is consistently evoked in every activity that carries the brand mark and remains consistent over time. Experts encourage managers to act as stewards of the brand's timeless identity.

A Short Genealogy of Corona Beer

The Mexican beer Corona was one of the most successful American iconic brands of the 1990s. Now the leading imported beer in the United States, Corona enjoys sales that have far outpaced the number two import, Heineken.[4]

Mind-share advocates prescribe that to build a strong brand, the company must first stake out a distinctive claim for an important category association, one that competitors haven't captured, and then consistently deliver on this brand essence over time. Yet Corona executed neither of these steps.

Corona's first brief climb to iconic status came in the mid-1980s and peaked around 1988. At the time, Corona was one of the cheapest beers in Mexico, the price brand of the large Mexican brewery Cerveceria Modelo. U.S. distribution was mostly limited to the Southwest, where Mexican Americans tended to live and where Mexican culture influenced the Anglo population.

In the 1980s, the idea of a hedonistic spring-break vacation had caught on spectacularly across U.S. colleges and was widely celebrated in the media. Students from across the country stormed Daytona Beach, Florida; South Padre Island, Texas; and—most popular of all—the beach resorts of Mexico. These vacations were carnivals of excess: 24/7 drinking, wet T-shirt contests, dirty dancing, and sexual escapades, real and imagined.

At about four dollars per case, the price of Corona was certainly appealing. In addition, Corona had a leg up on other Mexican beers for two reasons. First, it had a distinctive package design, with all the right connotations. A clear, returnable bottle with the logo roughly painted straight on the glass, this package was understood as an authentic Mexican beer (read: offbeat, noncommercial product of a less industrialized country) compared with the foil labels and brightly colored cans used by the more expensive Mexican beers. Second, somewhere along the way, American students started putting lime in their Coronas. This was a beer analogue to another favorite party ritual: licking some salt, drinking a shot of tequila, and sucking on a lime wedge.

As college students returned to campus with stories of libidinous fun in the sun, Corona was frequently a prop. Distribution followed the students as they entered their professional lives in major metropolitan areas, particularly in places like Texas, California, and Arizona, from where a disproportionate number of college kids traveled to Mexico for spring break. As Corona-laced myths of sun and debauchery spread, the beer soon became the drink of choice among young professionals throughout the nation. Corona was the quintessential beer for an evening of partying at bars and clubs.

Mind-share advocates would explain that Corona owned the beer category's partying associations and attendant user imagery. This explanation, however, does not work. At the same time that Corona became popular, Bud Light was beginning an extraordinary sales climb with its Spuds McKenzie, "the official party animal," campaign. Bud Light apparently owned partying, too. Nor were these two brands alone, as other beer brands tried to convey a partying attitude, albeit with less good fortune.

Beer drinkers didn't value partying as a generic concept associated with the brand. Rather, they valued beer brands when the brands told the partying story that best resonated in American culture. In the 1980s, Corona and Bud Light had the most compelling partying myths. Other brands did not. Partying was one of several category benefits available to brewers as a platform on which to build culturally specific myths. Corona's success came from its authentic role as a key prop in the Mexican spring-break myth. The beer won out because it embodied one of most resonant party-centered myths then circulating in American culture.[5]

What happened next is a good example of what often happens when customers act as the primary authors of the brand's myth. As Corona became popular, the trend-leading consumers who had initially propagated Corona's myth watched the insider coolness of their Corona drinking evaporate. The Corona story lost its cachet, and so they moved on to other beers.

Because Corona's U.S. distributor was not airing ads that advanced Corona's myth, the brand effectively lost its myth when these insider customers moved on to other beers. Corona became a short-lived fad. By 1990, sales had collapsed, returning to pre-1987 levels. For five years the brand struggled to return to growth, but without success. Other beers had replaced Corona as more desirable party drinks for young people. Corona became the Mexican beer that used to be cool.

Corona's next move directly violated mind-share principles. The brand team ditched the brand's supposed partying brand essence and concocted the "Change Your Lattitude" campaign. The ads depicted an idyllic beach scene—what Americans understood as a Mexican beach—viewed through the eyes of a couple lounging beachside. The ads had little in the way of action and no music. Time stood still. Instead, the audience was gradually introduced to a simple setting: a beach, a couple relaxing, and Coronas.

The campaign's breakthrough spot, "Pager," opened with a long shot of the blue ocean, a gentle surf washing onto white sand, and the familiar sounds of the sea—seagulls, wind, and waves. Then a rock skipped across the water. As the camera pulled back, we saw a woman lounging on the beach next to a table. On the table rested a Corona, a man's watch, a half-dozen small saucer-shaped rocks, and a pager. The arm of the woman's male companion reached into the frame, grabbed a rock, and skipped it across the surf. The man began to repeat the motion when the pager went off; the vibrating beep made the pager bounce around the table. His arm hesitated, changed direction, grabbed the pager, and skipped it across the surf, just as he had skipped the rocks. Unperturbed, the woman swept her hair back and stared mindlessly out at the ocean. The tag line told us "Miles Away from the Ordinary." As the campaign developed, the tag line was switched to "Change Your Lattitude."

Corona immediately took off, soon hitting sales numbers far beyond the 1980s peak. Unlike what happened with its first fifteen minutes of fame, Corona sustained extraordinary sales growth for a decade, becoming far and away the leading imported beer in the United States.

How do we explain Corona's success? Mind-share advocates would argue that Corona succeeded because the brand now owned the relaxation benefit. Again, however, Corona's association with relaxation does not explain the brand's success. Relaxation had been a central benefit in the beer category for many decades, long before Corona had significant distribution in the United States. Budweiser had emphasized a relaxation theme as far back as the 1950s, and other beer brands followed Bud's lead. Since other beers shared Corona's generic connection with relaxation, what, then, made Corona's particular expression more resonant than those offered by other brands?

When Corona's American consumers slapped down seven dollars for a six-pack of the former bargain-basement beer, they were buying a chance to experience, through the ritual gulp of the yellow liquid, a glimmer of the American ideal of a tranquil beach vacation. The new advertising campaign had grabbed hold of Corona's valuable but dormant cultural estate—the Mexican beach—to develop a different and more meaningful myth. With its roots as a working-class Mexican beer and its spring-break reputation, Corona was still indelibly etched in the collective American imagination as a key prop in a winter beach vacation. This asset, however, lay dormant, underutilized.

Mexican beaches had another meaning that Corona's managers adapted. Sitting on a beach relaxing with a beer or margarita had become one of the most salient American dreams for getting away from it all. This ideal, equating relaxation with escaping to a beach in a less developed country, a place far removed from the highly competitive company life, a place where time slowed down, was tremendously appealing to overworked Americans. To tap into this cultural opportunity, Corona authored an evocative myth that used the Mexican beach stories to imbue its beer with the idea of escaping from everyday routines.

Corona's new campaign registered so powerfully because the United States had just undergone a profound shift in its labor market. Process engineering techniques and outsourcing were applied to once secure white-collar jobs. For the first time in the twentieth century, middle-class salaried jobs were now routinely subject to layoffs and firings. Work became intensely competitive, and work-related stresses dominated everyday life. In this environment, relaxation took on a new, historically specific meaning. No longer did relaxation mean simply kicking back at the end of the day to chill out with a cold beer—a common relaxation story told by Budweiser, Schlitz, and Pabst from the 1950s through the 1970s. With job demands following workers into their homes, this simple tale no longer made sense. Relaxation required more radical escapes. Professional men and women now dreamed of going someplace far removed from the rat race.

In thirty seconds of film, Corona used its authority to represent the Mexican beach to encapsulate these desires for a sanctuary from the hectic pace of work life. Corona gave beer drinkers the perfect antidote that they could now gulp down, even while sitting at home on a Wednesday night after a frantic day at the office.

To accomplish this feat, Corona branding violated the rules of mind share by shifting its supposed brand essence from wild partying to tranquil relaxation. But consumers didn't seem miffed. Instead, the story connected, and Corona came to embody one of the most potent expressions of relaxation in American culture. The brand didn't represent relaxation in a generic way, as an abstract concept stripped bare of connotations, reduced to its dictionary definition. Rather, Corona owned a particularly evocative representation of relaxation in American culture: doing absolutely nothing on a faraway Mexican beach.

Why Can't Mind-Share Branding Build Iconic Brands?

Corona's iconic value resided in the particulars of its distinctive myths, not in the abstractions that mind-share advocates emphasize. Further, Corona succeeded only when it radically shifted its myth, from a story about partying in Mexico to one about relaxing in isolation on a quiet beach. Rather than stewarding the brand to maintain consistency at all costs, as mind-share advocates advise, Corona succeeded when managers attended to historical changes and made the appropriate adjustments to better align the brand's myth with important tensions in American society.

Mind-share branding can be an effective approach for utilitarian, low-involvement brands like Dove and Crest, because distilling the product to a handful of key benefits simplifies decision making for the consumer. On the other hand, the reduction of the brand to a handful of abstract concepts will never lead to the building of an iconic brand.[6]

Why, then, does mind share maintain such a tenacious grip on all branding activities today? Managers hold on to the mind-share model because it allows for easy rationalization of the branding task. If the brand is a timeless, abstract entity, then creating a brand strategy is a painless process. Once you've got it, you've got it. And, if the management task is to express this brand essence in everything the brand does, then managers can make quick decisions, brand bible in hand, on whether proposed branding activities are on-strategy. Metrics that measure the brand's success flow easily from these assumptions, as well. In general, mind share is attractive to managers because it allows them to coordinate and control brand strategy throughout their organizations and with their business partners.

As we shall see in the coming chapters, the problem with applying mind-share principles to identity brands is that the impulse to conceive of the brand in abstract terms, and then to focus on keeping these abstractions consistent over time, necessarily overlooks what makes identity brands valuable to their consumers. Identity value exists in the details that managers who follow mind-share principles routinely consider extraneous executional issues. By simplifying the brand so dramatically, managers treat the brand's most critical assets as strategically irrelevant.

From Emotional Branding to Cultural Branding

Consultants have recently peppered the management book market with promises of a revolutionary new branding model, what I call *emotional branding*. Emotional branding is less a new model, though, than an extension of mind share. In emotional branding, the basic mind-share assumptions—that the brand consists of a set of abstractions that should be maintained consistently in all brand activities over time—still hold. But as the name suggests, emotional branding emphasizes *how* this brand essence should be communicated: Managers should build emotional appeals into their branding efforts, which are used to spur emotionally charged relationships with core customers.

Emotions seem to sell. Consider consultant's books like Marc Gobe's *Emotional Branding*, or *A New Brand World*, by former Starbucks executive Scott Bedbury.[7] Gobe wants everything the brand does to be packed with emotion, personality, and sensory experience. Bedbury works within the mind-share paradigm, even though he discards seemingly old-fashioned terms like *positioning* and substitutes more au courant ones like *genetic code* and *brand essence*. But he argues for a more emotive and experiential slant instead of the hard, cognitive approach popular in previous decades. Managers should continue to stake out distinctive associations and consistently articulate these associations through everything the brand does. But a brand must emphasize its personality and forge an intimate connection with customers.

Pushing one step further, some experts today argue that, through the magic of internal branding, the entire organization should emote in unison the spirit of the brand. Organizations are to look deeply inward to truly understand their identity and then inculcate the brand spirit so that they can express this spirit in everything they do. Likewise, communications should work to build emotional linkages between brand and customers. Some consultants even argue that organizations must work to get both employees and customers to treat the brand as a religion. When the brand is communicated with supercharged emotion, a deep bond will form with customers.[8]

A Short Genealogy of Coke

Coca-Cola is a favorite example of emotional branding. Managers envy the extraordinary bond that Coke developed with its customers, particularly in the brand's halcyon days in the United States, from the 1950s through the 1980s. But how did Coke build and sustain these emotional ties?

In the United States, Coke was originally launched through mindshare techniques—as a nerve tonic, hangover cure, and stimulant for "brain workers." But, beginning with its innovative use of advertising and public relations during World War II, Coke was soon transformed into a potent iconic brand.

The Coca-Cola Company shipped Coke to the troops on the front lines and celebrated the war effort in a blizzard of print ads. The media reported that GIs were writing home from the battlefront, pining for Coke. This idea was picked up in Robert Scott's wartime best-seller *God Is My Co-Pilot*, in which he describes how shooting down his first "Jap" was motivated by thoughts of "America, Democracy, and Coca-Colas."[9] Troops would treat the scarce bottles of Coke with religious zeal, drinking in a ritual confirmation of their national pride.

As a result, by war's end, Coke came to represent American myths exemplified in the war effort: a country willing to sacrifice its sons and daughters to save the world for democracy, a country with a unique industrious spirit able to outpace the Axis powers in building war machinery, and a country with the tenacious ingenuity to out-science the enemy in the race to the atomic age. Downing a Coke, consumers could imbibe in collective feelings of national solidarity emanating from America's ethos as dramatized in World War II.

There is no question that Coke consumers formed a significant emotional bond with the drink during this period—a bond that continued through the 1980s. But the crucial strategic question is this: What spawned these ties? Even a glimpse at Coke's history in this period reveals that the source of customers' emotive relationships with the brand had to do with the identity myth that has been plunked into each bottle of Coke through publicity and advertising. The lesson we should learn from Coke's postwar success is straightforward: Imbue the brand with a compelling identity myth, and potent emotional ties will follow.

Throughout the postwar years, Coke rested on these laurels. As American nationalism surged around the country's postwar economic strength and Cold War containment policies, Coke served as the favored vessel for these ideals. Meanwhile, Americans were going to work for large companies and were moving into the new government-subsidized suburbias, and Coke was championing the new suburban-nuclear life in its most euphoric mode. In Coke ads, smiley all-American cola-quaffing girls exuded equal dashes of modesty and sex appeal, filling the drink's "pause that refreshes" with unquestioned patriotic good cheer about the new American way of life. Americans could experience a moment of national solidarity simply by sharing a spare moment sipping a Coke.

By the late 1960s, however, Coke's apple-pie celebrations of the American commonweal were wearing thin. Civil rights protests, a youth culture disenchanted with companies and middle-class life, and a very unpopular war in Vietnam were all tearing the country apart. Coke's suburban-nuclear myth had become naive, antiquated. Attempts to reconnect with consumers by means of a smorgasbord of tried-and-true Americana imagery failed.[10]

Here we see a common property of iconic brands. Since these brands derive their value from how well their myth responds to tensions in the national culture, when there are tumultuous cultural shifts, the brand's myth loses steam. I call these shifts *cultural disruptions*. When disruptions hit, iconic brands must reinvent their myth, or they fade in relevance.

Finally, the company and its ad agency hit on a resonant revision of the Coke myth.[11] "Hilltop," shot on an Italian hillside, began with two fresh-faced and short-haired girls singing, "I'd like to buy the world a home, and furnish it with love. . . ." As the camera panned, we saw that they were joined by other youth, men and women, whose facial features and dress showed that they were from different countries. As the camera included them, their voices joined the chorus, until finally we heard many dozens singing the next verse: "I'd like to teach the world to sing in perfect harmony." What had begun as a folk song had turned into an anthem for peace, one that placed Coke as the fulcrum: "I'd like to buy the world a Coke, and keep it company." Each held a Coke bottle as if it were a flag and stared slightly upward, singing with a sense of conviction and optimism that more than hinted at a church choir. As the camera pulled back to a shot taken from a helicopter above the hill, we saw that hundreds of youth had come together on this hilltop to sing with great idealism. "It's the real thing. What the world wants today is the real thing. Coca-Cola."

Again, the company had spun a myth that many Americans found useful as a symbolic resource to patch up their identities as citizens. Moreover, the myth's identity value renewed emotional connections between Coke and its core customers.

Coke had dramatically reinterpreted the product's refreshment benefit—the "pause that refreshes"—to perform a new myth of American solidarity. Coke drew on mass-media images of the hippie counterculture and the peace movement to address the conflicts of the era with a symbolic cure: a humanistic plea for understanding and tolerance. Through a folk song sung as a hymn, a song that longed for friendship and understanding across races and nationalities, the brand delivered a utopian sermon enjoining John Lennon's call for love to conquer all the world's problems. The brand's myth told consumers that an act as simple as sharing a Coke could heal seemingly intractable social divides. Now Coke was construed as an elixir of universal harmony. Sipping a Coke with a friend or stranger was a symbolic act of healing racial, political, and gender divides.

Americans responded. The ad was first aired in Europe, where it received only a tepid response. But the feedback in the United States was immediate and overwhelming. So many requests for the song poured in that the song was redone, without the Coke lines, as a single. It quickly jumped to the top of the charts.[12] Americans' heightened relationship and emotional connection to Coke arose from the myth's ability to symbolically heal acute cultural tensions tearing at American society.

A decade later, the company and its ad agency again shifted the focus of the Coke myth and again rekindled the brand's emotional connection.[13] In "Mean Joe Greene," a young boy encounters Pittsburgh Steeler "Mean"

Joe Greene as he leaves the football stadium after a game. Greene, nearing the end of a Hall of Fame career, was one of the most feared athletes ever to play professional football. As his nickname implied, Greene treated football like war, and he usually won. He was an immense and immensely talented defender, renowned for his ability to overpower offensive linemen and crush opposing quarterbacks.

In Coke's ad, the kid stopped the ferocious player by simply asking, "Mr. Greene?" Hobbling through the tunnel after a tough game, the massive Greene turned to the small boy and answered, "Yeah?" "Do you need any help?" the kid asked. Greene shook him off and continued his retreat to the locker room. Unfazed by the star's grave veneer, the kid asked, "Do . . . you . . . want my Coke?" "No no," Greene said. "Really, you can have it," the boy responded. Greene finally relented, took the Coke, and, parched from the game, chugged the entire bottle. The earnest and intimidated boy expected nothing in return and walked away, but Joe shouted to him, "Hey, kid!" When the boy turned, Greene offered up a gift, tossing his game jersey to the boy. "Wow, thanks, Mean Joe," the kid said. Greene's face lit up, his big smile revealing the warrior's humanity and his momentary bond with the boy. The text, "Have a Coke and a smile," concluded the ad.

By the late 1970s, America's Vietnam wounds were beginning to heal and youth culture was no longer as threatening. But racial strife had continued to increase. Highly segregated African American neighborhoods had formed in Northern industrial cities when sharecroppers migrated in masses to take unskilled production jobs after they lost their agricultural jobs to the cotton gin. In the 1970s, as American industries shed jobs, the African American workers were the first to go. Factories began an exodus from these cities to the suburbs, to the nonunion South, and overseas, leaving behind black urban ghettos that were increasingly jobless, isolated from the rest of society, lacking families, and lacking public investments. It was not surprising, then, that these ghettos became increasingly violent in the 1970s as a new underground economy dominated by gangs and drugs formed.[14]

The ghetto became America's most acute social problem. American mass media was filled with panicky stories of marauding gangs and so-called "welfare mothers." Suburban white Americans feared the imagined threat emanating from the ghetto.

Again, Coke offered a utopian moment of healing built around a "pause that refreshes." Drinking a Coke now provided a magical salve that symbolically healed the racial divide in American society. The confrontation in the dark tunnel conjured up the growing nightmare of the ghetto in the collective imagination of the majority white population: the physically intimidating black man who threatened an innocent white child. But we soon learned Greene's meanness was just an affectation, that he was actually a sweet guy who could show real affection for the small white kid. The ad offered a story of racial healing for a country that couldn't contain its racial conflict. In this way, Coke again helped the nation momentarily forget its real problems that were then devastating its cities.

In the two decades following this off-the-charts success, The Coca-Cola Company and its many ad agencies have failed to pull off another significant performance of the Coke myth. They've brought in a Hollywood talent agency to make the brand famous through entertainment. They've hired the hippest creative boutiques in the business to make ads that would appeal to younger generations. Along the way, Coke has aired many entertaining ads and many less impressive ones, but none of these ads have ignited a passion for Coke among the generations that came of age since the 1980s. In fact, considering Coke's monstrous equity and media weight, the brand has had some of the least effective advertising in the industry. How could this be?

Since Mean Joe Greene, The Coca-Cola Company has become a leading advocate of mind-share and emotional branding. The company's strategy focused on advancing Coke's abstract associations (refreshment, authenticity, and social bonds) and forging emotional connections with its audience, resulting in the most entertaining and heart-tugging communications its vast resources could buy. In its halcyon days, however, Coke did much more than combine copy points with Spielbergian cinematic tricks.

Coke's product benefits worked as a platform on which the brand built powerful identity myths that spoke to American ideals. In these myths, the irrepressible American spirit always overcame otherwise divisive problems. By sharing a Coke Americans of very different ethnic and class backgrounds could revive their commitment to a common moral charter. Coke called its followers into a world in which the ever optimistic and indefatigable American spirit overcomes seemingly intractable social problems. As these social challenges changed, Coke's myth changed accordingly.

Perhaps more than any other brand, Coke had earned the authority to promote a utopia in which American citizens come together to solve social problems that threaten the commonweal. Yet, since the 1980s, Coke has failed to engage social issues that are utmost on the minds of the brand's customers. Today the United States is a troubled empire, maligned by people throughout the world. These circumstances provide potent cultural material that Coke could forge into myth. Coke's managers, however, are so beholden to the logic of mind share and emotional branding that they've missed opportunities like this time and again.

Poignant evidence that the company misreads the value of the Coke brand comes from a much promoted ad that ran several years ago. Company managers wanted so desperately to recapture the magic of Mean Joe Greene that they commissioned a sequel. This time, however, the commercial used famed Baltimore Orioles shortstop Cal Ripken Jr., who gets a Coke from his son at the ballpark. The Ripkin ad suggests that Coke managers understood the Mean Joe spot as simply an emotional bond formed between a famous sports star and a kid, rather than a symbolic resolution to racial strife. They missed the ad's symbolic importance because they stripped away the particulars of the ad's story and yanked the ad out of its historically specific cultural context.

Today Coke exists as a nostalgic brand, harking back to the day when the drink enjoyed its peak iconic stature. Coke now stands for 1950s Americana. Not surprisingly, then, one of Coke's few recent bright spots occurred when it brought back its classic bottle design and redesigned its plastic bottles to mimic the glass, encouraging customers to indulge in the Coke myth of old.

Why Can't Emotional Branding Build Iconic Brands?

From the 1940s through the 1980s, no American brand did better than Coke in forging potent emotional ties with its customers. But the mere documentation of these strong attachments does not explain how they came to be. Gurus of emotional branding encourage managers to give their brand a personality, to build emotional content into communications, and to emphasize emotional benefits. While appropriate for some categories, these recommendations are wrongheaded for identity brands.[15] Observers have rashly inferred that the emotional connections between the brand and its customers are the result of emotional branding efforts. This erroneous conclusion has led to many misguided branding efforts that seek to build identity value by provoking an emotional reaction from the audience.[16]

Rather, the emotional connections we routinely witness between iconic brands and their core customers are the result of potent identity myths spun by the brand. Coke didn't compel its customers to form an emotional bond by airing generic emotional communications. Many sappy ads intended to pull at the audience's heartstrings come and go with little fanfare. Rather, Coke developed these emotional ties just like other iconic brands. The right identity myth, well performed, provides the audience with little epiphanies—moments of recognition that put images, sounds, and feelings on barely perceptible desires. Customers who find this kind of identity value in a brand forge intensive emotional connections. Emotional attachment is the consequence of a great myth.

From Viral Branding to Cultural Branding

Cultural branding also stands apart from another recent challenger to mind share, so-called viral branding (some authors and managers also call this approach *grass roots* and *buzz*).[17] As the name suggests, viral branding focuses on the paths of public influence: how noncompany actors influence customers to value the brand. The viral approach is a compendium of ideas rooted in the classic ideas about public influence—diffusion of innovation, word of mouth, and public relations—that responded to two major shifts in the 1990s: the increased cynicism toward mass marketing and the emergence of the Internet.

Viral branding assumes that consumers, and not firms, have the most influence in the creation of brands. Cynical consumers will no longer heed the missives of mass marketers, so instead must "discover" brands on their own. The Internet provided a means to accelerate this discovery. As a result, what was once considered an important process that marketers might want to stimulate has now often become an end in itself.

In addition, many experts today recommend below-the-radar marketing, which seeds the brand among the most influential people. The basic idea is that if the firm can convince these people to make the brand their own, and configure the brand, like a virus, to make it easy to talk about, these influencers will rapidly spread their interest in the brand to others through their social networks, just as a virus spreads. At the beginning of the new-economy era, Douglas Rushkoff warned the world about what he termed *media viruses.* Brand managers quickly turned the tables and decided that going viral was the quickest and cheapest path to brand heaven. The more velocity through the system, the better the brand does.

A related idea is what New Yorker writer Malcolm Gladwell has called the coolhunt.[18] In this view, brands are no longer led by corporate activities but rather given meaning and value on the streets by opinion-leading trendsetters who adopt the brands and give them cachet. Consumer goods companies send out cultural detectives onto the streets of cool territories, like the playgrounds in poor urban neighborhoods or underground clubs, to scout out new trends. The race is to grab the newest, coolest culture the fastest, before it becomes mass culture.

In viral branding, a covert public relations mode becomes the core of the branding effort. The ad agency Doyle Dane Bernbach (DDB) champions its ability to create "talk value" as its core competency, for instance. Many major ad agencies and consultancies have launched specialized groups, such as Young & Rubicam's Brand Buzz, to deliver viral branding plans to their clients. Streetwise research consultancies like Sputnik make a living hanging out with the right trendsetting fringes and filing reports with multinational companies.[19]

In sum, the viral approach presumes that consumers—not marketers—create identity value. Consequently, identity branding has turned into the task of stealthily seeding brands with the right customers so that they will take up the brand and develop its value. The company takes a back seat to consumers in forging what the brand stands for.

As we will see with Snapple, while viral processes are (as always) important for the diffusion of branding efforts, viral branding itself is not a viable approach for building an iconic brand. The primary source of Snapple's identity value comes from the company's marketing activities, not from its consumers. And, like Corona and Coke, Snapple's efforts created a potent identity myth.

A Short Genealogy of Snapple

Snapple is often used as a poster child for viral branding.[20] In the early 1990s, Snapple developed tremendous buzz among cognoscenti in New York and beyond, eventually spreading across the United States. In fact, Snapple's climb to iconic stature was due to its owners' idiosyncratic cultural branding strategy. The brand's viral characteristics—its buzz, its underground coolness, and the ragtag community of fans that formed around

Snapple—all are consequences of the resonance of the brand's myth, which became embodied in the large-mouthed bottles of juices and teas.

The Snapple line of teas and juices was founded by three Brooklyn entrepreneurs who, in the process of goofing around with their small company, eventually stumbled on the brand's myth. Through the company's new products, advertising, promotions, distribution, and even customer service, the founders authored a quixotic script about a radically different kind of company, one run by amateurs who shared their customers' cynicism toward how large companies were managed. Everything the company did was antithetic to marketing as practiced by The Coca Cola Company, PepsiCo, and other sophisticated marketing Goliaths. Instead of looking to grocery chains and fast-food franchises, Snapple distributed its products in restaurants, delis, street carts, and mom-and-pop groceries. For product, the founders continually rolled out odd and seemingly ill-conceived blends, a few of which became hits. They relied on their most zealous customers for product and packaging ideas, rushing oddball requests into production without so much as a focus group. For example, customer Ralph Orofino's affinity for melons inspired Ralph's Cantaloupe Cocktail, a drink that featured Ralph's face on the label. Customers loved to try these weird drinks, even the bad-tasting ones, which offered surprises compared with the least-common-denominator processes of corporate marketing.

For advertising, the company hired "celebrities" it liked and could afford. The ads were so poorly produced and odd that they became cult classics among the growing legion of New York Snapple groupies. For example, in one ad, less-than-charismatic tennis player Ivan Lendl, with his thick accent, mispronounced the brand's name "Schnahpple." Another spot featured Richie Sambora, the rock band Bon Jovi's only sort-of-famous guitarist, because one owner was a fan.

Especially critical to Snapple's rise was the hiring of "shock jock" talk radio personalities Rush Limbaugh and Howard Stern as spokespersons. Both men conveyed real affection for Snapple and gave the drink extemporaneous plugs on the air in addition to the paid-for sponsorships. It would be hard to pick two more different advocates: Limbaugh was the self-righteous voice of the reactionary right, leading a loyal following of angry white men who called themselves "dittoheads" to blast the liberal tendencies of Washington politicians (Hillary Clinton was a favorite target) and stem the tide of political correctness. Stern, on the other hand, was the comedic and paranoid voice of slutty anarchy. He thrived on a nihilist attitude that involved celebrating whatever polite society considered tasteless, and dissing whatever it considered important. Stern loved to call the bluff on America's puritanical tendencies by stuffing as much sexual innuendo into his program as possible. But, while diametrically at odds in terms of politics and tastes, the two radio jocks were united in that they were America's most provocative populist voices denouncing the priorities and tastes of American elites.

Snapple had ultimate credibility as an amateurish company because its three entrepreneurs knew nothing about professional marketing. Nor did they have any interest in learning. They ran the company according to what made sense and seemed like fun. Snapple's customers knew as much and loved them for it.

When private investors bought majority interest from the entrepreneurs in hopes of expanding the Snapple magic to Americans across the country, they faced a huge risk: How could they apply professional marketing to a brand that attracted legions of devoted followers for Snapple's amateurism? By hiring a young ad agency copywriter to run the marketing department, the new owners avoided brand management orthodoxy. The copywriter, in turn, hired an upstart New York ad agency, Kirshenbaum & Bond, to create a national branding platform for Snapple.

This unorthodox brand team did not attempt to reduce Snapple to a set of brand essence adjectives, seek out deep consumer truths, or plumb Snapple devotees' emotional connections to the brand. Rather, they searched for ways to further extend Snapple's odd, amateurish performances. At the time, Snapple's followers were so touched by the brand that they flooded Snapple's small office with fan mail. Over two thousand letters a week poured in, not to mention original videos, songs, artwork, and poetry, all odes to Snapple.

The team found a promising story in Wendy, a woman who did clerical work for Snapple. Wendy had taken it upon herself to respond to mail as best as she could. The brand team cast "Wendy, the Snapple Lady" as the letter reader in dozens of TV ads. The ads opened with Wendy seated behind the real-life Snapple receptionist's desk, throwing out an unselfconsciously friendly "Hi from Snapple!" Viewers could clearly see that the chatty and plump Wendy was the real thing, not a Hollywood actor. She would then read a letter from a customer with a fussy question about one of Snapple's products, a question that could only be of concern to a devotee. After Wendy answered the question, the ad would cut to a camera crew shooting documentary style in the customers' homes to capture their reactions. None of the spots were scripted, and various bloopers were often left unedited on the film. The tag line "100% Natural" captured the idea that Snapple was not only a natural product, but, even more important, a transparent company run by well-meaning amateurs. The company was run by eccentric people who shared their customers' enthusiasm for frivolous pleasures, not by M.B.A.'s and their spreadsheets and market research.

To complement the advertising, Snapple sponsored many events, but not the usual blockbuster sports, music, and celebrity spectacles of Coke and Pepsi. Instead, Snapple staged events that mocked big corporate promotions: Cherry spitting in Minnesota, yo-yo tossing in New York, and the Miss Crustacean contest in New Jersey were among the sanctioned contests.

The founders had stumbled on, and the brand team nimbly amplified, an identity myth that responded to a burgeoning contradiction in American society. To understand why Snapple connected so profoundly with a significant slice of the American public, we must place Snapple's amateurish brand performances in the context of social tensions that were becoming acute in the early 1990s. During the 1980s, most Americans, particularly men, had signed on to Ronald Reagan's call to arms to get tough again, like the pioneers of the West, to revive the country's economic and political stature. With gung-ho entrepreneurs, tougher business practices, and painful but necessary reorganizations, Reagan promised that the United States would lead the world again. By the late 1980s, the U.S. economy had been largely reinvented as a much more dynamic and much more cutthroat economy, with the constant threat of downsizing and reengineering disrupting labor markets. Profits began to surge, and the country found a new set of heroes in its swashbuckling entrepreneurs (e.g., Ted Turner, Bill Gates) and athletes (e.g., Michael Jordan), who exhibited the "Just do it" spirit. But, while companies and corporate elites profited handsomely, the constant restructuring pushed many other American workers into service-economy McJobs.

As it became clear that trickle-down economics wasn't trickling down, this dissonance bubbled to the surface in both popular culture and politics. The populist backlash of the early 1990s gained political expression in the massive defection of Republicans and Democrats to the populist candidacies of Ross Perot, Pat Buchanan, Jessie Jackson, and Jerry Brown. Americans suddenly had a tremendous appetite for highly cynical and nihilist counterpoints to Reagan's spin on American ideals. Television programs like *The Simpsons* and *Beavis and Butthead* became hits. *Wayne's World*, Nirvana, and the cartoon strip *Dilbert* painted culture-leading myths that responded to these tensions.

Snapple (along with Mountain Dew, as we'll see later) jumped into this swift current of discontent and devised a blissful rebuttal. Through its marketing activities, the company authored a myth that suggested that big corporations and the overpaid elites who ran them only gummed up the works. In the utopia Snapple acted out, companies were run by amateurs who cared more about having fun with their customers than in generating profits to stockholders. The amateurs inspired their customers to dream the craziest drink-inspired dreams, and they played around with products and promotions, however crazy. This myth of a world turned upside down—in which amateurs win over the bureaucratic elite—was plunked into bottles of sugary tea. Gulping down a bottle allowed customers to experience this fantasy as a salve for the identity anxieties they faced.[21]

As Snapple's myth engaged these emerging veins of social discontent, sales rose rapidly from less than $50 million in 1987 to over $200 million in 1992. A legion of hard-core devotees were inspired by Snapple's voice in the wilderness. Then, as mass culture responded to raise the populist revolt to a fever pitch in 1992–1994, with everyone from Wayne and Garth to Kurt Cobain joining the chorus, Snapple sales soared skyward, approaching $700 million in 1994.

The Quaker Oats Company purchased Snapple at this juncture, believing that Quaker's professional marketing operations could further leverage the brand. The company implemented a new strategy based on conventional mind share and emotional branding ideas. Quaker managers completely misunderstood what had generated Snapple's awesome identity value—its myth of anticorporate amateurism. They fired Limbaugh and Stern, scrapped Wendy and the "100% Natural" campaign for a more professional and conventional treatment, and instituted a rationalized new product development process. The company thought that it could optimize Snapple's value by applying its expertise in mind-share branding. Instead, Quaker killed Snapple's myth, and soon enough, Snapple lost its iconic stature. Because Quaker marketers failed to grasp the principles of

Iconic Brands Versus Fads and Fashions

The viral model is essentially a fashion branding model.[22] The model relies on taste leaders who set trends and create the brand's must-have desirability when they use it and talk about it. Viral efforts thus seek to influence tastemakers. While numerous fads and fashions have been established through viral processes, iconic brands operate above this cycle. In fact, getting caught up in a fad cycle can destroy an iconic brand. The once-iconic retailer Gap hooked into a fashion cycle when its innovative ads for its classic chino pants placed the brand at the epicenter of the swing music craze of 1997–1998. After enjoying its two years of fame and sky-high stock prices, the brand collapsed when it failed to package another hit. Meanwhile, the new young customers who hopped on the brand to be part of Gap's cool factor combined with Gap's newfound interest in delivering fashion hits scared away the brand's much more durable iconic consumers.

Identity brands that are developed through viral approaches have a fatal flaw—they are authorless. The firm relinquishes control of the brand to consumers and cultural tastemakers. The problem is that these authors thrive on influencing the next big thing. As soon as they make a brand famous, they move on. Fad brands are dumped by fashion-forward tastemakers as soon as their cachet has been depleted, as Corona's first flash-in-the-pan success attests.

When properly managed, iconic brands are much more durable than fads and fashions. Rather than ride boom-and-bust cycles of fashionability, icons address acute social tensions that usually last for many years.

cultural branding, the company lost some $1.4 billion when it had to sell off the Snapple brand in a fire sale as sales came crashing down.[23]

Why Can't Viral Branding Build Iconic Brands?

By 1994, Snapple had generated plenty of buzz, was considered by many to be a cool trendsetting brand, and had even attracted a hardy band of followers who formed an occasional Snapple community. But these viral effects were artifacts of the brand's success, not causes. Snapple earned these desirable qualities because the brand pushed a compelling new identity myth. Snapple's company of amateurs championed a fantastic populist alternative to the growing disgust with the new-economy labor market and the elites in government and business who were installing it. Consumers loved Snapple for acting this way, talked about the brand, considered it ahead of its time compared with conventional soft drinks, and even enjoyed gathering sporadically with people who felt the same.

The buzz that Snapple generated was the consequence of the power of its myth. Simply getting people to talk about something—say, repeat a catch phrase from an ad—is not a particularly noteworthy event. Most such talk quickly fades from memory and, regardless, becomes detached from the meaning of the story. What sticks are stories that affect how people think about themselves in the world. The problem with the viral model is that it assumes that any communication is good as long as it's retold. Much more important, however, is what people remember and use symbolically in their everyday lives. Snapple didn't just get people talking. Instead, the brand served as a role model, a rather absurd one, which provided a silly but meaningful critique of corporate life in the early 1990s.

The Path to Cultural Branding

All iconic brands enjoy the characteristics of strong brands described by the conventional models: They have distinctive and favorable associations, they generate buzz, and they have core consumers with deep emotional attachments. But these observed characteristics are the *consequence* of successful mythmaking, not the cause. The identity myth embedded in the brand leads customers to associate the product with category benefits, to spread the myth by word of mouth, to emote, and to gather together. Hence, while these measures serve as useful metrics for appraising identity value, they offer little strategic help in directing how companies should build iconic brands.[24]

Rather, managers can build iconic brands only if they apply the tacit cultural strategies that supported the success of brands like Corona, Coke, and Snapple. Initially, a company may have difficulty assimilating these principles because they differ so much from conventional branding ideas. To introduce the next chapters of the book, which will develop cultural branding strategy in considerably more detail, let me reprise three of the most difficult shifts in mind-set evident from the three case studies in this chapter.

From Persuasion to Mythmaking

Conventional branding models hold an instrumental view of brand communications. These models assume that the purpose of advertising is to influence consumer perceptions about the brand (e.g., associations tied to quality, benefits, personality, and aspirational user imagery). Communications should use whatever creative content will do the best job of persuading. But, ultimately, this content is instrumental rhetoric that shapes perceptions, not an end in itself. Customers presumably discard this rhetorical material once they believe what the communications was designed to make them believe.

Cultural branding turns this approach to communications on its head. In cultural branding, communications are the center of customer value. Customers buy the product to experience these stories. The product is simply a conduit through which customers can experience the stories that the brand tells. When consumers sip a Coke, Corona, or Snapple, they are drinking more than a beverage. Rather, they are imbibing identity myths anchored in these drinks. An effective cultural strategy creates a *storied product,* that is, a product that has distinctive branded features (mark, design, etc.) through which customers experience identity myths.

From Abstract Associations to Cultural Expressions

Conventional branding models propose that the brand consists of a set of abstract associations.[25] Consequently, managers obsess over the concepts that the brand should own. Strategy meetings extend for months in which managers debate which adjectives best suit the brand. Meanwhile, tracking studies meticulously measure whether consumers associate these words with the brand.

With cultural branding, in contrast, the brand's value resides in the specifics of the brand's cultural expression: the particular cultural contents of the brand's myth and the particular expression of these contents in the communication. For Corona, the brand exists in the Mexican beach and its "nothing's happening" style of advertising. For Coke in the 1970s, the brand existed in the idea that the hippie counterculture contained the seeds of peace and racial harmony. For Snapple, the brand was centered in loud-mouthed Wendy telling silly stories of Snapple drinkers and in the barbed political soliloquies of Howard and Rush. Abstracting these cultural expressions to the generic qualities of relaxation, friendship, and quirkiness, respectively, strips these brands of their most valuable assets.

It's impossible to build an iconic brand with mind-share principles. Mind share demands intensive abstraction. Managers systematically cleanse their strategies to rid the brand of the messiness of society and history in search of its purified essence. Endless haggling between brand managers, ad planners, and market researchers yield strategy documents consisting of montages of generic phrases. Mind share is driven by a logic of quantification—the drive to simplify the world so that it can be contained through measurement. The memorability of adjectives, unlike culturally specific stories, can be quantified and examined via benchmarks.

The distilled strategies of mind share, however, disable identity brands because they deny the brand a role as a historical actor in society. In their continuous effort to lodge a transcendental brand essence in consumers' minds, mind-share strategies fail to recognize that identity value is created and transformed in particular historical contexts. To create identity value, brand managers must instead detail the brand's stakes in the transformation of culture and society and the particular cultural expressions the brand uses to achieve these transformations.

From Consistency to Historical Fit

Conventional models assume that managing a brand is the art of insisting on consistency in the face of organizational and competitive pressures that push for zigging and zagging. Brand management is about stewardship: finding the brand's true essence and maintaining this compass point, come hell or high water.

Yet Corona and Coke both succeeded by moving away from their initial branding—their supposed brand essence at the time—to address shifting currents in American society. Of the iconic brands that I've studied with histories extending more than a decade, all have had to make significant shifts to remain iconic. These revisions of the brand's myth are necessary because, for a myth to generate identity value, it must directly engage the challenging social issues of the day. Coke celebrated America's triumphs against Nazi Germany in World War II, shifted to dramatize ways to heal internal strife around war in the early 1970s, and then shifted again to attend to racial divisions in the early 1980s. Corona, originally a brand that represented collegiate hedonism, later evolved to become a soothing antidote to the compression and anxieties of the networked free-agent work that came to a head in the 1990s.

Mind share assumes that brands exist outside of history, as transcendental entities. Managing a mind-share brand thus requires consistency, staying above the fray of changes in culture and society. Iconic brands apply precisely the opposite philosophy: The brand is a historical entity whose desirability comes from myths that address the most important social tensions of the nation. For identity brands, success depends on how well the brand's myth adjusts to historical exigencies, not by its consistency in the face of historical change.[26]

CHAPTER 3

Targeting Myth Markets

IDENTITY BRANDS COMPETE in myth markets, not product markets. For managers, as well as economists, this concept is hard to grasp. Markets usually form around concrete, material product characteristics. Economists think of markets in terms of substitutability: A market consists of those products that consumers view as substitutes based on their functionality. A television competes with other televisions based on its ability to deliver a sharp picture, its reliability, its features, and so on.

Identity brands are different. They compete with other cultural products to perform myths that resolve cultural contradictions. Identity brands participate in myth markets, competing and collaborating with films, music, television, sports, and books.

The first task of any brand strategy is to pinpoint the appropriate target for the brand within a given market. In mind-share branding, the product category is segmented according to benefits or user psychographics from which a target is chosen. In cultural branding, managers must instead identify the most appropriate myth market.

Targeting myth markets can be a complicated task, for they don't stand still. In fact, myth markets are routinely destabilized by cultural disruptions: Symbolic earthquakes pulse through society, shattering the value of existing myths and spurring the creation of new ones. Iconic brands not only target the most appropriate myth market; they are also sensitive to cultural disruptions, shifting their target when opportunity strikes. Successful iconic brands leap nimbly across cultural disruptions by deciphering the new myth markets created by the disruption and homing in on a new target.

One especially agile iconic brand has been Mountain Dew. The hands-down winner of the cola wars, this brand has built sales faster than any other carbonated-soft-drink competitor during the decades of the 1980s and 1990s. Today PepsiCo sells $4.7 billion of the sweet yellow liquid every year. In so doing, Mountain Dew has leapfrogged 7 UP, Diet Pepsi, Dr. Pepper, Sprite, and Diet Coke. Only Coke and Pepsi are bigger.

But along this march, the brand hardly stayed static. Mountain Dew was twice reinvented in the face of major cultural disruptions, targeting new myth markets as they emerged in American mass culture. These transformations were the key to the brand's stunning growth.

The Hillbilly Myth

Mountain Dew was first introduced in the late 1940s and was then pulled from the market because of a competitive conflict with its distributors. In 1960, a small Tennessee company rolled out the product as we know it today, initially in the Middle Atlantic states. Though competing directly with the likes of Coke and Pepsi, Mountain Dew nonetheless became a regional success out of the blocks, leading PepsiCo to buy the brand in 1964. Mountain Dew owed its quick popularity to the founder's strategy. They used the soft drink to create an identity myth that addressed one of the mightiest contradictions of the day.

National Ideology: Scientific Bureaucracy

American ideology of the 1950s and 1960s was deeply influenced by World War II and the Cold War. U.S. military success—which Americans understood to be caused by the precision of the military with its rationalized, hierarchical administration; the ability of new U.S. mass-production companies to gear up swiftly to support the war effort; and the massive organization of scientific efforts to win the race to develop the atom bomb—made a convincing case that a new era had come. The national ideology lauded scientific expertise and bureaucratic organization. Large, rationally administered, and professionally managed bureaucracies would unleash the power of science. Popular culture embraced dreams of technology that would create fantastic new futures. The United States now had the secret keys to win markets and defend the free world against the Soviet bloc.

In this ideology, old ideas about rugged individualism had become anachronistic. To contain communism, everyone had to step to the same beat. On the job, the employee who was mature enough to subsume his or her individuality under the umbrella of corporate wisdom was praised.

Outside the work place, these ideals found potent expression in the new modern living sold by Hollywood and Madison Avenue and practiced by nuclear families in planned suburbs. Americans saw suburbia reproduced on television programs and in ads that portrayed men who appreciated the synchronized routines of the new lifestyle. Paternal figures were expected to keep their emotions and impulses on a tight leash.

Cultural Contradiction: Conformity Erases Rugged Individualism

This new ideology produced a litany of contradictions for men and women. Men found these ideals coercive and emasculating when these principles were measured against America's historical rugged individualism. Books like William Whyte's *Organization Man* and David Riesman's *Lonely Crowd,* both of which damned the new conformity of corporate America, became best-sellers. Soon a myth market sprang up to ease these tensions.

American mass culture draws upon populist worlds to tell stories that both buttress (affirmative myths) and challenge (myths of resistance) the country's ideology. In the period lasting roughly from the mid-1950s through the mid-1960s, the country's most powerful masculine myths emanated from five populist worlds—the cowboy's Western frontier; the new world of rock-and-roll; the Beats' bohemia; the subculture of the outlaw biker; and the hillbilly way of life.

The Hillbilly Myth Market

As the United States rapidly industrialized, the pockets that remained relatively untouched, particularly in Appalachia and the South, were perceived by the rest of America as blights. These Appalachian families—pejoratively nicknamed hillbillies in those days—were portrayed as living a backward rural life. As a result, many urban metro Americans perceived these people as a national embarrassment that must be removed, but also as rebellious and even dangerous figures. The urbanites projected onto these people various innate animal qualities, qualities off limits to the corporate world. Endowed with such potent cultural power, the symbol of the hillbilly offered excellent source materials for mythmaking.

The hillbilly was used to create myths that both buttressed and challenged the national ideology. Affirmative myths made fun of the "backward" life of country people, the life that the United States was now happy to leave behind as the nation came to dominate the world. The hillbilly also became the center of an earnest and paternalistic policy discussion. Destitute mining communities of Appalachia were "discovered" in Michael Harrington's best-selling 1962 policy book, *The Other America.* Harrington framed for the nation a previously hidden "blight" that a newly rich nation couldn't tolerate. But for the urban metro middle class, they perceived Harrington to be reporting on a mysterious tribe of backward people who lived outside of time and who hadn't yet caught on to Tang or instant coffee.

But images of hillbillies were also used as a populist weapon to push against the emerging ideology. To make biting social satire in his *Li'l Abner* cartoon strip in the 1930s, Al Capp exaggerated the hillbilly's lack of civility. Elvis Presley, the poor Mississippi (and then Tennessee) hillbilly who brought black music to a white audience, oozed a primitive sexuality that titillated young women and sent young men in search of rock-and-roll records. With his uninhibited swagger and lascivious vocal renderings, Presley's mythic figure implicitly argued that real men were to be found out in the country, away from the emasculating new norms of suburban life.[1]

In 1962, CBS launched *The Beverly Hillbillies,* which became the second most popular television program of the 1960s. The formulaic episodes revolved around the Clampett family's encounters with the nation's elites, particularly their banker—the uptight and conniving Milburn Drysdale. The stark contrast of these interactions revealed the Clampetts' lack of any sort of guile, pretensions, or social graces. What made the program endearing and entertaining was that the Clampetts, living in the center of wealth, were unconcerned about their perceived shortcomings. They continued to wear the same beaten-up clothes, Granny made vittles and spring tonic, and Ellie May was more concerned with critters than men. While Jed and his clan weren't much for fashion and fancy words, they demonstrated time and again that they were more dignified, more resourceful, and often more clever than the business class of Beverly Hills. *The Beverly Hillbillies* was a populist allegory that championed pragmatic knowledge over book learning, character over self-presentation, and traditional hospitality over manners.

Mountain Dew's Hillbilly Myth

Mountain Dew's entrepreneurs picked a name from a popular old-time Appalachian folk song, which told of the pleasures of moonshine liquor known by the euphemism "mountain dew." They crafted the beverage to create a heart-pumping rush from caffeine and sugar and gave it a bright yellow color and fewer bubbles so that it was chuggable. Then they created a comic hillbilly character—Willy—who drank Mountain Dew to "get high." This branding was carried through advertising, packaging, and even the location of the bottling plant.

Invoking Appalachian stereotypes like the blood-feuding Hatfields and McCoys, the bottle's label featured a barefoot Willie pointing his cocked rifle at a neighbor running away in the distance. Tied to Willie's hip was a stoneware jug, the type associated with homemade booze. Print ads showed the same jug (labeled "Mountain Dew") having exploded in Willie's hands so that the cork ripped a hole through his hat. The tag line "Yahoo! Mountain Dew!" was accompanied by either "Thar's a bang in ever' bottle" or "It'll tickle yer innards." On each bottle label, fictional illicit distillers' names were printed. For example, "Filled by Mary & Kathy."

When PepsiCo bought the brand in 1964, the company kept the hillbilly character, renamed him Clem, and put him in animated television ads. One ad, called "Beautiful Sal," featured an all-barefoot cast set in the country. A pair of rural Southern men courted Sal, a zaftig redhead clad in a brief, tattered dress. Sal refused flowers from both bumpkins and tugged their hats over their faces before she strutted away. Enter Clem. Half Sal's height, Clem appeared an unlikely mate. But from under his ten-gallon hat Clem revealed a tall bottle of Mountain Dew. Sal swiped the bottle from Clem's flat head and threw back a few quick gulps of Dew. As Clem gazed lustily, Sal lifted a leg and hollered, "Yahoo, Mountain Dew!" Her long hair snapped into curls beside her head. If the audience failed to understand that Dew held the power to immediately change attitudes, the muzzle flash that exploded from Sal's ears sealed the deal. She growled like a panther in heat, squeezed Clem into her considerable nooks and crannies, and smothered him with an arresting kiss. The spot then cut to a single-toothed old man who reached behind his head, lasciviously wiggled his finger through a bullet hole in his hat, and said, "Mountain Dew'll tickle your innards, cuz thar's a bang in ever' bottle."

Mountain Dew created a fictional manhood that stood against the buttoned-up emotions and routines of organization men. The brand celebrated what Freud called the id and what Robert Bly called, in his bestselling book, *Iron John,* the wild man—man's primitive animal nature, in which libido, violence, and sensual pleasures are unleashed, free of social sanctions. Mountain Dew's hillbilly was a juvenile prankster who, with a devilish twinkle in his eye, called onlookers to let loose their wild man.

During the 1960s Mountain Dew sales took off among white working-class people from the southeastern United States, through Kentucky and Tennessee, through the Great Lakes states, and into the Northern Plains of Minnesota and the Dakotas. The spread of the brand was distinctive in that, as if by radar, it bypassed every major urban-metro population center. Dew's myth resonated in America's predominantly white smaller cities, towns, and rural areas, an area that PepsiCo brand managers came to call the NASCAR Belt, after the stock-car racing circuit so popular in the same regions. When Mountain Dew's customers guzzled the sweet yellow liquid, the brand allowed them to imagine themselves as a bit of a wild man in a world in which the organization man reigned supreme.

Cultural Disruption Destroys the Hillbilly Myth

Unfortunately for PepsiCo a series of devastating national failures buried the American ideology that provided the grist for Mountain Dew's myth. Massive urban riots dramatized the limitations of the Great Society programs. Japanese corporations showed that U.S. companies were hardly world leaders, while Arab oil tycoons demonstrated the vulnerability of U.S. economic power. The Viet Cong made something of a joke of U.S. military superiority, and Watergate undermined Americans' confidence in their political system. Beginning in the summer of 1967, the hippie counterculture took over the airwaves. Alongside the peace movement and civil rights protests, the media were particularly interested in telling America about a new cultural phenomenon, the epicenter of which was the corner of Haight and Ashbury in San Francisco. Popular culture soaked up "the summer of love," and soon *Laugh-In* had become the top TV program, the Volkswagen Beetle became America's favorite car, and kids in Peoria were wearing bell-bottoms imprinted with the American flag. The nation experimented with new ideological possibilities inspired by the most radical populist challenges of the day: the black power movement, the peace movement, the hippie counterculture, and the women's movement.

Against this backdrop, the hillbilly celebration of the wild man became irrelevant. Instead, people began to associate the hillbilly with a more reactionary strand of American politics: they were viewed as white Southerners who stood against racial and sexual equality (as depicted in the 1972 film *Deliverance*).

Television programs featuring hillbillies, *The Beverly Hillbillies* and *Hee Haw*, were canceled. Mountain Dew sales slid. A variety of new branding initiatives failed to stem the fall. The hillbilly was ditched for new creative ideas that placed the idea of the Dew "bang" in a variety of contemporary scenes showcasing current trends, but these new ideas didn't increase sales. Entering the 1970s, the brand was in trouble. Pepsi's plans to convert Mountain Dew into another powerhouse national brand seemed to be a pipe dream.

Traversing Cultural Disruptions

Contrary to intuitive ideas that culture is constantly in motion, ideology must be relatively stable for society to function effectively. National ideology works something like Stephen Jay Gould's idea of punctuated equilibrium: Extended periods of relative stability are occasionally disrupted by radical changes. As citizens lose faith in the nation's ideology, experimentation ensues, historical ingredients are reworked, and society finally arrives at a new consensus. When such a shift in ideology occurs, people are forced to adjust their self-understanding and their aspirations.

New myth markets grow up around these new desires. Culture industry texts that perform the most successful new myths become icons, basking in the aura bestowed on those who have the foresight and charisma to provide cultural leadership in times when identity desires are the greatest.

PepsiCo has used disruptions in ideology to increase Mountain Dew's identity value, crossing cultural chasms rather than allowing the brand to be dismantled by them. But Mountain Dew didn't recover overnight. As the nation experimented with these populist challenges, so too did Mountain Dew, though with little success. Finally, Mountain Dew found a new cultural toehold in the late 1970s.

The Redneck Myth

In the late 1970s a new ideology began to take shape, the Wall Street Frontier, which created a new myth market that aligned well with Mountain Dew's prior stories. Through considerable experimentation, PepsiCo eventually recast Mountain Dew's advertising to perform a redneck myth, a myth that created even more identity value for the drink's customers than its hillbilly predecessor.

National Ideology: The Wall Street Frontier

Ronald Reagan galvanized the United States around a new ideology that resuscitated Teddy Roosevelt's turn-of-the-century vision of America: the idea that the country should rally around its frontier values to expand its global power. Reagan used the cowboy on the Western frontier as the rough-and-tumble new hero for the economy—an idea that he argued would, if pursued vigorously, save the U.S. economy from overseas threats. Reagan cajoled American men to stand up to the nation's twin threats: Soviet communism and Japan's economic prowess. To do so, he relied on his many actor friends who had portrayed cowboys and man-of-action heroes in films: John Wayne, Clint Eastwood, Charlton Heston, Arnold Schwarzenegger, and Sylvester Stallone. Stallone's second Rambo film—*Rambo: First Blood, Part II,* which depicted a rebellious Vietnam vet overcoming an ineffectual government bureaucracy to save soldiers missing in action—became the signature film of Reagan's administration.

While Reagan trotted out effective metaphors from the past, the mass media soon retooled them to make sense of the dismantling of the U.S. economy. Economic restructuring was led—in the popular imagination, at least—by a new Machiavellian type of business executive, represented by Donald Trump and Ivan Boesky on Wall Street and *Dallas*'s J. R. Ewing on television. Reviving the economy seemed to require a new breed of aggressive manager chasing after wealth and power with ruthless guile. Urban professionals quickly picked up on their role as the economy's new cowboys and, by the mid-1980s, were decked out in cowboy boots and heading out to urban cowboy bars on the weekends. The media celebrated these M.B.A.'s and lawyers who put in eighty-hour weeks orchestrating high-pressure, billion-dollar, leveraged buyouts.

Cultural Contradiction: Yuppies Aren't Heroes

From 1978 on, the working class faced the most rapid decline in earning power since the Depression. Among Mountain Dew's constituents, the result was increased unemployment, falling real wages, and disappearing benefits. Workers' youthful dreams of the good life, of rising pay in secure industrial jobs, were disappearing. Men could no longer imagine themselves as successful breadwinners; women increasingly had to find part-time work to make family ends meet. Much of the North became the Rust Belt. In places like Flint, Michigan, unemployment approached 20 percent.

From Reagan to automotive executive Lee Iacocca, leaders responded to this crisis by calling on working men to accept sacrifices to support their country in a time of need. This call awakened an older patriarchal order—to "take it like a man"—and was largely heeded. Patriotism became the order of the day. "Buy American" bumper stickers adorned cars. Working men, by and large, accepted this challenge as a duty of American citizenship and sided with Reagan in a historic flip-flop of party loyalties in the 1980 and 1984 elections. But these same men had trouble seeing the people celebrated in the media as the new frontier heroes. These yuppies weren't patriots (they had no problem with sending their jobs overseas), they weren't tough (they ate quiche and Lean Cuisine and liked to jog), and worse, they worked hard to get their BMWs and Rolexes, rather than work hard because that's what a man does for his country, community, and family.

The Redneck Myth Market

Instead, many working men aligned with emerging new myths of resistance based on the populist world of the redneck, the progeny of the hillbilly. The redneck was a reactionary, standing against the cultural changes wreaked by the 1960s and the economic changes of the deindustrializing United States.

In the fertile imaginations of the urban metro middle class, the rural South constituted an insular, backward society of these rednecks. Members of this disparaged group were thought to possess the same problematic values to which the hillbilly allegedly subscribed. The urban middle class understood rednecks as parochial, crude, and slothful. They were backward folks who resisted the social reforms, such as racial and gender equality and environmental protection, favored by the middle class.

The nonurban working class reversed the redneck insult and turned the epithet into a badge of honor, following the same pattern as the hillbilly. The confederate flag became the group's coat of arms. A host of redneck myths sprang up. Southern rock arose as a popular new genre, featuring bands like Lynyrd Skynyrd, the Charlie Daniels Band, the Outlaws, and Black Oak Arkansas. By the mid-1970s, songs like Skynyrd's

"Sweet Home Alabama," which spoke with pride and defiance of men who communed around a tough, hard-living machismo, became radio hits.

In 1978, a new television series, *The Dukes of Hazzard*, quickly became a huge hit outside major metros. The Dukes were an extended family living in rural Georgia. Hunk cousins Bo and Luke built a hot rod, the "General Lee," from junkyard parts and painted a confederate flag on its top. Bo and Luke loved fast, dangerous driving and spent most of their time in thrilling car chases, taking death-defying jumps as they eluded the corrupt local sheriff. The program delivered the same myth, week after week: Guys who thrived on perilous excitement—rather than dedicate themselves to company jobs—were sexy and heroic.

Mountain Dew's Redneck Myth

PepsiCo and BBDO retooled Mountain Dew's hillbilly from the 1960s to deliver a redneck perspective on Reagan's Wall Street frontier. The brand team borrowed directly from other redneck myths, particularly the *Dukes of Hazzard*. For example, an ad called "Rope Toss" (1981) presented an informal teen outing in lush, hilly terrain. A sinewy young man dressed only in brief shorts and running shoes stood on a ledge far above a river. He waited with his young buddies for the perfect moment to swing out, Tarzan style, over the river on a knotted rope. On the opposite bank four teenage girls swung another empty rope out to meet him halfway. Filmed in slow motion, he executed the switcheroo perfectly, his lithe body taut and rippling as he released the first rope to grab the second, after which he swung safely to the other river bank. The enthusiastic girls cheered his rite of passage and greeted him with excited, pogo-stick bouncing. Intercut with the action, we saw the hero in close-ups, soaking wet, chugging a bottle of cold Dew. By the spot's end, he'd polished off the entire green pint without coming up for air. Shaking the water from his hair like a Labrador retriever, he faced the camera, eyes shut but mouth wide open. The film froze as he seemingly shouted, "Ahh!"

Throughout the 1980s, in ad after ad, Mountain Dew performed variations on this new version of the wild man in which the centerpiece was the rural watering hole. The action revolved around boys peacocking for girls by taking exciting, watery plunges whose thirst-quenching connotations could easily be redirected by viewers in more libidinous directions.

When corporate executives donned cowboy gear as fashion in the mid-1980s, Mountain Dew responded even more assertively with a new campaign called "Doin' It Country Cool." Handsome, scantily clothed young men still performed athletically to impress the young women who lined up to watch them. But this time, the guys wore cowboy hats and were considerably more clever in their adventures. "Horse Ski" began with shirtless, cowboy-hatted guys riding horses down the bank of a river. Or so the audience was led to believe. With a co-ed crowd gathered on the bank, one of these guys tossed a lasso to another who floated in the water. A horse was spurred, a "Yahoo!" shouted, and the horse raced down the riverbed. The guy in the water (Brad Pitt, in one of his first acting gigs) popped up on water skis, and away he went, towed behind the horse. A dozen similar vignettes were produced, which combined to offer a powerful new installation of the redneck myth. Rather than buy the cowboy as a fashion, as yuppies supposedly did with their expensive toys, these were real cowboys, guys who were inventive enough to create their own fun, making do with what they had. Like "Rope Toss," these performances celebrated the virility of redneck populists, but with a message that pushed aside Wall Street's wannabe cowboys. Mountain Dew implicitly argued through these mythic mini-dramas that virile guys live to play dangerously, not to sweat it out on the job.

Cultural Disruption Destroys the Redneck Myth

Mountain Dew's story of virile, athletic working-class guys who had access to a type of manhood unavailable to the flaccid, indulgent Wall Street yuppie had traction as long as American ideology heroized Wall Street's buccaneers. But, in 1987, the nation became rapidly disenchanted with the Wall Street frontier as Reagan left office, scandals rocked Wall Street, and the stock market crashed. The quest to hoard the most goodies did not jibe with the frontier ethos. Neither did the fact that privileged insiders were the stars of the economy, rather than the adventurous entrepreneurs promised by Reagan. A deluge of popular books and films like *Barbarians at the Gate* and *Wall Street,* which excoriated arbitrageurs for their greed and indulgence, punctuated the end of this era. As a new, more aggressive and more individualistic version of the frontier ethos took hold, Mountain Dew's redneck myth shrunk to naive irrelevance like the hillbilly myth before.

The Slacker Myth

Responding to this disruption, PepsiCo ditched Mountain Dew's redneck myth and worked with BBDO to experiment with new advertising. Three years of trial-and-error finally yielded a new myth that addressed new contradictions faced by Mountain Dew's constituents.

National Ideology: The Free-Agent Frontier

As Wall Street finished dismantling the conglomerates in the late 1980s, a new organization form—the networked firm—began to take shape. These especially agile companies continued to outsource production on a global basis. They also aggressively outsourced all other functions that were not core to the firm's business, boldly invested in technology to replace labor costs, and used process engineering techniques to rationalize white-collar work. Workers of all stripes now faced a Hobbesian, winner-take-all labor market. Every company job was up for grabs to the most talented and most tenacious worker, as firms threw out seniority systems in favor of performance-driven meritocracies.

As this new economy emerged, a turbocharged version of Reagan's frontier myth took hold, this one lauding heroic individual achievement. Gone were Wall Street's buccaneers. In their place came the most successful adventurers, entrepreneurs, and athletes. The United States celebrated heroic individual achievement, explorers who conquered new territory, and athlete's victories in the most competitive battles. Michael Jordan and his brand of in-your-face NBA basketball was the iconic hero of the time. Professionals no longer savored expensive dining and Rolexes. Now they groomed their bodies for heated competition by heading into the wilderness for tests of will against white water and mountains. Sport utility vehicles exploded in popularity, and Montana ranches were the new frontier dream. The aptly named Ford Explorer told us that life had no boundaries. One's manhood was revealed in the tackling of extremely difficult and sometimes dangerous challenges, which demanded both mental and physical toughness.

Cultural Contradiction: Manhood via Work Is a Joke

This new version of the frontier galvanized managers and professionals in top positions, as well as those who competed for these positions. But many workers were pushed into a secondary labor market with depressed wages and no job security and into service-economy work that promised a serial progression through stifling, micromanaged McJobs. The lower tier of middle-class jobs was pinched by these forces as well. Continual downsizing and restructuring transferred workers' stress from the shop floor to the office. College no longer guaranteed a professional career. Working hard to pursue a solid career became increasingly like playing the lottery, a game with poor odds in which the distance between winning and losing widened each year.

Tensions between the free-agent frontier and the realities of work were extraordinary. At the moment when many young men were moving into jobs as telemarketers and retail clerks, mass culture was lauding executives who conquered markets, technology, white water, and rock walls, all in a week's work. To make matters worse, in households across the United States, parents pushed even harder to keep their children's hearts and minds dedicated to making it in this fiercely competitive job market.

Popular TV programs like *Roseanne* and *The Simpsons* expressed a new cynicism toward work and corporations. The cartoon strip *Dilbert*, which satirized the McJob life, became the nation's favorite. Populist diatribes from the likes of Rush Limbaugh, Pat Buchanan, Jerry Brown, Howard Stern, and Ross Perot attracted millions of fans.

Parents' insecurities created a new epithet: *slackers*. They applied this term to Peter Pan–like young adults who would rather pursue quixotic cultural activities than grow up and become serious about a career. Slackers were caricatured as directionless zombies lacking the maturity to accept adult challenges.

This epithet was a double whammy for youths lacking good career prospects. First, the nation now championed executives and celebrities with the physical vigor and daring-do that was previously ascribed to the working class. At the same time, being called a slacker was a sucker punch. Youths were responding rationally to downshifted economic incentives by investing less energy in work and education, yet society told them that they were immoral for doing so. These tensions produced a tremendous swell of demand for myth products capable of reconciling these new tensions.

The Slacker Myth Market

An enormous myth market sprang up to feed these anxieties, reclaiming the slacker as a hero of sorts. In his quasi-novel *Generation X*, Douglas

Coupland provided an ironic slacker lexicon (such as *McJobs*) and envisioned the heroic possibilities of pushing as far away from the new work ethos as possible. The same year, Richard Linklater's documentary, *Slacker*, told a compelling story of a community of quirky, charming folks who come together around their lack of interest in pursuing the American Dream. Television networks like Fox, MTV, and ESPN2 quickly picked up on the slacker ethos and delivered programming that emphasized what would become the key tenets: do-it-yourself, melodramatic iconoclasm, extreme manhood, and recycling pop culture.

> *Do-it-yourself:* Rather than the rule-bound, domineering competitions found in professional team sport leagues like the NBA, slacker culture favored do-it-yourself (DIY), improvisational athletics, new sports that participants pursued with a minimum of corporate interference. Skateboarders, for instance, favored outdoor spaces many nonskaters would find dangerous: concrete staircases and embankments, tall curbs, ramps, fountains, and sculptures. They sought public spaces—access to which was free but often forbidden—to scrape their boards down handrails and flip from statues in the town square.
>
> The DIY sensibility applied to music and other entertainment, as well. Rock and roll had always been DIY. Surf started as outlaw music, as did the rockabilly rockers of the 1950s and the psychedelic movement of the 1960s. But these once marginal genres soon became part of mass culture and big business. Not until the 1970s punk movement, ignited by the Ramones in the United States and the Sex Pistols in the United Kingdom, did we see a defiantly DIY movement that took on resistance to mass market-commodification as central to its ethos. This idea took root in the American indie (independent) music scene of the 1980s and finally burst into national attention with the meteoric rise of Nirvana in the early 1990s. The DIY aesthetic asserted that, rather than listening to a Janet Jackson CD, youths should make their own music. Slacker culture found synergy with its urban African American analog, hip-hop, in which anyone with a turntable and some old records could make vital music; anyone could be a musician.
>
> *Melodramatic iconoclasm:* Slacker culture ripped apart the most cherished values and norms of American ideology. *The Simpsons*

launched a genre that dominated youth TV in the 1990s. Other offerings in the genre included *Beavis and Butthead, Wayne's World, South Park, Jackass,* and the tabloid talk shows, led by Jerry Springer and Jenny Jones. Pleasure now came from grossly violating the norms of middle-class society for a good laugh. Whereas 1960s counterculture experimented with new norms, slacker took a more nihilist tact, sneering at civility rather than revolutionizing it.

Extreme manhood: The slacker took the masculine expressions of the new American ideology—competing in the toughest contests and willingness to take on risk—and turned up the adrenaline to a melodramatic extreme. So-called extreme sports became the rage, with MTV and ESPN promoting "sports" that featured guys fearlessly risking bodily harm to perform crazy, never-before-attempted stunts. All-star wrestling on *WWF Smackdown!* became a top entertainment choice of the day. And ultraviolent video games allowed guys to spend hour after hour reveling in manhood fantasies.

Recycling pop culture: What marketers called *retro* consumption in television, fashion, and music was deeply inspired by DIY. In the late 1970s, the DIY counterculturalists had begun rummaging through artifacts of the postwar culture, finding kitschy clothes, peculiar home decor, and odd music genres that marketers had bypassed. Later, slackers added television programs and esoteric film genres to the list. The underlying aesthetic, regardless of the particular style in play, was the same. Rather than accept what corporations marketed, slacker counterculturalists reclaimed what had been discarded as worthless. In the ultimate act of one-upsmanship, slackers showed corporations that they could take the most worthless stuff and make it valuable with the power of their creativity and imagination. No marketing needed, thank you. The hit 1993 movie *Wayne's World* moved this idea from the underground to youth culture, proposing an ironic, DIY one-upsmanship over corporate marketing. In the same period, the rock band Nirvana broke through with its anthemic jab at youth branding, "Smells Like Teen Spirit." The massive hit in which Kurt Cobain taunted marketers and the mass media—"here we are now, entertain us"—in the end told them to go away: "Oh well, whatever, never mind."

Mountain Dew's Slacker Myth

Mountain Dew's redneck myth was reformulated to speak from within the new populist world of the slacker. A hugely successful ad campaign, featuring the tag line "Do the Dew," drew on the plethora of source material available in the slacker myth market. An ad called "Done That" was the first breakthrough. The spot opened with a hair-raising shot of a guy jumping off the edge of a cliff to take a free fall toward the narrow canyon's river bottom. Accompanied by a thrashy metal soundtrack, a stomach-tightening shot trailed behind the jumper's feet as he fell away from the cliff. The music stopped abruptly and the camera zoomed toward four young men, dressed like low-rent gym rats, standing in the Mojave Desert. The guys hung on each other in a kind of casual street camaraderie. In rapid succession each mugged for the camera and commented on the skydiving the viewers had just seen: "Done that." "Did that." "Been there." "Tried that."

The camera returned to live action, following an athlete diving off a twenty-foot waterfall on a boogie board and "surfing" the rapids on his belly. The four dudes returned, still among Mojave cacti, and quickly announced their boredom with that high-risk activity. The dudes' dismissive words painted only half the picture. Their cocky body language betrayed no fear of the camera; each leaning toward it to make absolutely certain that no one could mistake his feelings. The guys, parodying the testosterone-induced jockeying of young bucks in business, played at being cocksure daredevils for kicks.

The loud soundtrack resumed as abruptly as it had stopped as the camera cut to a Mountain Dew dispensing machine in a jungle setting. "Whoa!" "Never did it." "Never guzzled it." Dew cans blasted like cannon shells from the machine's delivery slot. Each dude snatched a can from the air and chugged it down under the desert sun. Sated, they repeated in rapid succession: "Did it." "Done it." "Liked it." "Loved it."

In the three sequels that followed, the stunts became increasingly fantastic and absurd: water skiing behind a helicopter past icebergs in the North Pole, in-line skating off the Sphinx in Egypt, wrestling an alligator in the Amazon, taking a platform jump off London's Big Ben clock tower. With less preposterous stunts, the dudes' tastes became fickle. After a skier shot off of a cliff and fell precipitously with no landing in sight, he somersaulted and opened a parachute. The dudes appeared in front of a sun-washed sand dune to dismiss the move: "Blasé." "Passé." "Okay." "Cliché." A rock climber rappelled head-first, a mountain biker leaped in front of a wall of flames, a surfer launched off a desert sand dune, a scuba diver hand-fed a voracious shark, and a snowboarder tumbled mercilessly head over heels down a steep slope, but the dudes' posturing grew only more aggressively indifferent: "Obvious." "Frivolous." "Tedious." "What a wuss!"

Why were these ads so commanding? The celebrated spots used extreme sports with dramatic action film cinematography, but so had prior Mountain Dew ads, with little impact. The campaign's success was due to *how* the ads presented these daredevil stunts. With this campaign, Mountain Dew's redneck ethos was revamped into the vernacular of the slacker. Three slacker elements woven into the mix made all the difference.

First, the extreme sports were presented as DIY quests, not as competitions. The most admired protagonists weren't the most buff or competitive athletes, but the most creative guys who pursued their dangerous quests as whimsical art. In the land of Dew, guys played a game of goofy one-upmanship, in which nothing mattered except inventing the craziest and most death-defying stunts. The ads suggested that although professionals may have thought themselves as heroes through their world-changing innovations and their weekend warrior escapades, they took themselves way too seriously and possessed little imaginative flair. The dudes even used corporate buildings as their playgrounds to emphasize the point.

Second, the Dew guys didn't just face down dangerous situations that came their way. They sought out insane risks, well beyond what the ideology was then serving up. They lived for the adrenaline thrill of life-threatening feats. This posturing upped the ante on risk taking to absurd levels, which, in the end, made fun of the whole idea that manhood has anything to do with such feats.

Finally, the ultimate heroes of the ads were not extreme-sports enthusiasts or even the whacked-out slacker extremists. In Mountain Dew's warped worldview, the people with real power were consumers who asserted peculiar tastes. The Dew dudes weren't particularly athletic. But as extreme-sport connoisseurs, they had nuanced opinions about great stunts. And they enforced these standards as exacting gatekeepers, like Olympic judges. Slackers had no power as workers. But they could assert their will over companies and their managers by exercising their opinions. Mountain Dew's new view of manhood proclaimed, with heavy satire, that guys who had lost out in the new labor market still had potency because they could hold court with their ultrachoosy tastes. They could force companies to respond to their every whim.

How Myth Markets Work

PepsiCo and BBDO built Mountain Dew into an extraordinary financial success because they twice reinvented the brand's myth. Each time American ideology shifted, the brand located a new cultural contradiction that had created anxieties for its constituency: from masculine conformity, to the celebration of yuppies as America's heroes, to the preposterous ideals of hyperaggressive masculinity in a dreadful labor market. Myth markets formed around each of these tensions, which drew from populist worlds: hillbillies, then rednecks, then slackers. The culture industries mined these populist worlds to create identity myths. And Mountain Dew did likewise (figure 3-1).

The first step in a cultural strategy is to map out the myth markets currently in play in popular culture and to target the myth market most appropriate for the brand.[2] To do so, managers need to understand the three basic building blocks of a myth market: national ideology, cultural contradictions, and populist worlds.

FIGURE 3-1

Mountain Dew's Myth Reinvented Across Three Myth Markets

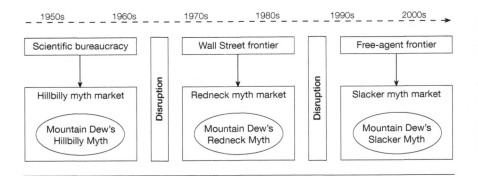

National Ideology

Nations require a moral consensus to function. Citizens must identify with the nation, accept its institutions, and work toward its betterment. Nations are organized around a set of values that defines what is good and just. These moral imperatives propel people to pursue national goals as they strive to meet society's definition of success and respect. This is national ideology, a system of ideas that forges links between everyday life—the aspirations of individuals, families, and communities—and those of the nation. To be effective, a nation's ideology can't be coerced or learned as though from a textbook. Rather, it must be deeply felt, taken for granted as the natural truth. National ideology is usually the most powerful root of consumer demand for myth; though national ideology often intersects and competes with other bases of group identity, especially religion and ethnicity.

Ideology is never expressed directly, as a declarative statement. Instead, ideologies are conveyed through myths. A variety of American myths are critical for the nation to function: the self-made man (which addresses the path to the country's idea of success grounded in economic status), the frontier (which addresses the nation's mission to "civilize" other peoples of the world into its utopian ideals), the melting pot (which expresses ideals about how immigrants can integrate into society), and so forth. Far and away the most important myths concern how citizens are linked to the nation-building project: how Americans, as individuals, see themselves as part of the team to build the nation's economic and political power. These myths are usually constructed around ideals of individual success and manhood—what it takes to be a man. Tracing the evolution of such myths as they are updated to address contemporary social issues is central to charting myth markets.

Cultural Contradictions

Americans don't naturally inhabit the nation's ideology simply because they are citizens of the United States. Rather, it takes work to build these identifications. And life circumstances can make it easier or harder to do so. Many people aspire to the nation's ideals, but have trouble seeing how their lives match up.

These tensions between ideology and individual experience produce intense desires and anxieties, fueling demand for symbolic resolutions that

FIGURE 3-2

The Structure of a Myth Market

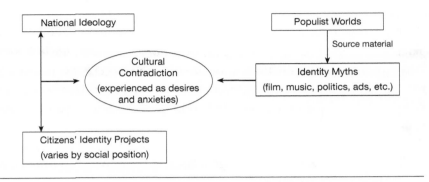

smooth over the tensions. National ideologies create models for living. The distance between that model and everyday life acts as a cultural engine, creating demand for myths that manage these differences.

These tensions are particularly acute when the nation's ideology shifts.[3] Periods of cultural ferment produce myriad contradictions, which in turn create veins of intense consumer anxieties and desires that ripple throughout society (figure 3-2).

Populist Worlds

Myths rely on populist worlds as raw ingredients. Mountain Dew employed the populist worlds of the hillbilly, the rebel, and then the slacker, as did other cultural products in these eras. Populist worlds are groups that express a distinctive ideology through their activities. They are potent cultural sites because the public perceives that populist world ideologies are authentic. This perceived authenticity stems from three characteristics:

1. Populist worlds are perceived as "folk cultures"—their ethos is the collective and voluntary product of their participants. The ethos has not been imposed upon them.

2. The activities within the populist world are perceived as intrinsically valuable to the participants. They are not motivated by commercial or political interests.

3. Reinforcing these perceptions, populist worlds are often set in places far removed from centers of commerce and politics. For worlds that have been commercialized (sports and music are key examples), these populist perceptions are much harder to maintain because the participants must fight off the commercial attributions.

Populist worlds are places where the public assumes that people's actions are motivated by belief instead of interest. The source materials for American myths exist wherever populism takes its most authentic form. Populism thrives wherever people are thought to act according to their own beliefs rather than have their actions shaped by society's institutions: on the frontier, in bohemia communities, in rural backwaters, in immigrant and African American neighborhoods, in youth subcultures. Of late, childhood has become one of the most powerful populist worlds used for brand myths.

Populist worlds supply the raw ingredients that iconic brands draw on to create their myths. The people who consume these myths rarely inhabit the populist world. Rather, the myth provides them with an imaginary connection to the world. The authenticity of these populist worlds gives the myth credibility. Because the myth is grounded in a populist world, its consumers believe that it is not entirely fictional. Implicitly, they think "There are people in the world who really live this way, so I can bring some of these values into my own life."

Myth Markets

Contradictions in the national ideology create myth markets. A wide variety of cultural products compete to provide the most compelling myths: stories that will provide symbolic sustenance to shore up the contradiction. At any given time in American society, there are a number of acute cultural contradictions. And each contradiction spawns a distinctive myth market.

Think of myth markets as implicit public conversations centered around the national ideology. This ideology is taken up by a variety of contenders with different viewpoints. By contenders, I mean popular culture in all its forms: films, television programs, music, books, magazines, newspapers, sports, politics, talk radio, video games, and, of particular interest here, brands. We usually think of popular culture as light entertainment and a record of current events, economically important but culturally trivial. Most of the time, this characterization is true. Myths, on the other hand, are much more than mere entertainment or news; they are the primary medium through which we participate in the nation's culture. Like other cultural products, a brand performs myths through its associated stories, primarily through advertisements. Then, as the customers ritually consume the product, they relive these stories.

Iconic brands rarely develop their myths from wholly original cloth. Rather, these brands typically borrow and add to existing myths circulated by other cultural products. Generally parasitic, an iconic brand seldom competes head-on with other cultural products—films, television, and the like. In terms of myth performances, brands can never compete with films, politicians, or musicians. Even the best sixty-second ad (say, Nike's "Revolution" or Apple's "1984"), can't compete with John Wayne's films, Ronald Reagan's speeches, or Kurt Cobain's songs and concerts.

But brands have an advantage over these more ephemeral figures in that they provide a material connection to the myth. Because brands load the myth into products used every day, brands can provide for ritual action (the ability to viscerally experience the myth through one's actions) in a way that a poster in a bedroom or an occasional gathering for a rally or concert cannot.

With only a handful of exceptions (Volkswagen and Nike stand out), brands do not so much originate new expressive culture as they recycle materials placed into circulation by other media (e.g., film, television, music, journalism, books). Mountain Dew's hillbilly myth borrowed from the *Li'l Abner* cartoon (e.g., stereotypes about drinking moonshine and running barefoot) and was informed by other contemporaneous myths, like *The Beverly Hillbillies*. Likewise, Mountain Dew's redneck myth was substantially influenced by, and played off, the television program *The Dukes of Hazzard*. And the brand's slacker myth was tremendously influenced both by *Wayne's World* and by MTV's portrayal of extreme sports. Iconic brands leap into emerging myth markets usually led by other mass-cultural products. That said, chapter 4 explains that iconic brands do not merely imitate. They develop a distinctive point of view and aesthetic as they recycle these cultural materials.

Myth markets eventually crumble when cultural disruptions hit. As a result, iconic brands remain iconic only if they abandon their old myth and invent a revised version that taps into a new myth market. Mountain

Dew has maintained its iconic hold across dramatically different periods in American culture because—as the nation's ideology shifted from scientific-bureaucracy to Wall Street frontier to free-agent frontier—the brand reinvented its myth to target a new contradiction that each ideology produced.

CHAPTER 4

Composing the Cultural Brief

To become an icon, a brand must not only target the most advantageous contradiction in society, but also perform the right myth, and in the right manner. In mind-share and emotional branding, storytelling is left to creatives as an executional issue. In viral branding, influential customers are charged with telling the brand's stories. In cultural branding, the story itself must be the center of strategy, because the quality of the myth, not some set of abstractions, drives the brand's identity value. For the brand strategy to influence market results, it must direct what kind of story the brand will tell and how that brand tells it.

Conventionally, the positioning statement is the heart of the brand strategy. Positioning statements typically identify the set of associations (benefits, quality, user imagery, etc.) that the brand should own, the support for claiming these associations, and perhaps the tone or personality by which the brand should speak to its prospects about these concepts. For advertising purposes, the brand's positioning is expanded into *the creative brief,* but the content is much the same. Overall, positioning statements are arguments for the brand relative to other brands in the category and are based on abstracted associations. For example, consider this Mountain Dew positioning statement used by PepsiCo in the 1990s as the core of its creative brief:

> To 18-year-old males, who embrace excitement, adventure and fun, Mountain Dew is the great tasting carbonated soft drink that exhilarates like no other because it is energizing, [is] thirst-quenching, and has a one-of-a-kind citrus flavor.[1]

This statement defines the target in terms of age and psychographics and then directs the creatives to communicate a laundry list of benefits: its exhilarating and energizing effects, its thirst-quenching ability, and its distinctive citrus flavor. Compare this statement to Mountain Dew's slacker myth described in chapter 3, and note what is missing. The statement is focused on product benefits and product experiences. It contains no directions that might guide how creatives should concoct Mountain Dew's myth. As a result, the guidance offered by this statement lacks strategic value. Sure, the "Do the Dew" campaign fits within these guidelines. But so do hundreds of other mediocre ideas. Viewing strategy as a set of abstractions leads managers to focus attention on matters that will only trivially affect the brand, while leaving the most important strategic questions to fate and hunches. PepsiCo is certainly no exception in this regard. Historically, iconic brands have been built *in spite of* strategies that push the brand toward more mundane objectives.

Cultural branding requires strategic direction that pushes commercial artists toward creating the right kind of story for the brand and rules out inappropriate stories. In so doing, a cultural strategy must avoid imposing irrelevant guidelines that distort and artificially narrow what stories the brand can tell. In other words, cultural branding requires abandoning typical mind-share directives—sell this benefit, express that emotion, show the product in use in this way, cast these actors because our customers aspire to be like them, and so on. Instead, strategies should move toward prescribing what kind of story the brand should tell to address a particular cultural contradiction of the day.

Elements of the Cultural Brief

The cultural analogue to the positioning statement is the cultural brief. Cultural briefs have three components:

Myth treatment: In the film and television industries, where storytelling is at the center of the enterprise, stories are directed by *treatments,* a briefing document that sets up the plot, characters, and setting. In advertising, such treatments are usually found in the creative ideas that ad agencies present their clients. But for identity brands, creative ideas are not merely instruments to deliver benefits. Rather, they embody the brand's proposed role in the culture. Managers must be closely involved in working out these treatments— carefully considering how well the outlined story addresses opportune cultural contradictions. Otherwise, they necessarily surrender responsibility for the brand's strategy to other organizations.[2]

Populist authenticity: Brand myths draw from populist worlds to secure source materials that audiences perceive as credible. Brands cannot, however, simply grab elements of a promising populist world and repackage them for a mass audience. Many companies have tried this and failed. Rather, iconic brands earn through their actions a credible place within the populist world. The audience must perceive that the brand has authentic ties to the populist world, and is not simply acting as a parasite. Brands earn consumers' respect as authentic when they deliver on two qualities: *literacy* and *fidelity*. All populist worlds have their own idioms and idiosyncratic cultural codes. Brands demonstrate literacy through performances that reveal a nuanced understanding of these codes and idioms. The glue that holds together any populist world is its distinctive ethos. Brands demonstrate fidelity to the populist world by sacrificing broad-based popularity to stand up for this ethos.

Charismatic aesthetic: To win over audiences with their myths, iconic brands' communications must exude charisma—a distinctive and compelling style that epitomizes the populist world from which they speak. Just like a successful political leader or social activist, iconic brands compel audiences to enter their worldview by adopting a distinctive and compelling aesthetic style that's organic to the brand's populist world.

In sum, brand myths succeed when the brand performs the right story, which is authentically grounded in the brand's populist world, and is executed with a charismatic aesthetic. In this chapter, I reverse-engineer the cultural briefs for Volkswagen's original myth, crafted by Doyle Dane Bernbach (DDB), and then the second myth developed thirty-five years later by Arnold Communications in its "Drivers Wanted" campaign.

DDB's Bohemian Myth

In 1970, the Volkswagen Beetle was one of the most powerful iconic brands in the United States. Volkswagen was selling more than 400,000 Beetles each year, controlling about 5 percent of the auto market, and had earned a coveted place in popular culture. The advertising campaign that pro-pelled the Beetle to this heralded position was created by DDB and is leg-endary in advertising lore for leading the creative revolution. Compared to its predecessors, the campaign appeared to be smarter and, because it en-gaged its audience in a more humanistic interchange, more artistic. A host of overtly creative-driven campaigns followed—from Alka-Seltzer to 7 UP to Braniff—as did many spin-off agencies founded by executives who had earned their stripes at DDB.

Although DDB's impact on advertising was profound, the agency's work on Volkswagen also left an important but previously unnoticed legacy for branding. Along with Leo Burnett's contemporaneous work on Marlboro and a handful of smaller efforts, such as the regional Mountain Dew campaign, DDB helped invent the foundational mythmaking princi-ples that turn brands into icons. To understand these principles, we need to examine the Volkswagen campaign, not based on how the ads looked compared to other ads, but based on how the brand engaged American culture. How did the Volkswagen campaign imbue this odd vehicle with such extraordinary identity value?

Targeting the Conformist Contradiction

American ideology after World War II was orchestrated around a consen-sus view of the good life.[3] Promoted by the rising class of psychological specialists in family magazines, by Hollywood in prime-time TV pro-grams, by Madison Avenue ads, and even by the federal government with its subsidies, the good life supposedly could be found in the new planned suburbs. Americans dreamed of owning a ranch home filled with the newest household appliances; the advertised national brands like Coke, Budweiser, Campbells, and Maytag which embraced the nuclear life; and, of course, a new model auto parked outside that reflected the latest in tech-nology and design. Marketers hawked these goods with untethered enthu-siasm. Ads uniformly trumpeted the newest, most scientifically advanced products as the only way to truly enjoy the new American lifestyle.

Detroit automobile design and advertising worked lockstep with this myth. Americans would secure a place in the corporate pecking order, and GM, Ford, and Chrysler would supply them the right car. No need to worry about the choice, for Detroit would engineer a car just right for their place in life. As families climbed the social status ladder, General Motors provided vehicles for each step: A Chevrolet begets a Buick, which begets an Oldsmobile, which begets a Cadillac.

To ensure that demand kept up with the burgeoning supply of autos, the industry promoted autos as badges of contemporary style whose value quickly faded. Each model year, manufacturers changed features to make the older design obsolete, pushing it out of fashion so that people would want the new au courant stuff, just like the latest Parisian designs. Auto ads at the time were the paragon of hype. Glamor, status, and masculinity were the goals, and these ideals were conveyed with sexy centerfold shots of the auto, often accessorized with beautiful women on the hood (except for the new "woman's car," the station wagon, of course). The design and advertising emphasized ornament: flashy features of the car, the latest whiz-bang technical components, and creature comforts. Consequently, when Americans bought autos, they were quite literally buying a piece of the American Dream as it was then proffered.

Many people, particularly the young, urban, and educated middle class, experienced this consensus mode of consumption as overly scripted and conformist. For people put off by the pressures to adhere to the bureaucratic suburban standards, driving an auto prepackaged with these norms felt coercive. Because autos were one of the most visible symbols of 1950s conformity, the category offered a prime opportunity to target this contradiction as it became acute.

The Volkswagen Beetle was considered one of the ugliest and least reliable cars on the road. While it was cheap, maneuverable, and durable, it also broke down regularly and was very small and Spartan. Above all, the car was considered anachronistic and unattractive compared to sleek Detroit designs. Associations with Nazi Germany—as the auto that Hitler developed as "the people's car"—still haunted the brand. When DDB took the account in 1959, the Beetle design was already fifteen years old, this at a time when Detroit was making quick and dramatic design changes to its models. By the standards of America's new good-life ideals, the Beetle failed on every count.

DDB's campaign flipped this seeming deficit on its head, tacitly implementing the three elements of the cultural brief.

DDB's Myth Treatment

Consider a classic ad from the campaign: "Lemon" (1960) was a print ad describing the lengths that Volkswagen's quality control department took to minimize the defects of its cars. The photo of the Beetle appeared to be a product beauty shot typically found in print advertising. But the copy told the reader that this car was defective. The ad's text was about Volkswagen's finicky quality-control standards: A Beetle had come off the line in Wolfsburg, Germany, with a blemish on the chrome trim around the glove box. Company inspectors caught it and sent the car back to be fixed.

While the ad was explicitly concerned with quality control, the ad's subtext aimed squarely at Detroit and American consumer advertising more generally. Against Detroit's hyping of the style and performance of its technical wonders, Volkswagen had the audacity to profile a damaged car and trumpet the car's problems. Volkswagen used an ad as a medium to playfully poke fun at the conventional wisdom of the day.

In ad after ad, Volkswagen hawked the Beetle in terms of what textbooks now call functional benefits: good gas mileage, airtight construction, best-of-class engine, great resale prices, and so on. Volkswagen stood squarely for the practical and the frugal. But these strident, pragmatic claims—couched in self-deprecating humor—were also potshots aimed at the puffed-up posturing coming out of Detroit. Volkswagen's seemingly heavy-handed nuts-and-bolts hard sell was, in reality, a clever means to create Volkswagen as the antihype vehicle—the car stripped bare of all the manipulative marketing machinations that Vance Packard and others had warned about.

Volkswagen offered to its customers a car unencumbered by a Madison Avenue image, in effect telling its audience, "You're too sharp and too much of an individual to be suckered by mass-marketed images. We just supply you the canvas, stripped bare of any pretense, and it's up to you to put your identity into it." DDB's ads empowered Beetle owners to create their own stories with their cars rather than rely on marketers to do so. And owners did just this. Many treated their Beetle as a member of the family, and gave their Beetle a name as if it were a pet.[4]

DDB's myth treatment can be summarized as follows: Volkswagen stands against the imposed lifestyles and tastes of mass culture and particularly of Madison Avenue. Volkswagen creates a world in which the customers are intelligent and creative people who can define for themselves what is stylish and beautiful. So Volkswagen acts as a smart-ass friend, offering up the unvarnished truth about how its cars are built and sold.

Earning Authenticity in the Art World

When DDB received the Volkswagen assignment in 1959, the contradictions that had formed in response to America's new ideology had already stimulated several potent myth markets that organized around populist worlds of the day. While Mountain Dew made use of the hillbilly to address conformity at work, Volkswagen targeted another populist world: the bohemian art world centered in New York City and other large cities to take on conformity in mass culture.

The most acerbic rebellion against the 1950s scientific-bureaucratic ideology came from intellectuals and artists. Social critics like C. Wright Mills, William Whyte, and David Riesman lambasted the new ideology for its lemming-like conformity. Literary critics like Dwight MacDonald fretted about the debasing of high culture. And artists such as the abstract impressionists spawned art movements that posed a direct aesthetic challenge to the new instrumental personalities of the day.

DDB's advertising quickly captured the imagination of the literati in the major coastal cities. This is not surprising, as DDB creatives hobnobbed in social circles that intersected with the avant-garde. DDB's key staffers were Jewish urbanites in a heretofore staid business dominated by Ivy League men. With the Volkswagen campaign, the creatives sought to make ads that their art-world peers would find hip and interesting, an absolutely novel approach that violated the customer-centric approaches that ruled then as now. Beetle branding was a concerted effort to create advertising that would actually impress New York's jaded bohemians, a group notoriously hostile toward Madison Avenue advertising of the day.

DDB's Literacy. To be perceived as authentic, the campaign had to adopt the art world's disdain for mass culture and its advertising. Moreover, Volkswagen had to heap scorn on Detroit with the élan expected of a leading member of the intelligentsia. The criticism had to be ironic and under the table, not simply a direct assault. The real trick was to avoid substituting a new, more bohemian-centric image for the car. Bohemians would easily see through this sleight of hand. Rather, Volkswagen ads had to make bohemian insiders conclude that, since Volkswagen was "one of us," the company didn't want to push any sort of commodified associations onto the car.

And this is what DDB did. In one seminal early print ad, "Think Small" (1960), Volkswagen attacked the patriarchal undercurrent of the existing hierarchy of auto models, in which the bigger and more expensive the car, the more status the owner has. In Detroit's symbolic competition, the size of the car and its engine were emblems of manliness. The psychosexual innuendoes were everywhere and rarely oblique. Every year, the stakes were raised. Advertisers even used photographic tricks to make the cars look bigger.[5]

DDB took a different tack. It photographed the Beetle from above and from the dead-square front of the auto, making a very small and rotund car look even smaller, more feminine, and more un-car-like. The declaration to think small was a devastating left hook to Detroit's macho posturings. In two words and one unadorned photo, Volkswagen mocked the car industry's ethos and replaced it with a more feminine and bohemian sensibility.

The magic of the DDB campaign was that, rather than promote nonconformist ideals, the advertising spoke from within the bohemian milieu as an insider to comment on what was going on outside in Detroit. There were no smoky underground jazz clubs or poetry readings. Instead of trying to hop on to the counterculture through imitation, Volkswagen acted like a particularly clever and creative insider.

DDB's Fidelity. Volkswagen never tried to stretch its point of view to reach a broader mass audience. If anything, Volkswagen turned up the volume of its critiques. For example, in response to Detroit's efforts to get customers to trade up to a more expensive model, Volkswagen chided the audience to "Live below your means." In ad after ad for over a decade, the brand heaped more and more puns and clever tongue-lashings on Detroit's propensity to dictate consumer tastes.

This willingness to defend a particular set of ideas, even when they offend a substantial fraction of the buying public, is a consistent thread among iconic brands. The longer Volkswagen stuck with its artworld-influenced values, the more respect it engendered for its commitment to this vision. This wasn't a company trying to sell a line; this was a committed philosophy that Volkswagen happened to express through a funny-looking car.

The campaign was so compelling in championing the anti-mass-market view that, when bohemia later exploded into the full-blown hippie counterculture, the Beetle was the obvious choice as the standard-bearing vehicle. For hippies, the creative reconstruction of the self—through drugs, philosophy, new living situations, and experiments of all kinds—was the order of the day. Cultural experimentation was in. And the Beetle quickly became the choice ride for these experimenters. The car provided the mobile space where free-spirited people pursued existential experiments. People started calling the car "the love bug," for its associations with the hippies and their "make love, not war" mantra. A film by the same name became a hit.

Volkswagen didn't make much money on hippies. Rather, as the hippie ethos became extraordinarily influential and valued in 1960s American culture, the Beetle became a symbol through which other Americans could access the hippie world. The Volkswagen Beetle had become an icon: In condensed form, the auto embodied a creative, sensual, and libertarian sensibility that allowed people who owned one to transcend the anxieties they felt with the bureaucratic-scientific ideology.

As mainstream Americans began to respond to hippie ideas and experiment with them—growing their sideburns, throwing away their bras, listening to rock music—the Beetle was an apt container for these ideas. Thus, when the counterculture became mainstreamed, when it moved from a fringe populist activity in coastal cities and college towns to become the zeitgeist of the times, Volkswagen sales exploded. Now you could drive a Beetle as a sales rep in Peoria and feel as if you were at the center of a whirlwind of cultural change in which all social norms were subject to challenge.

DDB's Charismatic Aesthetic

Automobile advertising of the 1950s and early 1960s was all hype: glib pronouncements claiming the biggest, shiniest, newest, sexiest, most modern, most sophisticated. Print advertisements were styled to glamorize the auto, like a model in a fashion magazine. Volkswagen offered up the antithesis: an aesthetic that combined a cutting sense of humor with the minimalist aesthetic of high modern design.

Volkswagen print ads became famous for their clever headlines that poked fun at Detroit. But some of the television advertising carried an even more powerful sting. One of Volkswagen's most provocative ads, "Auto Show," presented a fictional account of an auto show set in 1949. Crowds packed around car displays of Volkswagen's competitors: A slick announcer selling DeSoto intoned, "The car of the future, the car everyone wants." A high-society maven pushing the Studebaker advised, "Long skirts will be the next look on the fashion scene and the Studebaker will be the next look on the automotive scene." A scientist lectured, "Next year every car in America will have holes in it." A female a cappella group harmonized, "The Forty-nine Hudson will be the car for you." Meanwhile, an earnest salesman standing in front of an empty Volkswagen showroom declared, "So Volkswagen will constantly be changing, improving, refining this car, not necessarily to keep in style with the times, but to make a better car." The Volkswagen on display was identical to previous years. The fashion-seeking crowd ignored him. Volkswagen acted as a dry, tongue-in-cheek muckraker, revealing for all to see that Detroit wore no clothes.

The predominant codes for the print ads—an uncluttered layout featuring a black-and-white "beauty" shot of the car with a short and punchy declarative headline—reflected in form Volkswagen's high-brow stance against the lowest-common-denominator pitches of its competitors. While other manufacturers used glossy, stylized portraits and bombastic copy, Volkswagen responded with the austere minimalism then found in the form-equals-function high modernism of Mies van der Rohe skyscrapers and Eames furniture.

Volkswagen television spots carried these same aesthetic elements into film. One of the most famous spots, "Snowplow," told the story of "the car that the snowplow driver drives to work" (in a snowstorm), ostensibly to highlight the Beetle's better traction resulting from the rear engine placement. But, what struck the viewers was the twenty-five-second shot of the snowplow driver driving his plow through a storm before they heard the payoff voice-over that revealed that they were looking at an ad. DDB had delivered on the same striking, minimalism in a television spot.

Mind Share Buries an Icon

DDB and the rest of Madison Avenue learned the wrong lessons from Volkswagen's success. All believed that the Volkswagen campaign proved that if you let ad agencies act as artists rather than as Pavlov's helpers, audiences will connect with the advertising and the results will be stunning. Unbridled creativity became an industry norm. Ad executives fancied that they had joined the avant-garde. But, by the mid-1970s, creativity was dead. Ad agencies that followed the new principle—creativity drives great advertising—didn't generate uniformly good business results. There were the same hits and misses as before. Agencies and their clients learned that creativity was a necessary, but nowhere near sufficient, component in creating brand value.

By the early 1970s, the scientific-bureaucratic ideology that Volkswagen had used as a whipping boy to set up the Beetle campaign had ruptured, and with it the power of the Beetle myth. As the United States entered a period of ideological confusion and soul searching, Volkswagen remained one of the premier cultural authorities for the educated middle class and, thus, could have offered new direction. But this approach would have required that Volkswagen and DDB retool the advertising to offer a new myth that would direct ideological traffic to face up to the meltdown of Vietnam, the Arab oil embargo, and Watergate.

Instead, Volkswagen entirely abandoned the precious cultural authority accumulated over the previous decade. Working on the assumption that creativity alone drove Volkswagen's success, DDB first tried new variations of clever advertising. Then, as the brand team lost confidence, its advertisements reverted to mind share techniques, ditching all efforts to tell stories to the American public that would help them manage their identities.

In 1972, Volkswagen introduced the Super Beetle, a larger version of the Beetle. At a product level, the line extension made perfect sense. After all, one of Volkswagen's outstanding weaknesses compared with the competition was its small interior and trunk space. But Volkswagen was selling a worldview, not comparative product features. A bigger Beetle was fine, but denouncing the "think small" ethos was not. Nevertheless, that's what Volkswagen did. In one spot, comedian Jimmy Durante, he of the very large nose, proclaimed that the new car was big enough for him, his nose, and his lady friends. The new Super Beetle "is so big inside that you won't know it's a Volkswagen until you're outside." Volkswagen had conceded to Detroit's conception of vehicle size, which stated that a small car is a deficient car. Instead of an in-your-face antiestablishment attitude, Volkswagen was now apologizing for its smallness! What's more, the antagonist of quotidian marketing was now using a celebrity spokesman!

After the Super Beetle, the company launched the "Beetle Estate"—an extraordinary branding oxymoron. The advertising used Zsa Zsa Gabor to hawk a luxury Beetle. Zsa Zsa was a film star who played the sophisticated European noblewoman to the hilt. ("Dahhling" was her favorite line. Her sister Eva had become famous on the television series *Green Acres,* in which she played a similarly aristocratic, elegant, and urbane city woman who couldn't quite fathom how farm life worked.) This new limited-edition model was nicknamed "La Grand Bug." Here was a no-winks effort to sell a Volkswagen as a status vehicle using French imagery! For believers who'd traveled with Volkswagen for the past decade, the brand had abandoned ship. For those who hadn't, Volkswagen was simply incoherent.

For the first time, the brand was competing for mind share against the Detroit and Japanese makes, instead of for culture share among the newly liberated middle class, where it had previously encountered no competition at all. In 1975, Volkswagen introduced the Rabbit as the Beetle's replacement. The Rabbit was a great improvement: The new design handled much better, was more functional with its hatchback design, and didn't break down so easily. The Rabbit should have been a great success. But that success required that DDB reinterpret the Volkswagen myth for the new era. Instead, the brand team opted for long-standing clichés of the American auto industry, bragging about the vehicle's greatness and popularity:

- A 1975 Rabbit launch ad artlessly bragged with a huge header consuming the entire page, "The Rabbit is the best car in the world for under $3500."

- The 1978 campaign slogan for the Rabbit was "Volkswagen Does it Again." The copy for one print ad read, "It's just a wonderful car. True, we had a big advantage. We started with a wonderful car and made it even better. Over a million people all over the world have been impressed enough to buy them."

Ten years earlier, Volkswagen could have parodied these puffery-laden ads. Now Volkswagen was just a car claiming that it had the superior benefits at the right price. As such, measured against the Hondas and Toyotas of the day, consumers found Volkswagen lacking. DDB would struggle with the Volkswagen account for the next twenty years, never able to revive Volkswagen's myth originally expressed through the Beetle.

Throughout the 1980s, Volkswagen introduced new models—notably the Golf, Jetta, and GTI—which were well received by the auto press. Though these models didn't amount to much in terms of sales, they helped add a new dimension to the Volkswagen brand. These autos all featured taut handling that Americans were beginning to associate with German makes. Volkswagen succeeded in trading on the engineering prowess of its more expensive brethren—BMW, Mercedes, Audi, and Porsche. Using the tag line, "The German Engineered Volkswagen," Volkswagen successfully framed its models as inheritors of this German performance tradition, but at a more affordable price. Volkswagen was still competing on category benefits and not doing particularly well at it. But in the 1990s, this new benefit positioning provided an important platform for the myth that would revitalize the brand.

By 1990, Volkswagen management had grown desperate. Its American dealer base had shrunk considerably, and many dealers that remained had joined some senior managers at Volkswagen to call for DDB's head. Volkswagen North America's president decided to give DDB one last chance to deliver a breakthrough creative idea.

After five months of misfires, a DDB copywriter happened across an obscure technical term in a German dictionary. *Fahrvergnugen,* which meant "pleasure of driving," anchored an entire campaign based on the idea that Volkswagen should be a driver's car. The brand should champion people who loved to drive rather than simply drive to get somewhere.

The ads presented a family in a Volkswagen driving, not on a road, but on a black line surrounded by simple black-and-white cartoon scenery (with cows, for instance). The music was an electronic drone that can only be described as elevator music. A mechanized voice-over lectures:

> It starts the moment you start the car. An experience that's distinctly Volkswagen. The quick acceleration, the sense of control, the surprising responsiveness as if it were an extension of you. There is a word for this experience: *Fahrvergnugen.* It's what makes a car a Volkswagen.

While the campaign attracted considerable attention, much of it was not positive. The Prozacked feeling evoked by the ads was not exactly what the audience associated with the pleasures of driving, regardless of the translation.

Arnold's Indie Myth

By 1993, senior management at Volkswagen AG in Germany had all but decided to pull out of the money-draining American market and revert to a global strategy that excluded the United States. In a last-ditch effort, the company decided to allow American management to fire DDB and take one last shot at salvaging the business. Volkswagen North America ran an account review and selected Arnold Communications, a dark-horse regional agency from Boston with no particular creative reputation or auto industry experience.

The campaign developed by Arnold—"Drivers Wanted"—eventually became one of the most compelling branding efforts of the 1990s, restoring the identity value of the Volkswagen brand to levels approaching the late 1960s. Today, Volkswagen North America sells almost as many automobiles as the company did at the peak of the Beetle's run, and at a considerable price premium to competitors. How remarkable that one of the century's most successful iconic brands suffocated under decades of inept branding, then returned to health in just four years.

The new Volkswagen myth adopted the key elements of Volkswagen's earlier bohemian myth of creative individuality, but revised the story appropriately to fit the particular cultural circumstances of the United States as it entered the new economy of the late 1990s. Like Mountain Dew, Volkswagen targeted a powerful new cultural contradiction appropriate for the brand and chose the right populist world from which to reinterpret the brand's myth. This targeting, however, was a necessary but not sufficient condition for success. As the genealogy reveals, Volkswagen succeeded within this target only when it crafted an original new myth with the appropriate authenticity and charismatic aesthetic.

American Ideology: Bohemian Frontier

The timing of Volkswagen's move was fortuitous. A new national ideology was then rising to dominance: the bohemian frontier, an ideal perfectly suited as a foil for Volkswagen's revival. The United States was rapidly converting to an economy in which knowledge products—finance, software, entertainment, law, medicine, and education—dominated hard goods. This economy placed an extraordinary premium on highly trained and motivated professionals whom labor secretary, Robert Reich, termed symbolic analysts: consultants, engineers, scientists, lawyers, bankers, programmers, accountants, and commercial artists. This new, knowledge-centered organization of the economy brought about a new set of values that were functional to this work. The most valued knowledge work required creativity and nonroutine problem solving. Companies could not approach these tasks with rationalized processes, breaking down work into discrete pieces, and routinizing how it was accomplished. They needed to allow their employees to take a more independent and entrepreneurial approach to their work.

In response, a new tangent of the free-agent frontier formed. The bohemian frontier combined the intensely competitive winner-take-all labor markets of the early 1990s with the artistic inclinations of bohemia. For businesses that required creativity to spur innovation, managers had to weave the values of the artist into the workplace. For inspiration, the myths that formed around the bohemian frontier drew heavily on the hippie counterculture of the 1960s. Once a revolutionary countercultural challenge, the music, dress, and values became the mythic center of a new economic philosophy based on business as creative revolution.[6] Now, every good entrepreneur—especially those lodged in Silicon Valley—used the 1960s as a battle cry against staid institutions and rigid ways of thinking that kept economic value on a leash. New media like *Wired* magazine spurred this radical creativity, and the Burning Man Festival became the obligatory pilgrimage for Bay Area techies.

Leading-edge knowledge firms, such as software makers, Hollywood production houses, ad agencies, and other companies that specialized in creative content, began to reinvent work as artistic play. The ultimate work place was now modeled on bohemia: a job where you could arrive when you wanted, in full slacker regalia, and work like hell on projects that you thought were flat-out cool. No hierarchies, no formality. Corporatism was designed out of existence. All hints that the organization had anything to do with commerce were tucked in a back room so that creative employees could pretend that they were inventing for art's sake. This was business as theater troupe; the conflict between art and commerce had ended and art had won. New-economy workers were to devote themselves to projects geared to their own internal creative and technical standards of excellence ("insanely great," in Steve Jobs's words), the passion of which would necessarily drive marketplace acceptance. The new heroes of the bohemian frontier pursued quixotic avocations, but applied their creative wanderlust to capitalist pursuits to conquer commerce with the same enthusiasm found among the Wall Street deal makers of the 1980s.

Targeting the Bobo Contradiction

At the center of this new ideology lived people whom journalist David Brooks has called *Bobos* (short for bourgeois bohemians).[7] These were highly educated professionals—upper middle class by conventional definitions, approximately the top 5 percent of the country—people at the center of the knowledge economy. Bobos were entirely wedded to the idea that life was about individual expression and self-actualization, whether at work or at play. They crafted idiosyncratic lifestyles that expressed delightfully whimsical tastes. Life should be a creative and adventurous enterprise. The person was the canvas, and one painted it with extraordinary experiences. Passionate projects were the rule; everything that one did was to be a personal statement.

Although the bohemian frontier ideology promoted work as a forum for individual expression, most of the prior characteristics of bureaucratic life remained in place. Some had even intensified. While upper-middle-class Americans became wedded to Bobo values, the percentage of jobs that actually allowed for the Bobo work utopia—wherein commerce became art and everyday life was a quest for self-actualizing projects—remained minuscule. News reports hyped cool jobs in the commercial arts where the CFO was indistinguishable from the bike messenger. But most Bobos still worked at mainstream companies—as doctors, lawyers, publicists, and bankers. And most of the work at these companies, regardless of relaxed dress codes, became in the 1990s increasingly rationalized as management sought to squeeze higher productivity out of professional-managerial labor. Bobos found it difficult to retain an artistic self-concept when their work life was bent on satisfying customer demands, the assignments were routine, and their roles were often to execute orders handed down to them from above.

Once they committed to a professional career path, Bobos had to compromise the bohemian ideals they had treasured in college. Work suppressed the pent-up bohemian in them. As a result, these tastes took full expression in leisure and consumption, as Bobos grasped for symbolic expressions of the ideals that they no longer had time to actually live in their eight-to-eight jobs. This contradiction created an enormous indie myth market for cultural products that allowed Bobos access to the new bohemian world of the indie/alternative artists: noncommercial musical genres, independent films, artisanal foods, and experiential vacations.

Arnold's Myth Treatment

Arnold had won the account review with a campaign built around the tag line "On the road of life, there are passengers and drivers. Drivers wanted."

Volkswagen launched the "Drivers Wanted" campaign with seven spots, all of which depicted thirtysomething professionals, trapped by work and technology, who finally experience freedom by driving their Volkswagens fast in the countryside with the music blaring. The driving scenes relied on images styled like an MTV video, depicting rides full of rock-and-roll whims and pleasures. Despite the splashy introduction with substantial media weights, none of these spots caught on.

Instead, the first breakout ad was a promotion for lease packages. Ostensibly a product testimonial for the Golf, "Cappuccino Girl" featured a young woman with abundant energy and apparently working retail accounts for a specialty coffee distributor in New York City. As she traveled through lower Manhattan's cramped streetscape, she described her duties at a caffeinated pace: "I just moved into the city, right? And I need a very flexible car. So I leased a new Volkswagen Golf. It's great. I sell cappuccino machines. Sometimes I have to move big things, sometimes I have to move little things. But I always have to move." She chatted with the staff at a café that she serviced, walked in the middle of a narrow, brick city street, and drove maniacally through hectic urban traffic. As she stashed large coffee urns into the hatch, she said of the Golf, "Everything fits into it." She aced out another car about to sneak into her parking space and said that the Golf "fits into everything." To ward off the other car, she leaned out the driver's window and shouted, "Hey!" Perky as ever, she appeared again on the street and addressed the camera, "I've got to cut back on the caffeine." In the final shot we saw her red Golf, two bikes on the roof rack, speeding out of the city.

Viewers understood that she was a well-educated young woman. She was articulate and confident, suggesting a middle-class upbringing and a good college education, exemplary Bobo material. Her performance hinted that she could easily have landed a much more prestigious and better-paying job, perhaps downtown on Wall Street or uptown on Madison Avenue. Yet instead she had chosen the bohemian life, selling coffee to support her passions.

This unassuming ad struck a chord because it spoke to the key existential dilemma in Bobo life: the devil's pact requiring that one trade in Bobo ideals—the pursuit of passionate projects and personal creativity—for career success. Here was a woman who possessed the confidence to just say no to the corporate career track. "Cappuccino Girl" portrayed a woman with the guts to reject the professional career path for a downshifted life in the city. She thrived on her noncareer job's hustle and bustle, its street life. And because it didn't eat up her time or mental energy like a professional job would, she could focus her energies on other pursuits.

In these thirty seconds, Volkswagen demonstrated persuasively that the brand identified with one of the central anxieties in Bobo life. Yet the world that "Cappuccino Girl" created with her Golf lacked mythic power. Just like the uninspired launch spots for the campaign, Volkswagen's ads presented the world of driving as throttling a car through the countryside. Since the rise of rock and roll in the 1950s, the image of getting in your car and driving fast out in the country with the rock music blaring to rebel against bourgeois norms has been a cultural constant. Musicians from the Beach Boys to Jonathan Richman to Bruce Springsteen have painted this scene as the quintessential rebellious moment. The exhilarating rush of driving a car fast with loud music was neither an original nor a compelling solution to Bobo anxieties.

Beginning in 1997, Arnold corrected this deficit, creating an entirely original and compelling myth that reinterpreted DDB's work in a way that worked to resolve the Bobo contradiction. Amid a slew of smart advertising, four ads stood out as exemplars of the new myth.

"Sunday Afternoon." This ad, also known as "Da-Da-Da," was one of the most influential ads of the decade. It featured two young men on a Sunday drive, picking their way slowly, aimlessly, through working-class neighborhoods and industrial zones. Though shot in Los Angeles, the spot eschewed the usual television-commercial Los Angeles, the city of tanned, lyposuctioned actors. Instead, the ad showcased sprawling, empty, concrete Los Angeles, the city of empty bus stops, where a car could wait at a stoplight seemingly forever even though no other cars were visible. This was L.A. at noon, but the poor air quality prevented the high sun from inspiring a single shadow.

From the first shot, the hook on which the audience hung its hat was the incredibly droll and facile 1980s club hit, "Da-Da-Da." The song, by German minimalist popsters Trio, was a jangle of repetitive, percussive tones overlaid with a simple two-chord melody. You could not have entered a dance club anywhere in North America or Europe in the early 1980s without hearing the catchy tune. But by 1997, the tune had disappeared from the radar screen. Consequently, its use was entirely unexpected, neither hip nor retro. Accentuating the flat pictures, the banal but catchy tune provided lackadaisical propulsion.

Riding shotgun, a clean-cut, nondescript African American guy opened and closed his right thumb and forefinger to the music's beat, his fingers dancing between his eye and the sun. An equally tidy white guy at the wheel ignored him. The next shot showed the passenger mocking a martial arts combat pose with his arms and hands, chopping the air, mimicking a kung-fu movie. The driver still ignored him.

With a single hand, the passenger then manipulated a familiar child's toy—a small, multijointed figurine of the type that moves when someone pushes the underside of its plastic base. As with the other understated stunts, the figurine's dance was performed to the music's beat. The car paused at a stoplight, and the turn signal flashed to the beat. The driver briefly searched for his bearings in the unfamiliar territory.

The men returned to a residential neighborhood, still on a narcotic meander. The driver reached to the dash and with a finger wiped away a smudge, again back and forth to the song's rhythm. A wide shot showed the red car crossing a bridge over a particularly bleak section of a Los Angeles river, a sun-baked, nearly empty concrete drainage ditch. Slightly smiling now, and ever so gently moving with the music, the passenger popped a bubble he'd blown with his gum, still to the soundtrack's beat.

They spotted a well-worn green armchair, abandoned next to a trash can on the curb. In the next shot, the chair is in the back of the car, but the characters remained manifestly dispassionate. Suddenly, the driver sniffed a few times, looked sourly at his friend, who got his drift. They glanced back at the chair.

In the next shot, the car pulled away from another curb, revealing the newly abandoned chair. A female voice-over added a proviso to the standard "Drivers Wanted" refrain: "The German engineered Volkswagen Golf. It fits your life. Or your complete lack thereof."

"Sunday Afternoon" was the ultimate anti-ad. It wallowed in ugliness (the squalid scenery, the smelly chair) and unspectacular events (toys, kung-fu, smudges). The car was driven with no impressive turns or acceleration. Precious ad seconds were "wasted" showing the vehicle waiting at a stoplight. The Trio song became the improvisational skeleton on which the ad's makers built creative responses to the plain vanilla environment.

The passengers were absolutely stoic, thoroughly absorbed by the trivial. They flailed, swabbed, and karate-chopped to the beat.

The ad worked because it presented a novel and compelling idea of what it meant to drive and to be a driver, from a Bobo worldview. Gone was the literal interpretation of driving in the earlier "Drivers Wanted" spots. Now, to be a driver meant that one engaged life as a creative actor, as an iconoclastic producer of one's own cultural experiences. Whereas passengers were spectators who inertly absorbed mass-media spectacles, drivers were creative people who found all sorts of little pleasures in the world that they happened upon, improvising as they proceeded. "Sunday Afternoon" asserted that, with a sufficiently offbeat worldview and a will to create, one could find many small pleasures in what others found dispiriting.

Volkswagen's new hero was the creative misanthrope, the outsider who whimsically confronted the regimented world with an idiosyncratic, imagined world of his own. The auto became an autonomous space, free from institutional structures, where the hero could create. Following this pioneering effort, the brand team produced three more ads that embellished this myth.

Synchronicity. The sequel to "Sunday Afternoon," "Synchronicity" again featured two people in a Volkswagen, observing seemingly mundane life around them. In the ad, an early-thirties couple cruised slowly in their Jetta down a narrow, old-quarter New Orleans street. The art direction spoke to the educated, urban creative worker. Both characters were brunettes, both wore only black, and their car was black. Shots alternated between the couple in the car and what was happening on the street.

The driver, a man, popped in a CD, and a slow, hypnotic electronic dance beat began. Thereafter, each action that surrounded the couple was mysteriously synched with the beat: the windshield wipers (it was drizzling), people's footsteps, a broom that a man pushed to sweep the sidewalk, a yo-yo tossed by a kid leaning against a lamppost. They passed the traffic light, and the "Don't Walk" symbol flashed to the beat. So did the basketball a kid dribbled on the sidewalk. Periodically, the viewer saw the couple's faces looking around with increasing bewilderment. Men unloaded a truck, tossed boxes in rhythm with the music. At the corner, the car's turn signal light maintained the beat until a red pickup truck splashed a giant puddle's worth of water onto the Volkswagen's windshield. As though a bucket of cold water had awakened the drivers from their dream, the synchronous effect disappeared. The man said in a flat, straight voice, a conclusion that could have been spoken in an *X-Files* episode: "That was interesting." His partner nodded agreement. The car turned right and drove on. The closing shot provided an elevated look down the empty street before them. No vehicles were in sight—certainly no red pickup.

Volkswagen's new driver sensibility was on parade here. The couple peered from inside their car-as-cocoon to see the world as an odd aesthetic pleasure, which could be had simply by observing and interpreting the seemingly banal activities of everyday life. Volkswagen called out to all those who imagined themselves as an artist. The brand proscribed that everyday life could be anyone's canvas.

"Great Escape." The "Great Escape" spot was Volkswagen advertising at its most confident and adventurous. It placed Volkswagen values in an entirely new and unexpected place: a geriatric African American man in an old-folks home. The spot began with a confident, elderly man standing before a mirror in his room and adjusting his tie and hat. He grabbed his cane and stepped gingerly from his room into the home's institutional corridor. Proceeding spryly down the hall, he tipped his hat to a passing nurse and then, unable to resist temptation, turned somewhat furtively to admire her derriere. Evidently she knew the old codger, because she too looked over her shoulder and shot him a semiplayful scowl. Above reproach for such a minor infraction, he smiled and continued sneaking down the hall until he came upon a horrible sight—a geriatric calisthenics class. He took a quick detour, sneaked past the nurses' station, and pushed through a door with a sign that he ignored: "Please use the front door." He stepped into a desert parking lot's bright sun. A silver Jetta skidded to a stop in front of him. The old fellow beamed recognition. In the car, a young black man looked dead ahead, smiled mischievously, and greeted the fugitive hero, "Grandpop." The old man climbed in and said with a grin, "Hey Boo-boo. I'm glad you're on time."

The car disappeared down a desert highway. Boo-boo opened the sunroof. Grandpop tilted his head back, soaked up some sunshine, and reached his hand out the window to play aerodynamic games with the rushing wind, a playful gesture that obliquely referenced the "Da-Da-Da" guys. With nothing around but the Mojave landscape, the car raced past a

83

road sign that put Las Vegas 134 miles in their future. The old man tossed his hat out the window.

The cantankerous old man, trapped in the old folks home, was an effective metaphor for the Bobo professional suffocating in rationalized corporate life. He was yet another hero who escaped regimented daily life in favor of the freedom of expression to be had while driving. His enthusiastic toss of the hat and playful hand surfing, combined with the subtle intimacy he shared with his grandson, told the audience that a simple act—like sharing a drive through the desert—could be transcendent.

The ad's soundtrack music was a classic free-jazz composition by Charles Mingus, a renowned jazz iconoclast who invented a textured ensemble style of jazz. Mingus was a fiery personality who lived the bohemian life with gusto. The old man possessed similar tendencies, a mature but still vigorous spirit.

"Milky Way." The final addition to this quartet, "Milky Way," told the story of a racially integrated carload of meditative teenagers cruising under a full moon in a Cabrio convertible on lonely rural roads. The images were cold and blue, accompanied by Nick Drake's haunting ballad, "Pink Moon." As the teens quietly pondered the moon reflecting off a creek, the fireflies, and the dazzling rural starscape, they seemed to be simultaneously realizing that quiet moments with friends and the moon possessed unseen relevance, emotional gravity.

The kids pulled into the dark driveway of a summer cottage that was alive with a summertime party, but no one got out of the car. They washed each other tenderly with their eyes, trading quiet, subtle glances. None of them spoke. The driver put it in reverse, the turn signal flashed, and they headed back out onto the road. They leaned back and soaked in the moon.

The kids had skipped out on the usual suspects of teen culture—loud music, partying, and sexual conquest—for the simpler yet much more profound pleasure of soaking in a perfect night. Teenagers blowing off what seemed like a cool party for a more soulful and imaginative experience staring into space with the wind in their hair was yet another original context to illustrate that Volkswagen championed personal autonomy and sensitivity to aesthetic experience. In this advertising masterpiece, the automobile again became a medium for the pleasures brought by an aesthetic sensibility and the iconoclasm to break with "normal" behavior. "Milky

Cool Can't be Hunted

Malcolm Gladwell helped popularize an idea—the coolhunt—that has become a key identity branding tool. But a hunt for cool is a contradiction in terms. The genesis of cool is to lead culture as part of an artistic vanguard. If you have to hunt it, you're not cool. Cool hunting is a parasitic strategy. Brands compete to tap into sites of hot cultural value and try to grab on to these coattails. This approach cannot, by definition, build icons.

DDB's advertising never tried to ride the trends and fashions of the Beat or hippie countercultures. There was no rock music, no sex, none of the druggie Peter Max pop art style in graphics and design that other brands of that era pilfered. In fact, the ads were resolutely unhippylike. Yet, Volkswagen became the most potent and enduring branded symbol of what was cool in the hippie counterculture. Similarly, Arnold's "Drivers Wanted" ads relied on seemingly mundane plots with drab settings that had little to do with trends in the indie scene. In both incarnations, Volkswagen didn't imitate what was cool. Rather, the brand established itself within the art worlds of the day as a literate fellow traveler. In each case, the brand absorbed the countercultural ethos and created from within.

Iconic brands don't mimic existing culture, nor do they grab on to emerging trends. They are *cultural innovators* that beckon to their audiences, using artistic techniques, to change how the viewers think and act. Leading trends is a superficial approach to cultural change. Iconic brands help to change culture at a deeper level, influencing how people understand themselves in relation to the nation's ideals.

Way" became so popular that Volkswagen continued to broadcast the ad two years after its original release.

The myth treatment for Arnold's campaign can be summarized as follows: Volkswagen champions a world of drivers: people who treat whatever mundane situations they find themselves in as a canvas with which they improvise to create personal aesthetic statements, everyday art.

Authentic Populist Voice: The Indie Art World

Arnold located Volkswagen's new myth in the contemporary incarnation of the artist's bohemia. As in the past, bohemias had sprung up primarily

Staged versus Organizational Populism

There are two distinctive paths to developing populist authenticity: *staged populism* and *organizational populism*. We find staged populism used for brands like Coke, Marlboro, Mountain Dew, Volkswagen, and Budweiser. These brands advance myths that have nothing to do with the companies that produce the product. Their authenticity comes from how well the brand portrays the populist world in its performances, not whether the company is in fact a real participant. In contrast, brands like Snapple, ESPN, Patagonia, Harley-Davidson, and Nike in its formative period have relied on organizational populism. In these cases, the company exists within the populist world, and the myth is an expression of the company's ethos (as well as its fellow insiders within the populist world). Brands that rely on organizational populism develop the brand to express—in a distilled and stylized dramatization—the core ethos of the company.

As more and more brands compete to be perceived by consumers as authentic, Americans have become increasingly cynical about staged identity brands. They are placing a sizable and increasing premium on brands that can actually "walk the walk." Not many companies have a credible position within a populist world. So those that do have a tremendous mythmaking advantage in terms of authenticity.

in big U.S. cities and college towns. At the center of new bohemian life was indie, or simply *alternative* culture. Indie began in the early 1980s as the American transplant of the British punk counterculture of the late 1970s. The punk movement never caught on as a working-class political expression in the United States, because American class politics was much more reticent. Instead, punk inspired a bohemian underground that simmered through the Reagan years, just as the Beats had in the Eisenhower years.

Because mainstream American life had changed dramatically since the 1960s, the bohemian critique had shifted as well. The bohemia that DDB tapped in the 1960s had stood against the stultifying conformity enforced by mass marketing and corporate bureaucracies. By the 1990s, much of the cultural agenda of the 1960s had been absorbed into mass culture. The market had easily adapted to Volkswagen's stinging critique—the desire to express individuality in one's consumption—with microsegmented markets and rebellious brands. But, regardless of the countercultural frosting, work life had become even more rationalized.

So, in the 1990s, bohemia pushed hard against the routinization and passivity of everyday life. Beyond merely rejecting cultural conformity, bohemians pushed a step further, rejecting the idea of being consumers. Indies were well aware by now that marketers used their anticonformist values to hype their brands. And they wanted nothing of it. The new bohemians rejected consumerism as a passive approach to life. Instead, they claimed the role of cultural producers. They were intensely involved in music, film, and other forms of popular culture. Rather than purchase mass-marketed products, they preferred to support their fellow nonconformists who produced music, film, and art at the margins of commerce. They also rescued and reused odd cultural detritus that they found gathering dust at thrift shops.[8]

Central to the indie sensibility was a mix-and-match eclecticism: the more obscure and absurd, the better. Alternative culturalists began rummaging through artifacts of post–World War II United States. Thrift shop fashion quickly spread to kitschy, mid-twentieth-century interior style. Interest in less-known music genres spread to the odds and ends plucked from the twenty-five-cent bins: Hawaiian guitar music, 1950s country, show tunes, torch singers, Latin jazz—the list is as deep as the bin. Playing in a band was cool, part of everyday citizenship in the indie world. But really impressive is taking up something that hasn't been explored before—Japanese cartoons, tube amplifiers, Kurdish folk songs—and digging into these cultural materials with the never-sated enthusiasm of a 19th century aristocratic amateur.

Arnold's Indie Literacy. In the second year of the "Drivers Wanted" campaign, Volkswagen established its indie bona fides with a spot that had little impact on the mass audience, but won considerable credit in bohemian circles. "Speed Racer" featured the GTI in a take-off of a 1960s cartoon. Speed Racer, the cartoon's earnest young race driver protagonist, lamented that his car, the "Mach 5," broke down before a race. He believed his competitors had sabotaged it. As a replacement, he was given a GTI. He and his cohorts were surprised at the GTI's speed and handling, and they won the race. This silly, stilted spot ended with the theme song from the original cartoon.

Set against the conventional show-the-metal car advertising of General Motors and Toyota, Arnold's choice to animate an ad was audacious, reminiscent of DDB's communication-code jabs of the 1960s. The choice seemed to be a spoof, denying serious interest in promoting the GTI. And the particular choice of "Speed Racer" was a mighty nod to indie tastes. The Japanese cartoon had been dubbed into English and had played on afternoon television for a generation of American kids. In the 1990s, Japanese animation had become quite popular in the commercial arts scene, creating a cult following for this animated Japanese cartoon, which even played on MTV.

Aside from "Speed Racer," Arnold established Volkswagen's literate understanding of indie culture through purposely eclectic and discriminating music choices as soundtracks for the ads. The Nick Drake song "Pink Moon," which set the mood for "Milky Way," is a case in point. The ethereal melancholy ballad was ideal for the ad, but it also performed important work as a means to build authenticity. Drake was a mysterious figure in the British folk rock scene of the early 1970s. At an early age, he perfected new detuned guitar chords and a haunting vocal delivery. He made a few albums, and then, a depressed and possibly schizophrenic individual, he died of a drug overdose in 1974. Ever since, his reputation in the indie underground grew. In 1999, when Volkswagen chose his song, Drake's music had just been released on CDs. Using the Drake track in a creative and appropriate way, as the centerpiece of a moody ad that fit the song, gave Volkswagen tremendous authority as an authentic indie voice. Volkswagen's tastemaking capability was demonstrated by the tremendous sales of Drake CDs that followed the broadcast of the ad. "Pink Moon" sold more copies in three weeks after the ad's first broadcast than it had in the previous twenty-five years.[9]

Most of Arnold's musical choices reflected this kind of discriminating taste. Occasionally, however, Volkswagen ads purposely dipped into songs of dubious merit. These odd choices were also subtle nods to the indie sensibility. Just like the indie bohemians cruising the bins at the Salvation Army, Volkswagen confidently played songs that were decidedly unpopular. In addition to "Da-Da-Da," another spot infamously featured the Styx song "Mr. Roboto Man," a schlocky AOR hit by a 1970s band whose albums most discerning music fans would be ashamed to admit they stored in the attic. Such confidently oddball choices demonstrated that Volkswagen inhabited the indie world rather than pilfered from it as an outsider.

Arnold's Indie Fidelity. Iconic brands demonstrate their fidelity when they are willing to take chances to uphold the populist ethos. Sacrifice of this sort is one of the most effective vehicles for earning authenticity. Brands that claim an affiliation with a populist world, but then behave in ways motivated by commercial rather than populist interests, are perceived as shallow and opportunistic.

Volkswagen's "Driver's Wanted" spots consistently stood up for indie values. For example, Volkswagen earned authenticity points when it launched "Sunday Afternoon" on the famous episode of the television program *Ellen,* in which Ellen Degeneris came out as a lesbian. Many advertisers had backed out of this show fearing that audiences might infer that the advertised brands condoned lesbianism. The publicity around the ads that did run made the program a huge media event, and eyes were not only on Ellen but also on which advertisers were willing to be associated with lesbians. In this charged atmosphere, Volkswagen won many new admirers, just as it made enemies among social conservatives.

The *Ellen* placement also precipitated an unintended reading of the ad that further added to its indie credentials. In the gay community, "Sunday Afternoon" was interpreted as depicting a gay couple. These additional connotations only served to enhance Volkswagen's credibility among the very prodiversity bohemians.

Volkswagen's most successful performances of its fidelity have come from how it presents its vehicles in advertising. Auto industry conventions have always been guided by the assumption that ads persuade when they glamorize the auto. Showing off the graceful good looks of the car is supposed to convince prospective owners that they will be recipients of this borrowed glory. Nodding to the DDB campaign, Arnold's ads also pushed against this convention. For example, one ad showed a Golf with a dirty mattress tied to the roof.

Volkswagen's most audacious act of fidelity came in an ad broadcast at the 2000 Super Bowl, the first time the automaker had placed a commercial on advertising's biggest event. "Tree" was a static spot, even for Volkswagen. Most of the sixty seconds featured two men standing around a big maple tree, occasionally throwing various objects into the tree to knock out what could be a ball or Frisbee. A disheveled kid looked on curiously. Finally, the man knocked out his target with a stone. But, rather than dislodging a toy, he had succeeded in freeing a full-sized GTI hidden in the branches. The car landed with a massive crunch, and as the GTI came to rest, leaves and small twigs fell onto it. The thrower's friend offered the punch line as sarcastic advice: "Next time, don't let the clutch out so fast."

"Tree" fared poorly according to the *USA Today* poll. Industry observers called the ad a failure, citing Volkswagen's lack of Super Bowl savvy. Just the opposite was true, however. Volkswagen pulled off the ultimate symbolic coup. In the most-watched media event in the world, in which all advertisers were more than willing to bend their strategic goals to play to what the audience would rate as most entertaining, Volkswagen refused to play this game and instead offered an ad that was defiantly Volkswagen. "Tree" was Arnold's rendition of "Lemon," the 1960 print ad for the Beetle. The brand declared its allegiance to indie values by showing the company's best performing auto in the least flattering manner, and by refusing to play to the mass-market production values demanded by the event.[10]

Arnold's Charismatic Aesthetic: Independent Films

To make "Drivers Wanted" work, Arnold had to invent a charismatic aesthetic that would overcome the indie counterculture's inoculation to mass marketing. Rather than the formalism and wiser-than-thou humor of the Beetle ads, "Drivers Wanted" instead opted for an aesthetic centered on the conventions of art house independent films.

In the mid-1990s, the auto category provided plenty of low-hanging fruit for a brand looking to develop distinctive production values. Governed by the product-centric logic of conventional brand management, General Motors, Ford, Chrysler, and Toyota all produced predictable ads governed by the only rule that seemed to matter to auto executives: Show the metal. The ads emphasized cars over their passengers. There were images, but no characters or plot. Instead, the auto was a hero looking for a story, portrayed majestically on a winding Pacific Coast road or in the middle of an amazing, mountainous wilderness. The ads were lushly produced; glamorous shots put the auto in its best light.

Volkswagen produced ads that turned this aesthetic on its head. The spots emphasized character and plot over steel. Volkswagen displayed its cars as they would have been shown in a film, as if they were a prop in a movie rather than the stars of ads. The brand team developed characters worthy of an intelligent film-goer's time, in scenes selected to support interesting story lines rather than to show off the car. The ads used intriguing, off-kilter characters and abandoned the glib acting style common in advertising. Evidencing the automaker's distinctive approach, "Milky Way" received a nod as one of the Top Ten Films by an influential member of the bohemian press, the *Village Voice*.[11]

Another good example is a series of four spots Arnold commissioned from independent filmmaker Errol Morris to direct for Passat. Morris was one of the most respected indie documentary directors, famous for *The Thin Blue Line* and the quirky *Pet Cemetery*. Famous directors, including those of an indie persuasion, had been employed many times before in advertising. What was impressive, Arnold demonstrated the interest and knowledge to use Morris properly. Rather than grab a famous director and trade on his credibility, Arnold instead crafted ads to fit within the director's oeuvre, much as Apple had done years earlier with Ridley Scott for the ad "1984." Using the tag line "Our Secret's Safe with You," the brand team developed a set of confessional stories that allowed Morris to deploy his trademark eccentric interviewing style. In his movies, Morris had coaxed eerily uncomfortable deadpan confessions from his subjects, in which they matter-of-factly described their lives' odd and intimate details. Each ad in the series also used the curious music that Morris favored: Composed to make the audience expect that something profoundly interesting was about to be revealed, the clarinet and Theremin music sounded as if it were stolen from an old silent film or prewar traveling magic show. Oddly framed camera angles decomposed the subjects by putting them anywhere except in the center of the frame, where the eye usually expects to find them.

Most ads use metaphors of some type, but they are often clichés, analogies that beat the viewer over the head. The Volkswagen aesthetic was built on a literary style that used challenging metaphors, devices that forced the audience to engage their imaginations. Consider, for example, "Dawg," an ad produced to drum up anticipation for the new Jetta and Golf models that were due out in 1998. A shaggy mutt entered an informal dining room and sat beneath the table on which whirred a desktop fan. For a long pause, all that the audience heard were the fan's blades and the dog panting. Unsatisfied, the dog hopped onto a dining chair and sat so that the fan blew directly into its face. Volkswagen finally provided the punch line to resolve the mysterious story: "Get ready, the new Volkswagens are coming." Volkswagen's aesthetic exemplified the ethos of creativity and spontaneous improvisation that its myth championed.

Linking Creativity to Strategy

To build iconic brands, managers not only must target the appropriate contradiction in society, but also must develop a compelling myth to address this contradiction. Particularly revealing in Volkswagen's return to iconic status is that the brand team had the appropriate contradiction in its crosshairs from the beginning, at the agency pitch in 1994. But the group did not cobble together a successful new Volkswagen myth until 1997, three years later. When the ads finally delivered a myth that fired on all three cylinders of the cultural brief, Volkswagen's identity value took off.

Today's strategies are irrelevant for identity brands because they fail to direct what consumers value most about the brand—its myth. The cultural brief can provide creative partners with the strategic direction necessary to build a valuable myth.

DDB's Volkswagen campaign has been universally praised, but just as universally misunderstood. The DDB Volkswagen campaign is routinely hailed by management texts as leading the creative revolution. Advertisements no longer followed the advertising science rule books of the 1950s, as set out by Rosser Reeves and David Ogilvy's "unique selling proposition." Critics hail DDB's advertising for injecting smart humor and artistry, rather than Pavlovian repetition, into advertising.

Interestingly, managers are again crying out for great creativity. Brand managers pound their fists for it, and ad agencies flaunt it. Recent books have documented the rapidly expanding centrality of creative and entertaining stories and staged experiences in the contemporary economy. But managers who use the mind share, emotional, and viral models also understand creativity as something magical, outside their control.

As the Volkswagen genealogy demonstrates, however, in branding there's no such thing as pure creativity. DDB's ads, as well as Arnold's later work, are sparkling examples of the advertising art. Yet what makes these campaigns noteworthy is not their pure creative genius. Many other contemporaneous ads rivaled these ads in creative verve and production values, as a tour through any of the major industry awards will show. Rather, these campaigns stand out because they harnessed creativity—placing it in the service of a tacit cultural strategy. As many imitators who sought to follow DDB's lead found out, advertising that seeks to be extremely creative rarely works. Treating generic artistry as a branding formula is no better than the formulaic scientism of Reeves's unique selling proposition that preceded it.

Today, the pursuit of creativity in branding is an anarchic pursuit because existing models lack a framework for systematically managing creative content. Cultural branding directs creativity to fit strategic objectives. Managers choose the most opportune myth market for the brand. They then direct the development with the creative brief: guiding creative efforts toward particular kinds of stories, communication codes, and populist world expressions that will yield the most compelling myth.

CHAPTER 5

Leveraging Cultural and Political Authority

CRAFTING BRAND STRATEGY requires stepping back to view the brand as a strategic asset. The economic value of a brand—its brand equity—is based on the future earnings stream the brand is expected to generate from customers' loyalty, which is revealed in their willingness to pay price premiums compared with otherwise equivalent products. Managing this income stream into the future requires a sophisticated understanding of how the brand has acquired its current value.

In the mind-share model, brand equity is based on the strength and distinctiveness of brand associations. The brand essence, lodged in the consumer's mind, is its source of equity. The more firmly rooted, the stronger the brand.[1]

In the viral model, brand equity is located in the brand's hold on influential people. Brands well entrenched among the most influential and fashionable people have high equity. Managing equity in this model involves the precarious business of continually ingratiating the brand into the short list of the most fashion-forward set.

How should we understand an iconic brand as an asset? And how should we deploy this asset to enhance its value? For iconic brands, the brand is a symbol so equity is a collective phenomenon, rather than a product of the brand's hold on individual consumers. The success of a brand's prior myths establishes a reputation. The brand becomes renowned for telling certain kinds of stories that are useful in addressing certain social desires and anxieties. In formal terms, from the brand's prior myths grow two kinds of assets—cultural authority and political authority. Identity brands succeed when their managers draw on these two types of authority to reinvent the brand's myth. I will use a genealogy of Budweiser to develop this cultural model of brand equity.

Budweiser Genealogy

Few companies have responded as deftly to American cultural changes as Anheuser-Busch. Yet, for much of the 1990s, the company's flagship brand, Budweiser, was in a tailspin. Since iconic brands earn their keep by creating mythic resolutions to societal contradictions, when these contradictions shift, the brand must revise its myth to remain vital. Budweiser faced just this situation in the early 1990s. Bud had soared in the 1980s with "This Bud's for You," one of the decade's most influential myths. Yet the branding began to misfire around 1990, and Bud went into a seven-year funk. Anheuser-Busch struggled to recover from this disruption with various mind-share strategies and failed each time. Budweiser finally recovered its iconic value with two overlapping campaigns—"Lizards" and "Whassup?!"—which together created a new Bud myth that spoke precisely to the social tensions of the 1990s.

The financial results were impressive. From 1997 to 2002, Anheuser-Busch's operating margins climbed from about 18 percent to nearly 24 percent, and Wall Street responded with enthusiasm, bidding up the stock by 140 percent in a five-year period during which the Standard & Poor's 500 index was flat. Bud's branding efforts increased the perceived value of the brand, protecting sales as Anheuser-Busch aggressively pushed Bud pricing from an historic low in real dollars to price points that approached the major import rivals.[2]

Anheuser-Busch rolled out Budweiser to national markets at the beginning of the twentieth century, one of the earliest beers to do so, and began advertising Bud extensively in national magazines. By the 1950s, Bud was crafting a myth that encouraged working men to share in America's new idyllic life of suburban leisure. Budweiser ads showed men how good times were to be had with their family and friends in leisurely activities. With this advertising, Bud became the best-selling beer in the United States. But the brand's leadership would soon be challenged by Schlitz and upstart Miller High Life. We pick up the brand genealogy in the 1970s, as Bud's postwar myth fell apart in the face of Vietnam protests, economic decline, and Watergate.

Beers Battle with Reactionary Manhood Myths

Like Mountain Dew and Volkswagen, Budweiser also stumbled when it hit the cultural disruption of the late 1960s. Budweiser's myth of the suburban good life was wiped out by a laundry list of devastating national failures. Massive urban protests and civil disobedience demonstrated that the post-war good life was not very good for African Americans. Japanese corporations began to prove that American companies were no longer world leaders in major product categories. The Arab oil cartel showed that U.S. economic power was much more fragile than previously understood. The Viet Cong made the Pentagon's technical superiority a moot point. Watergate undermined Americans' confidence in their political system. And the burgeoning women's movement threatened the traditional male role as head of the family.

Many middle-class American men, particularly on the coasts, gave up on the idea of the American empire and took up the cultural revolution. They embraced a loosening of social mores and equality for women and African Americans.

However, the response in so-called Middle America—what Richard Nixon would famously call the silent majority—was quite different. In particular, white working-class men became attracted to aggressively masculine ideals that defensively proclaimed men's power in the face of U.S. economic and political decline. These men experienced America's difficulties and the rising influence of women as a crisis of manhood, a loss of control that produced considerable anxiety. Many of these men felt that the nation was becoming too feminine.

The beer market was particularly swift to respond to these emerging sentiments, as the core drinker was male and working class. Budweiser, Miller (with its "Miller Time" campaign), and Schlitz (with its swarthy adventurers in its "When You're Out of Schlitz, You're Out of Beer" campaign) all battled fiercely to create a new American myth that would respond to the desires of these men to regain a sense of masculine power.[3] Budweiser ditched the leisurely beer-swilling scenes portraying men at home, with friends at dinner parties, and in pool halls. Instead, Bud was now was the chest-swelling "King of Beers," and daredevil race-car drivers and marching band music celebrated Bud as a champion and encouraged the beer's drinkers to likewise think of themselves as kings.

Budweiser offered up the company itself as a role model for men who yearned for the return of U.S. military and economic might, and the return of the man as the king of his family. Ads declared over and over, simply, that Bud was "The King of Beers." Anheuser-Busch said, in effect, "Look at us as a model! We're successful and here's our secret: We have the winning attitude. While the government, the military, and other companies may be failing to meet your ideals of manhood, Bud is doing great!" Anheuser-Busch had the winner's spirit and, to prove it, used the highest-quality ingredients and the most labor-intensive and expensive processes because the product had to be perfect. Anyone who approached life with this spirit was a winner, a king. Bud drinkers, of course, were the first in line to be so ennobled.

This chest-puffing myth kept Bud in the hunt, but did not stand out against myths offered by Schlitz and Miller. It wasn't until Budweiser swiped Miller's work-reward concept and did it one better that Bud soared to iconic status.

"This Bud's for You"

Budweiser's climb to iconic stature was made possible by the new American ideology championed by Ronald Reagan. The Unites States bottomed out in the late 1970s: Inflation hit double digits; then, a deep recession resulting from inflation-correcting measures sent unemployment soaring. Japanese companies continued to make inroads, and the United States suffered through the embarrassment of the year-long wait to rescue American hostages trapped in the Iranian embassy. Cultural tensions ran at feverish levels, especially for men. Demand swelled for new national myths that would inspire the country to return to its former glory. And answering that call, along with the films and television programs of the day, was Ronald Reagan.

Reagan connected with men of all classes when he called for the United States to return to its roots as a frontier nation. He revived the idea of the man of action, calling out for American men to emulate John Wayne's portrayals of frontiersmen in Western films, as well as the modern frontiersmen like Clint Eastwood's Dirty Harry and Sylvester Stallone's Rambo. The United States needed new man-of-action heroes: individuals with the vision, the guts, and a can-do spirit to transform its wobbly institutions, invent wildly creative products, build fantastic new markets, and conquer distant infidels. Reagan presented himself as a modern-day man of action who stood up to government bureaucracies and the communist threat. As Reagan went after Mu'ammar al-Gadhafi, Manuel Noriega, the Sandinistas, and the Soviet Union, American men of all classes rallied around his heroic vision, forging a historic shift in the electorate. Inspired by his call to arms, white working men, many of them lifelong Democrats, shifted their allegiance to Reagan.

Managers and professionals interpreted Reagan's call for men of action in terms of the new "gold rushes" on Wall Street, in Texas oil country, and in the high-tech corridors of Silicon Valley and Boston. Cutthroat, individualistic competition was now admired and the quest to make money reigned supreme.

Working-class American men responded to this call more collectively. Reagan's manifesto was understood as a nationalist call to reverse the deterioration of domestic industry, to restore U.S. power through the collective efforts of American men rallying around a national cause. These men heard a call to war, but an economic war rather than a military one. Many working men blamed the disappearance of industrial work on aggressive competition from abroad. Japan especially had more efficient industrial production and was aggressively taking share in the United States. Consequently, American men were told they had to push their game up a notch. Reagan, Lee Iacocca, and other business and political leaders challenged them to help restore U.S. might with renewed vigor and sacrifice for their country. For the most part, men heeded these battle cries. "Buy American" bumper stickers appeared from coast to coast.

Yet even as workers rallied to this national project, many large corporations continued to aggressively ship production jobs to locations overseas, where wages were lower, and to substitute technology for labor. American workers wanted desperately to believe in a resurgent United States that relied on their labor, but they were faced with considerable evidence that corporate America had other intentions. This contradiction between Reagan's new ideology and the actual state of working-class jobs produced an enormous demand for new myths.

Myth Treatment: Working Men are Men-of-Action Artisans

Budweiser picked up Reagan's battle cry from the point of view of working-class men, many of whom were being laid off, forced to take sizable wage and benefits cuts, or were being pushed into the low-wage service economy. Adopting the persona of a powerful leader, Bud lauded workers for their heroic efforts and exhorted them to approach their jobs with the right values.

In the launch spot, "This Bud's for You," the narrator patted workers on the back: "To everyone who puts in a hard day's work, this Bud's for you." The jingle, a peppy pop salute, fleshed out the narrator's proposition.

> *This Bud's for you.*
> *There's no one else who does it quite the way you do.*
> *So here's to you.*
> *You know it isn't what you say, it's what you do.*
> *For all you do, the king of beers is coming through.*

The ad paraded a collage of blue-collar workers from all walks of life, each of whom practiced his trade with consummate skill and enthusiasm. Viewers saw train conductors, lumberjacks, construction workers, truck drivers, farmers, cooks, fishermen, welders, window washers, a boxer, a barber, a produce hauler, a meat cutter, and a policeman. In a scene borrowed from Sylvester Stallone's *Rocky,* a butcher used a cow carcass as a punching bag. Bud championed every man—race, region, and age were all irrelevant—who worked with his hands. The working men were all pictured as determined guys who loved their jobs and approached work with can-do attitudes.

As the campaign developed, the jingles became ever more encouraging, sometimes lapsing into cornball sentiment: "You are the power, the man of the hour, you really get things going," and "You keep America going, you keep the juices flowing, you are muscle, the hope and the hustle, you keep the country growing." But Bud was adamant about whose side the brand supported. Bud saluted men who industriously pursued work as an intrinsically satisfying calling, men who applied their craft skills with good humor and determination. The result was that America "worked," and work made the man. Bud implied that when working men participated in American enterprise together, the country would hum. Reveling in their contributions, working men formed a heroic brotherhood, gathering with other men in friendship and solidarity at the end of a working day. Bud gave men hope for a revival in the centrality of skilled manual labor.

Budweiser's myth treatment can be summarized as follows: Working men are men of action too, artisans whose talents and gung-ho spirit are crucial for America's comeback. Budweiser salutes these men by painting portraits of their industry and skill, revealing that these "back stage" jobs play a central economic role.

Authentic Populist Voice: Skilled Artisans

Bud's vision of work directly opposed the economic realities of the times. America was becoming a postindustrial society as technological advances and global outsourcing made many industrial production jobs obsolete. Bud used television ads as a bully pulpit to argue that the old guild ideals of craft labor still existed and could be revived. To make the work supremely important, Bud dramatized projects in which men labored industriously in backstage skilled crafts that, we learned, supported cities, sports teams, and the nation:

- A bicycle craftsman who built custom bikes for the U.S. Olympic team because "You can't build a bike for the Olympics by machine. Each tube has to be custom fit, to transfer weight and forward momentum. After all, a champion should ride a champion."

- The welders and riveters who worked on scaffolding surrounding the Statue of Liberty: "This Bud's for the crew restoring America's pride in liberty."

- The workers in a failing industrial city who overcame adversity and put together a plan to bring the city back to life. "They said this city was through. You said, 'No way!'"

- An African American baseball umpire who worked his way through the minor leagues. When he was promoted to the major leagues, he had to stand his ground against an angry veteran manager who contested the ump's call. In the end, the umpire earned the manager's respect and together they enjoyed a postgame Bud.

Bud championed a revival of artisan work and the heroic pursuit of challenging collective projects. To build optimism that this kind of work could again flourish, Bud celebrated occupational pockets where these values still existed. In these populist worlds, which harked back to the previous century, before the rise of mass production, workers still earned tremendous respect because they pursued their labor with skill, selfless dedication, and enthusiasm. These men were heroes because they were absolutely committed to getting the job done right in order to contribute to America's health. Bud could credibly champion this salt-of-the-earth myth on the basis of a long-term demonstration of fidelity by the parent company, Anheuser-Busch. Throughout the 1970s, Anheuser-Busch had asserted its commitment to the brewing craft as a family-owned company, with each generation of Busches dedicated to brewing as an art, using a team of Clydesdale horses as a symbol of this heritage. In unspoken opposition to its arch rival Miller Brewing Company—owned by Philip Morris to diversify its portfolio—Anheuser-Busch asserted that the huge company was in reality a family of craft brewers. Ads showed members of the Busch clan, narrating the history of the company with black-and-white photos, proudly documenting the brewing process, and lecturing the audience on the right way to pour a beer. Throughout the 1980s, Anheuser-Busch ads reminded the audience that Budweiser was made by artisans, no different really than its beer-quaffing constituents. The Busch men stood for the same values as did America's working men, because they, too, were craftsmen.

Charismatic Aesthetic: Epic Films

"This Bud's for You" used an epic film style to make seemingly mundane work heroic. This gravitas was enhanced by the announcer's voice, a slow deep baritone, reminiscent of NFL Films' football highlights. And the camera admired the workers from below, framing them as larger than life. Seemingly mundane work—building a bike, sanding metal, calling balls and strikes—was portrayed as a life-or-death drama.

Through the narrator's voice, Bud spoke—much as a boss would—with almighty authority to extol the work of Bud drinkers. This persona was crucial. In effect, Bud replaced the voice of corporate America, which at the time showed little interest in workers' skills and instead was exacting wage concessions and downsizing. In the Bud myth, workers finally get a boss who respected their contributions, who understood labor's value, and who distributed praise appropriately.

In an economy rapidly moving from industrial to service jobs, "This Bud's for You" connected powerfully with working men. And these workers rewarded the brand by making it a valued component of the symbolic armor with which they faced work-place uncertainties. The campaign firmly established Budweiser as an icon, one of the most persuasive and cherished cultural leaders of America's working men.

Cultural Disruption: Cynicism to Downsizing

By the late 1980s, American companies were reasserting a dominant position in the global marketplace. Workers had accepted difficult sacrifices in the process: lower pay, longer hours, and tougher production benchmarks. "Neutron" Jack Welch had furloughed fully 25 percent of the General Electric work force, over 100,000 workers. Earnings for nonmanagement workers declined by more than 10 percent in real terms.[4]

So when the economy finally began to perform well and productivity advanced past key rivals Germany and Japan, American workers expected repayment for the sacrifices they'd made over the previous decade. What they found instead was even more aggressive labor rationalization under the aegis of reengineering. Rather than settle back into a paternal model that gave workers a secure livelihood, American CEOs—motivated now with sizable stock options to do whatever it took to increase stock prices—squeezed even more productivity from their organizations. The result was a decade in which the rationalization of all corporate expenses—through technology investments, process engineering, and outsourcing to secondary labor markets—became a primary driver of corporate profit growth.

With the recession and jobless recovery of the early 1990s, nonprofessional men finally lost faith and rapidly abandoned their belief that their work would ever return to the respected, secure calling that they dreamed of. Bud's heroic artisan myth was shattered once and for all. Populist politics surged.

Anheuser-Busch was slow to respond to this tectonic shift. Instead, the company dragged out all the old symbols in a bet-the-farm run to revive the collective work-centered ideals of manhood. "Made in America" juxtaposed images of a bald eagle flying above Niagara Falls, Clydesdales running in slow motion, military men, and an American Olympic champion on the awards stand. Amazingly, the Bud narrator acknowledged the beleaguered state of American workers:

> If I thought that no one cared about the things I do in life, I'd still care about working hard and making it turn out right. Made in America, that means a lot to me. I believe in America, and American quality. Here's to you America, my best I give to you.

Bud used the ad as a confessional: Corporate America no longer cared about its workers, and it was pointless to pretend otherwise. Nonetheless, men of honor should continue to work hard because they're patriotic. Perhaps Anheuser-Busch thought that the Gulf War provided enough cover to stir such sentiment, but lauding "Made in America" seemed only to remind Bud drinkers of the jobs that were continuing to move overseas. The growing cohort of Wal-Mart shelf stockers could only grimace.

Failed Experiments with Conventional Branding

As the artisan myth lost traction, Anheuser-Busch began to experiment with replacements. For seven years, the brand team struggled to locate a resonant, new advertising campaign. Rather than reinvent Bud's myth, though, the brand team reverted to conventional mind share and viral branding models. The team generated a wide variety of creative ideas that worked through every trick in the branding book, only to come up empty each time.

Brand Essence. The brand team first pinned its hopes on a campaign called "Nothing Beats a Bud," which abandoned the epic dramas of American work and instead tried to revive Bud's branding from the 1970s. The ads presented a generic montage of "typical" American scenes: jogging in a small town, a barber shop, a college girl waving her diploma, young men in military uniform, a guy washing his car and making a muscle, some cowboys, guys watching a ball game on TV, a deaf woman talking in sign language, a woman blowing a kiss, a woman wrapped around a guy, and, of course, a few seconds of the indefatigable Clydesdales. This patchwork quilt of Americana was intended to communicate Bud's brand essence as a quintessential American masculine classic. The chest-beating lyrics harked back to the 1970s:

> *Here's to you America, for being strong, for coming through.*
> *Doing all that you can do. We send our best to you.*
> *Nothing beats our best, Budweiser.*
> *Nothing beats a Bud.*
> *And we'll toast and cheer with the king of beers,*
> *Nothing beats a Bud.*
> *I've seen 'em come and go. I've seen enough to know.*
> *So let your colors show. Nothing beats our best.*

Nothing beats a Bud . . .
(America's Best)

Brand Essence Again. A second campaign attempted the same idea, rekindling Bud's DNA, but with different (and better) creative. Because of the brand's success among American working men, Budweiser's dominant associations included "American," "masculine," "classic," and "for working guys." So, in "It's Always Been True, This Bud's for You," the brand team presented Bud as an American classic for real guys. One ad used a jingle to tell the audience that Bud was as classic and familiar to Americans as blue jeans, baseball, and beautiful blondes (imitating a famous Chevrolet campaign of the 1980s, but leaving out the apple pie). Another spot was set in a car garage, where some guys were working on their old, collectible cars. They held a verbal sparring match, arguing about the most classic make and model of all time. Budweiser, the audience was left to believe, was right up there in the pantheon.

Other Category Benefits: Sex Potion. While Bud was sinking, other brands were more successful selling beer as a sex potion for men. Budweiser tried co-opting this aspiration from its competitors with a variety of "Bud makes guy's dreams of babes come true" ads. One infamous spot showed two cool guys decked out in shorts and shades, imitating the feature film *Risky Business,* on a desert hike. When one guy opened a briefcase, a pool scene rolled out and inflated itself, complete with Buds and a young woman in a bathing suit. In a different ad, another cool guy unrolled a towel to reveal three more beautiful women in swimsuits. Viewed side by side from above, their swimsuits formed a perfectly rendered Bud logo.

Coolhunt. Other ads sought to make Bud relevant by weaving the brand into trendy pop culture currents. This strained effort involved a series of ads that traded on an odd juxtaposition: African American rap music and Bud. In "Auction," a touring rap group's bus got a flat tire "a jillion miles outside the 'hood," in the rural Midwest. The hip-hop-geared musicians worked their way through a cornfield in search of help and stumbled on a group of farmers at an animal auction. Deciding that the auctioneer "knows how to sell but's got no beat," the rappers took over. The lights dimmed, the turntables came out, and the group rapped the typical auction patter to the beat of record scratches. The spot ended with a rap shout-out: "Yo! MC Cowseller! Bud! Fresh!"

Buzz. Finally, Anheuser-Busch fired D'Arcy, Budweiser's agency of record for over three decades, and handed the business to DDB–Chicago, which had been doing breakthrough work on Bud Light. Ironically, the last ad that D'Arcy made before losing the account was the first ad in many years that attracted any attention. Set outside a log cabin tavern in the middle of a dark swamp, "Frogs" featured three mechanical frogs that croaked as crickets chirped in the background. While the audience waited for the action to unfold, the croaking became a promotion for the sponsor. The frogs were croaking the syllables, "Bud," "weis," and "er."

DDB picked up the concept and made a string of frog ads that audiences at least valued as entertainment and liked to talk about. It was a cute, one-hit joke, and the frogs got their share of laughs. Unfortunately, the ads did little to build Bud's identity value. DDB tried to extend the concept with ants that partied with Bud and a mischievous lobster that stole beer, but like "Frogs," these ideas also failed to perform significant branding work. The word of mouth failed to do much to the value of bottles of Budweiser beer.

"Lizards"

While Anheuser-Busch was trying in vain to revive Bud using conventional branding formulas, an enormous new slacker myth market had emerged, as described in the Mountain Dew genealogy. Budweiser's recovery was premised on inventing a new slacker myth that spoke to men who had become intensely cynical about the idea that their manhood hinged on putting in a hard day's work.

Lizards Myth Treatment

Budweiser's "Lizards" campaign was one of the decade's most effective and durable branding efforts. The ads were televised for four years and continued for years as a series of radio spots. The creative idea behind "Lizards" was deceptively simple. Anheuser-Busch had been running the "Frogs" campaign for two years. To extend this campaign, Anheuser-Busch selected work from another ad agency in their stable, Goodby Silverstein &

Partners. Goodby came up with an improbable concept: a jealous lizard who lived in the swamp wanted to rid the swamp of the celebrity frogs. The would-be assassin, Louie, hung out with his lizard friend, Frankie, on the perimeter of the frogs' swamp and commiserated. Louie wanted to star in the Bud ads and seemed ready to try anything to get his chance to step over the rival frogs. Frankie was the street-smart and world-weary friend who consoled Louie and tried to keep Louie's zealous ambitions in check.

All the action centered on these two alleged spectators who observed, and tangentially participated in, what transpired around them. Like *Seinfeld,* the campaign made a lot out of little real activity. Moreover, "Lizards," again mimicking shows like *Seinfeld,* was entirely reflexive: The ads were about how the advertising was made.

The "Lizards" ads were dead-on funny. But rather than the mindless silliness of the "Frogs" campaign, the humor was much more effective in terms of branding because it relied on wicked satires about working life. To understand how the satires worked, we have to dissect the ads to reveal the premises that the ads twisted for laughs.

The plots revolved around Louie's intense envy for the frogs' stardom and his quixotic mission to replace them. In his banter with Frankie, Louie resented the three Bud-weis-er frogs for having been cast in the ads, for becoming stars, and for their big salaries:

Louie: I can't believe they went with the frogs! Our audition was flawless. We did the look [postures for the camera]. We did the tongue thing [sticks out tongue].

Frankie: Frogs sell beer. That's it. The number one rule of marketing.

Louie: The Budweiser Lizards. We coulda been huge.

Frankie: There'll be other auditions.

Louie: Oh, yeah. For what? This was Budweiser, buddy. This was big. Those frogs are gonna pay.

Frankie: Let it go, Louie. Let it go.

Louie was so jealous that he fantasized about the frogs' assassination. In a spot shown during the Super Bowl, Louie hired a ferret to cut the support for the electric Budweiser sign that hung over the bar's entrance. As the ferret climbed the sign, Louie watched, secretly hoping the ferret was up to the task of sabotaging the sign and electrocuting the frogs. "I'm no electrician but that has got to be dangerous," Louie said with transparently fake concern. When the sign fell and sent a charge of electricity through the swamp, the frogs smoked and sizzled from the shock. It seemed that Louie's dreams were finally fulfilled. "Frankie, eventually every frog has got to croak," he intoned with a smirk. Unfortunately, the frogs proved hardy enough to survive the assassination attempt. In turn, the distraught Louie could only construct uglier plots to rid himself of the frogs and to steal their limelight.

To Louie's chagrin, Anheuser-Busch hired the ferret as a spokesperson, even though he could only screech gibberish. Exasperated, Louie condemned the ferret for his obvious lack of qualifications. Frankie, forever pushing Louie's many buttons, suggested that the ferret possessed star potential. Sporting a beret, the ferret looked, according to Frankie, "like a famous French director." Louie was beside himself.

Years into the campaign, Louie finally made it as a replacement for one of the frogs. But, even then, Louie wasn't the big cheese. The frogs revealed that they were actually tough guys who could talk, and proceeded to lash Louie with their long frog tongues, repaying him for the years he spent taunting them.

In the culmination of Louie's tragic quest for vainglory, he ran for president of the swamp. But he was up against a Kennedy-esque turtle who'd concocted an impressive platform, complete with a smear campaign that featured ads about Louie's seedy past. Louie lost the election and once more had to endure the pain of sitting on his branch and watching other mechanical beasts bask in power and fame.

Louie was the voice of the working man who'd allowed himself to be seduced by the new hypercompetitive U.S. labor market, where the winners became celebrities. He ached to get a piece of the action that he saw emanating from economic and cultural hot spots like Los Angeles; Silicon Valley; Washington, D.C.; and New York City. All that he attained, however, were equal doses of neuroses and self-absorption.

Frankie countered Louie with the slacker ethos, cool and aloof. He was happy to hang out in his back yard, the swamp, and take cynical swipes at the world beyond. Frankie understood how the game worked. He was unwilling to get sucked into a game he knew he probably could not win. The gates to fame and money were closed, so why bother? Ultimately, the only reasonable choice was to hang out on the sidelines and watch the proceedings as a spectator, emotionally distanced from the game.

Louie's passive-aggressive behavior wonderfully tapped the new zeitgeist of men who had trouble seeing causal relationships between hard work, dedication to craft, and society's respect. They sympathized with Louie's efforts to succeed in the new system and felt his pain when he failed time and again. That Louie couldn't resist stardom's temptations made for tragic comedy. But, in the end, they knew that Frankie was right. They delighted in Frankie's cynical worldview: better to sit on the sidelines, take it easy, and have a laugh. A guy could attain slacker manhood by asserting his sovereign prerogative to not participate, to reject the game's premises outright.

"Lizards" grabbed the audience because it used satire to make American men confront an idea that was hard to face straight on. Giving up on old models of manhood, these guys were still grasping for alternative toeholds. "Lizards" revealed a simple truth: You're not a hero, because society won't let you be. So what? The pressure's off. Revel in the absurdity of your situation! Sit back and enjoy.

The myth treatment for the "Lizards" campaign can be summarized as follows: Today only suckers strive for respect by chasing the American Dream, climbing the ladder of success. Now the only real option is for men to opt out of these man-of-action games and, instead, enjoy the show by mocking those who are conned into competing for success.

Charismatic Aesthetic: Borscht Belt Comedians in a Kid's Cartoon

"Lizards" was social satire. Like much great satire, the campaign was set in another place and another time so that the story could poke at cherished beliefs without alienating the audience. The set design and mechanical animals, lifted from the "Frogs" ads, reminded the viewer of a Disney-Pixar flick rather than an ad. Yet the lizards were nothing like swamp creatures. Their patter evoked something like Borscht Belt comedians trading one-liners or old Italian guys in the Bronx sitting on their front stoop commiserating.

By displacing the barbed lines, putting them in the bodies of mechanical lizards whose mouths were imperfectly synched to open and close to the match their words, Bud coaxed the audience to entertain otherwise taboo thoughts. These silly mechanical creatures were allowed to voice truths that were painful and deeply personal.

Authenticity Among Immigrant Enclaves

The campaign drew on the populist world of the immigrant enclave, a place far removed from the norms of the middle-class labor market. The choice was original and compelling. But how did Budweiser get away with this point of view after years of corporate cheerleading?

Populist authenticity can be garnered from the literacy with which one speaks from the populist world, and the fidelity with which one stays true to its values over time. At the time, Budweiser lacked the authority to champion the immigrant's cynical views. After all, Bud's earned its iconic value by motivating men to keep up the good fight, working hard for their company and country. So to switch sides, to move from a myth that celebrated hard work to one that mocked it, required not only that Bud deliver performances off the scale on authenticity, but Bud also had to be contrite, renouncing its old views. "Lizards" seemed like masochistic advertising. The ads seemed to go of their way to slam Anheuser-Busch's hard-won reputation. By conventional standards, the campaign's irreverent treatment of the firm was incoherent. Louie continually ridiculed the marketing decisions of Anheuser-Busch management: "Do you hear the script they wrote? Bud-weis-er. How creative! These advertising people just don't get it." He made fun of how much Anheuser-Busch spent on the spots. The ads blasphemed virtually everything that Bud had championed for the previous fifty years: the heroic qualities of achieving men, the devotion to hard work and enterprise, the homage to the Anheuser-Busch empire.

The ads even attacked the brand's other advertising. When the "Whas-sup?!" campaign caught on, Louie, true to character, was incredulous. He made fun of the campaign with a tongue-wagging demonstration of his own. Louie even mocked the August Busch III ads, in which the chairman of the board recounted the family history with the brewery. Mimicking August's unmistakable halting speech pattern, Louie recited the ancestry of the swamp master and the history of the swamp in epic terms.

Many ads have reflexively mocked the commercial conceits of advertising: old Volkswagen ads, the Energizer bunny, Spike Lee's pleas for Nike, Joe Isuzu, Little Caesar's, and Sprite's "Obey Your Thirst," to name the most prominent. But only the "Lizards" campaign had the audacity to deliver what seemed like a knockout punch to the company that made the product. "Lizards" was an act of flagrant disobedience in which Bud

The Power of Cultural and Political Authority

Iconic brands' own mythic turf that no other brand can touch. When Johnny-come-lately brands try to invade the storytelling terrain of an iconic brand, consumers summarily reject the newcomer as inauthentic and unoriginal. For years, The Coca-Cola Company's senior management watched jealously as Mountain Dew grabbed share points for its brands. When the company could stand the situation no longer, it launched Surge in 1996. The copycat soft drink was supported with a clever Leo Burnett campaign that delivered in spades on slacker masculinity allegories and was supported by a huge advertising war chest aimed at male teens. Teenagers flirted with the brand for a while, but soon abandoned it. Surge faded into oblivion in less than two years. The Coca-Cola Company had thrown away hundreds of millions of dollars in a vain attempt to squash its arch rival. Mountain Dew owned the slacker version of the wild man. The authority of the brand was unquestioned. Surge was an interloper with no credibility. Because The Coca-Cola Company did not understand how brand equity works for iconic brands like Mountain Dew, the company mistakenly tried to grab a piece of Mountain Dew's myth, rather than leapfrog Mountain Dew to chart out a new cultural opportunity.

Mountain Dew's potent display of its brand equity is typical for iconic brands. Customers will happily stick with their favorite icons, paying a premium even when attractive competitors enter the fray. What gave Mountain Dew such extraordinary traction that its customers so easily resisted Surge? Mountain Dew's brand equity did not stem from assets identified in typical mind-share models: the ownership of distinctive category associations.[5] Rather, iconic brands are valued because customers look to the brand to perform myths that resolve acute anxieties in their lives. Consumers don't care whether the brand owns adjectives. They care about what the brand accomplishes for their identities. The brand's equity derives from people's historic dependency on the brand's myth. If a brand's stories have provided identity value before, then people grant the brand authority to tell similar stories later on.

renounced its historic position as the champion of men's work. Bud gave up the mantle of omnipotent authority—the one that crowned Bud drinkers as kings—for the more humble but more valuable role of slacker confidant. The only way for Bud to credibly switch to this new role was to explicitly distance itself from its previous incarnation.

We can only understand how this self-immolation worked to advance Bud's identity value if we understand the corporation and the brand as two distinct characters in dialogue with the consumer. For many years, Bud and Anheuser-Busch spoke with the same voice: authoritarian, achievement-oriented figures that were proud of their accomplishments and sought to anoint beer drinkers with their power. Now that this model had been discredited among Bud's constituents, the strategic challenge was how to credibly jettison it and leap to the other side of the political divide.

Anheuser-Busch's tacit strategy was to allow Bud to run amuck, to attack the father company as would a Bart Simpson type of character. By taking wicked swipes at its own company, Bud joined its constituents who were doing the same. Anheuser-Busch didn't come out of this exchange beaten up, either. The audience was well aware that this was all a fiction, and the viewers gave Anheuser-Busch credit for this humorous confessional. They respected the company's willingness to be the butt of the joke, to absorb their hostilities toward the new economy.[6]

"Whassup?!"

With "Lizards," Bud rekindled its close identification with working men's anxieties. The brand had regained its authority by recognizing and responding to the jarring socioeconomic changes faced by its constituents. Frankie's solution, however—to sit back in the peanut gallery and observe at an aloof distance—lacked a satisfying resolution. Bud still needed a positive myth, an ideal world of manhood around which men could build solidarity. DDB's "Whassup?!", a campaign launched to complement "Lizards" in 2000, provided this missing link.

Whassup?! Myth Treatment

"Whassup?!" picked up where "Lizards" left off. The opening salvo in the campaign, a spot called "True," introduced a new Bud manhood myth into the space created by the "Lizards" satire. "True" was the first chapter of what became an ongoing saga that revealed how a group of childhood friends—African American guys around thirty and apparently single—socialized, how they hung out. The opening shot presented two of the friends, each in his own apartment, drinking Bud from the bottle and watching a game on TV. The action on the television faintly reflected off their faces. In the spirit of the consummate couch potato, each character was hanging out with his game and drinking Bud as a matter of habit.

One of the friends, a man with a large Afro and wearing bib overalls (we'll call him Bib Man), initiated the phone call to his friend as he slouched deeply in his easy chair. Though dressed in game-day casual, he was clearly a self-supporting, reasonably respectable adult. Bib Man's friend Ray, a slender man with shaved head and neatly groomed beard, appeared equally entranced—Bud, couch, and televised game—on a weekend afternoon. He answered the phone on the first ring. His performance suggested that while he was not optimistic about the conversation, he would have preferred it if someone called and gave him a reason to live.

The two men exchanged salutations, in the African American vernacular, intended to reveal nothing in particular:

Bib Man: Whassup?!

Ray: Nothing, B. [short for *bro*, which in turn was originally short for *brother*].

They admitted that they didn't have much of anything going on, which probably came as no surprise to most viewers, who could easily intuit from the vibe that this situation was typical.

Ray's roommate, Jersey Man—he wore a bright yellow football jersey—entered the kitchenette in the background, raised his hands, and delivered an exaggerated "Whassup?!" to Ray, which Ray returned in kind.

At the other end of the phone call, Bib Man couldn't help hearing the exchange and became suddenly animated, asking cheerfully, "Yo, who's that?"

In a second, Jersey Man picked up the kitchenette telephone extension, and the three men performed a cycle of joyous "Whassup?!" greetings for each other. Jersey Man interrupted and, inquiring about Bib Man's roommate, asked, "Where's Dookie?"

Bib Man responded with a "Yo, Dookie!" and a large, shaved-headed teddy bear of a man sitting at his computer picked up the phone extension.

Understated and serious compared to his pals, Dookie appeared to be working diligently. He offered a quiet "Yo."

Jersey Man shouted the most enthusiastic "Whassup?!" yet, which Dookie rebutted with his own, understated, slightly cool, and extended baritone, "Whassuuuup?!"

The cycle began again, each man delivering his own interpretation of "Whassup?!" into the phone, each man bobbing his head making sure that his tongue hung out in front of his chin as he spoke.

This chorus of "Whassups" had disintegrated into group laughter, when another interruption occurred. The intercom on the kitchen wall next to Jersey Man beeped, and he answered it. The next shot showed a leather-jacketed man standing on the apartment's stoop and toting a six-pack. He shouted his own stylized "Whassup?!" into the intercom.

The men all charged through one more round of "Whassup?!" which then ended suddenly, like a fire run out of fuel.

Jersey Man hung up and headed to the door to let in the guest with the six-pack. Dookie hung up and returned his attention to the computer screen, and Bib Man and Ray returned exactly to their original state, staring at the game on television. As if the crescendo had never happened, they started over with the same mundane conversation, one they'd probably had hundreds of times.

Bib Man: So, whassup?

Ray: Nuttin', B. Sittin' here, watchin' the game, havin' a Bud.

Like the earlier exchange, and perhaps countless others, they both nodded and repeated, "True. True." A black title card with the Bud logo announced the tag line: "True."

The closing sequence gave the audience access to what was really going on. Bib Man didn't phone Ray for any particular reason. He simply wanted to share empty time with his friend. The state of doing nothing was a central, and even profound, part of these guys' lives. It was a way for them to forge intimacy, to express deep affection without saying anything. Nothing needed to be said, because they all experienced the world in the same way, a way they'd built simultaneously through years of hanging out together. The game and the Bud became the firmament, fixtures through which these solidarities flowed.

Subsequent spots established the "Whassup?!" idea as a miniseries, in which, much like *Seinfeld* and "Lizards" before, not much ever happened. The ads were set in the same apartment, the same camera angles were employed, and the actors wore the same clothes. This *was* their life. The guys watched sports, drank Bud, and chatted each other up, albeit with precious few words. That all five men could not find anything to fill their time other than to phone each other and practice an in-joke they'd probably done hundreds of times begged the audience to interpret what was going on. More clues were given as the miniseries extended to include episodes in which our Whassup guys collided with people outside their fraternity.

Women Can't Whassup. In the Whassup world, life revolved around allegiance to the close-knit circle of friends. Whassup was a guys-only club. Girlfriends were barely tolerated, and there was no sign of a wife in any of the spots. All other relationships and commitments deferred to the guys' elemental bond. Some of the funniest and most strategically effective "Whassup?!" ads took advantage of the tension between guy solidarity and girlfriend desires.

In "Girlfriend," Dookie snuggled with his girlfriend on the couch. Since they were at her place, the television was tuned to figure skating. The show elicited only a benign stare from Dookie. She, however, was enraptured. She hovered at the brink of tears and clutched his arm as if to brace herself from being overwhelmed by emotion. When the phone rang, Dookie coolly answered it and his pals at the other end of the line all shouted, "Whassup?!" into the phone. The three buddies were at the bar watching a game on television and, missing their fourth wheel, had tracked down Dookie at his girlfriend's place. Dookie responded with as much enthusiasm as his situation allowed. He turned his head away from his girlfriend, and whispered a "Whassup?!" that he hoped she wouldn't hear. Unfortunately, his effort stood no chance of convincing his buddies that he was still a member of their club. The buddies knew Dookie was understated, but not this understated.

Sensing that his pals were losing faith in him, Dookie pried his arm from his girlfriend's grip and turned away from her so that he had a better chance to convince the friends that he was still on their side. He told his friends that he was watching the game and having a Bud. Before his pals had a chance to process Dookie's words, his girlfriend destroyed his alibi.

"Yes, yes!" she squealed as the TV announcer described a skater's great move. Still looking away from his girlfriend, Dookie grimaced. He did not want to have to explain her noise. At the bar, the friends heard the shrill shriek and, breaking out of their usual bantering slang, inquired seriously, "What game are *you* watching?" At this point, the guys found it difficult to believe that Dookie was watching the game. Back on the couch, the girl-friend's high-pitched wail grew more intense. "Yes, yes!" she cried. Dookie could only grimace, keep his mouth shut, and hope that his friends' mis-interpretation kept him out of their doghouse.

The joke worked because the Whassup ritual was a clever way to demonstrate how these friends constantly affirmed their commitments to each other. In many men's social circles, checking up on an MIA member and hearing a woman squealing "Yes, yes!" in the background would be reason enough for the members to smile knowingly at their comrade's sex-ual conquest. In this case, they were only concerned that Dookie wasn't watching the game they thought he should have been watching. He wanted to finesse his two competing commitments, to have his cake and eat it too. His difficulty gave the audience their laugh.

Similarly, in "Girl Invasion," the Whassup guys watched an apparently big game. In contrast to their earlier couch-potato routines, they actively rooted during this particular game. Dookie's girlfriend was perched on one of his massive thighs. When the men erupted into high-fives to cele-brate a big play, the girlfriend was accidentally jostled around as though they had forgotten she was there. The intercom buzzed, and when one of the guys answered it, a bunch of women screamed, "Whassup?!" The guys were confused. They'd clearly not expected any more guests, nor had they invited women to watch the game. Each man asked the other if he'd in-vited anyone, and each responded with a shoulder-shrugging denial. Dookie's girlfriend grinned coyly. The men groaned. Shamed, Dookie hung his head. Jersey Man stood at the open apartment door as the women charged in, handed him their coats, and squealed like tipsy sorority sisters as they hugged Dookie's girlfriend.

The next shot showed all of them cramped into the living room, still watching the game. The men's faces registered grin-and-bear-it expres-sions of a good day ruined, a feeling no winning team could correct. Stand-ing behind the couch, one of the women pointed at the television and said, "Oooh, he got a big head. Look at his head!" The picture cut to the black screen with the title, "True." In voice-over, the same woman screeched, "Number thirty-four!" Dookie moaned, defeated, "Oh man."

Both ads played on the idea that the "Whassup?!" salutation was a passkey into a shared worldview, that it wasn't a mere catchphrase. Dookie couldn't shout it out in front of his girlfriend. The idiom was such a complete sign of brotherly solidarity that to use the word in front of her would be totally inappropriate. Likewise, while the guys' girlfriends could imitate the word, they neither knew about nor cared about the meaning that lurked behind it. Their oblivious, reckless use of the word made the guys cringe. By protecting both how the term was used and its connotations, the men demonstrated that theirs was a boys-only club.

Professionals Can't Whassup. Likewise, Whassup was a club for working guys, not for professionals and bosses. In Goodby's contribution to the DDB campaign, "What Are You Doing?" guys who drank imported beers, Heineken in particular, were presented as the antithesis of the Bud ethos. Three satirized men, young Wall Streeters or Silicon Valley professionals, replaced the crew of African American young men. One yuppie was Indian, just back from the club, with tennis racket in hand. He stood in for the new immigrants—from Bombay, Delhi, or even Seoul—who'd joined the nation's economic elite in droves during the last high-tech expansion. He was incorrigibly cheery. All three wore Ivy League costumes, the clothes that defined preppy in the 1980s: loud plaids, stiff golf shirt collars protruding from beneath yet another shirt, and sweaters, either worn normally or draped around the shoulders.

In sharp contrast to the "True" crew, these men spoke the King's English and replaced "Whassup?!" with "What are *you* doing?!" Rather than "watchin' the game, havin' a Bud," the man on the couch was "watching the market recap and drinking an import." And instead of the hipster-correct "True, true," response, the yuppies replied to each other with "That is correct, that is correct." When the Indian man entered the scene from the kitchen, he was told to "pick up the cordless." When he did, he shouted an enthusiastic "What are you doing?!" with an Indian accent. The shtick unfolded just as it did with the young African Americans, but with hyperbolic versions of the habits and the phrasing of junior executive frat boys. The men were painfully stiff and lacked even a modicum of improvisational skill. They were the Whassup guys' social opposites.

This parody slammed men who still found identity and solidarity in corporate America. The ad proposed that import drinkers were guys who found fulfillment through their employment and thus devoted all their energies to their professional lives. As a result, they were social misfits; they had no knowledge of, or connection to, popular culture. And because they'd been so heavily socialized in the mechanical interpersonal style of the corporation, they were unable to improvise a conversation. Because they hadn't a clue about the subtle shades of meaning behind "Whassup?!" they could only parrot it. They treated the phrase like the latest Top 40 radio hit, as a cool fad that they could appropriate to impress each other that they were street savvy. The intense solidarity produced by a few choice slang words proved elusive for professionals whose energies were focused on getting ahead at the office.

The final shot showed two of the original Whassup men sitting on a leather couch. They looked puzzled, even vaguely offended. They'd just watched the same yuppie Bud ad on their television. By laughing at the yuppies with the Whassup crew, viewers could imagine themselves as more interpersonally savvy and graceful than the young professional ciphers. By extension, viewers could feel good about their association with the Whassup guys and their separation from the nation's elite professional cadre.

Whassup was available only to men who truly shared a brotherly camaraderie, a social bond that could only develop among guys who avoided the instrumental dog-eat-dog work of middle-class occupations to spend "quality time" together hanging out. Although women and professionals desperately wanted to participate in the brotherhood of Whassup, they only understood it as a surface code of slang rather than a deeper intimacy based on years of shared experience. This impenetrability, an exclusion borne of class and gender, formed the core of Whassup's credibility as a "true" expression of working men's manhood.

This parable was expanded in a spot called "Wasabi." Dookie, who emerged as the star of the campaign, was again with his girlfriend, this time at a sushi restaurant. The audience saw only her back. The Japanese waiter presented their food and routinely announced, "Wasabi," as he placed a small bowl of the green horseradish on their table. With a wry grin Dookie repeated, "Wasabi," with a touch of the "Whassup?!" delivery style. After the waiter innocently nodded, "Wasabi," Dookie again repeated the word, this time with more "Whassup?!" gusto, his tongue flapping. The waiter, still blind to Dookie's playful framing, repeated another innocent, "Wasabi."

In the background, the sushi bar chefs—stereotypically always eager to shout an incomprehensible phrase in unison—raised their knives and shouted, "Wasabi!" Dookie jumped on this bandwagon, upped the chefs' enthusiasm, waggled his tongue, and generally played the fool as though he were alone with his Whassup brothers. The cycle repeated, the volume increased, and the camaraderie between Dookie and the Japanese men escalated. And it was all based on improvisation around the silly phrase. Dookie's girlfriend finally had enough. With her hand, she rapped the table like a judge pounding a gavel, hard enough to bounce the dishes. Dookie snapped to her attention and cut short his boy's play.

The spot worked by playing on the tension between the natural bonds of working guys championed by Bud, and Dookie's female relationship. The girlfriend convinced her man to take her out for dinner, finally dragging Dookie away from his Whassup buddies. Yet, even here, among strangers as culturally removed from African American life as one can imagine, Dookie connected in a way that eluded her. She found it neither funny nor worthy of participation.

In clever fashion, "Wasabi" expressed how working men, even strangers, instinctively shared a distinctively masculine intimacy. The bond was based on a shared appreciation for their place in the world, a place in which few words need to be spoken. Additionally, the spot showed that localized pockets of work—in which the joie de vivre of Whassup-styled interaction can be woven into work—still existed. Sushi chefs were craftsmen whose labor was on display for their customers. Instead of the old Bud myth, which celebrated the heroism of craftsmen, the myth in "Wasabi" presented new Bud ideals. Now work was merely an occasion, one of many, in which men could find intimacy in freestyle play.

In the Whassup world, friends created intimacy around their secret code, the different phrasings of a single salutation. The friends knew each other so well that they could practically grunt and groan a generic phrase to communicate everything they needed to say. Different inflections reflected not only men's different personalities, but a wide range of emotions as the situations demanded. It was a distinctly masculine way of communicating, saying everything by saying not much of anything.

When men had difficulty finding solidarity and affirmation in what they made or in their contributions to society, where were they to look? Whassup provided a humble, yet affirming answer. In this worldview, masculinity needn't be modeled on the heroic pursuits of soldiers, athletes, cowboys, or even supposedly heroic welders working atop the Statue of Liberty. Manhood lay in the love, loyalty, and intimacy that one shared with one's mates. Whassup retooled slackers' scornful mocking into something profound. The ultimate center of gravity for men's self-esteem flowed from a tightly knit circle of male friends.

The myth treatment for "Whassup!?" can be summarized as follows: Today men find brotherhood and intimacy hanging out together, creating their own hermetic culture that they use to perform for each other. They can't depend on job success to earn respect, because heroic efforts are no longer rewarded as such. So identity must grow out of the camaraderie of close friends.

Authenticity Among Urban African American Men

Anheuser-Busch set the "Whassup?!" stories in social environs that were virtually the inverse of the prior myth. In "This Bud's for You," Bud had championed the heroic efforts of a melting pot of American men who made things happen behind the scenes at work. Bud's heroes had included the urban, the suburban, and the rural; blacks, whites, and Hispanics; and those in production jobs and those in service jobs. African Americans played a statistical rather than strategic role. In contrast, African American life is the focus of "Whassup?!" Bud's populist world, recast as the leisurely life of single, urban black men, leaned exclusively on their lifestyle and vernacular for its effectiveness.

The Beats of the 1950s had built their aesthetic around worship of the raw sensuality and stylish sensibility of the inner-city black hipster. Since that time, the African American ghetto, and particularly the single, urban black man, has been one of the most potent populist worlds used in American mythmaking. Urban black culture has been represented as hip and freewheeling, while the white middle-class males thought to inhabit the center of professional-managerial life have been showcased as staid and reserved.

Because they'd developed a deeply ironic counterculture that stood up to racial discrimination, urban black men were understood by whites to be among the most successful at insulating themselves from American ideology's pressures toward conformity and instrumentality. As such, this cohort of black men became, for a white male audience, a perfect populist world for rebellious masculine myths. In recent decades, the nation's upper-middle-class elite has included African American men who are every bit as committed to American ideology as their white counterparts. Yet black men have remained—in the nation's cultural imagination—more able to escape the daily grind to create their own culture and pleasures.

"Whassup?!" presented five African American guys whose work lives were out of focus. They seemed to be neither blue-collar nor white-collar. Only Dookie apparently had some vague attachment to a desk job. Rather, because of their vernacular, the audience presumed that these guys grew up in an urban black neighborhood and were still ensconced in hip-hop culture, even though they were self-sustaining adults.

For their fraternity, the friends depended on personalized appropriations of black vernacular: *Whassup, B.,* and *true* were all colloquial African American expressions. The idiom *whassup* had circulated in black urban culture since at least the 1920s. More recently, the comedian Martin Lawrence regularly tossed out *whassups* well before the Bud campaign broke. Like *phat, in-the-house,* and *word,* before, young white men had appropriated these expressions to pilfer some of the rebellious attitude associated with black men. The "Whassup?!" ad gave white guys privileged access into the everyday lives of hip black guys and how they interacted.

For younger men who'd grown up in a generation in which much popular culture was dominated by urban African American genres, looking to black guys as mythic figures was commonplace. But for Bud drinkers over the age of forty or so, and particularly men who lived away from big cities, the ads were tremendously polarizing. Older white Bud drinkers didn't like the "Whassup" spots initially and flooded Anheuser-Busch customer centers with complaints. While many marketers would have pulled the ads, Anheuser-Busch senior managers stuck to their guns. They decided to air the spots with low media weights to see how the campaign would build. After several months, the resonance with the younger audience was so strong that the elders caved in to the emerging consensus. When the company went back to research the elder white drinkers, their opinions had flip-flopped. The Whassup guys turned out to be desirable after all.

This antagonism demonstrates a crucial property of the myths spun by iconic brands. These myths lead culture rather than mimic it, so they necessarily take a provocative stand against conventional ideas. If the advertising doesn't alienate people who are resolutely tied to a competing ideology, the political vibrations running through the ads are probably not sufficiently compelling to build an icon. Just as Elvis Presley and Marlon Brando disturbed people who wanted to hold on to cultural orthodoxy, so too did Bud's Whassup guys in their own way.

Utilizing the style and sensibilities of urban black men is an old trick for identity brands, one that often backfires (witness Bud's "Auction" ad described above). It's initially puzzling that Bud was able to get away with it. Bud was still strongly identified with the Midwestern heritage of the Busch family and its St. Louis headquarters. The brand's advertising had always comprised a middle-American vibe, despite its regular nods to racial and ethnic diversity. So why did Bud's audience quickly accept that Bud was a committed player in urban African American life?

Further complicating Bud's problems on the authenticity front was the origin of the "True" spot. Before it was turned into an ad, "True" was a popular, independent short film. Anheuser-Busch bought the rights to the film from its writer and director, Charles Stone III. It would not have been surprising if the campaign had been castigated as yet another example of cultural appropriation, in which authentic expressions from black folk culture had been crassly lifted for commercial aims. Once the campaign became popular and the subject of media coverage, the origin of the spots became common knowledge outside advertising circles. Why, then, wasn't Bud taken to task?

Casting Stone and his friends rather than professional actors was the crucial strategic move that granted the campaign the requisite authenticity. Bud established the credibility to represent the world of "True" because the audience quickly learned that the actors in the ad were real friends, not part of the ad world, and that the film had been "discovered."

The Anheuser-Busch public relations machine leaped on the public's interest and launched a campaign within the campaign. The inside story—the making of "Whassup?!"—was repeated in *USA Today*, and the crew appeared on *Entertainment Tonight*, *The Tonight Show*, and *The Late Show with David Letterman*. Anheuser-Busch pushed the back story one step further, sending the Whassup guys on a nationwide tour of local talk shows and media events. This story became just as important as the ads themselves. The public relations campaign helped suggest that Anheuser-Busch was not using Madison Avenue chicanery to trick us into falling for some fun-loving black guys. These guys were real friends, they were charismatic in real life, and they'd chosen, of their own volition, to join forces with Bud.

Charismatic Aesthetic: Ensemble Acting in a Low-Tech Production

The verisimilitude of "Whassup?!" relied entirely on the cast's performances, on the actors' ability to convince viewers that theirs was indeed a brotherhood of truly hip and fun-loving guys. Persuasive ensemble acting made "Whassup?!" tick. These guys acted as if they'd known each other forever (later on, viewers found out they had). They were entirely comfortable communicating with the most minimal of body language. They mixed in idiomatic phrasings without effort or pretense. They seemed to be actually hanging out rather than reading lines.

In addition, "Whassup?!" incorporated the most minimal production values, precisely the opposite of Bud's previous advertising. Rather than spectacular shots, editing, and music that suggested a $100 million Hollywood blockbuster, the spots relied on a single, static shot in the apartment, with the characters presented in a flat, democratic manner. The ads were low-budget, one-camera documentaries, not Spielberg. This style established the Bud persona as an intimate, down-to-earth peer rather than a voice from on high.

Managing Cultural and Political Authority

With "This Bud's for You," Budweiser delivered one of the most powerful brand myths of the 1980s. When a massive cultural disruption caused the value of this artisanal myth to plummet in the early 1990s, the brand team tenaciously worked to revive the brand, wielding a variety of conventional brand strategies, from mind share to coolhunt to buzz. Despite years of experimentation supported by an enormous media budget, these efforts failed.

Budweiser finally recovered when the "Lizards" and "Whassup?!" campaigns combined to deliver a new myth. The campaigns targeted an acute contemporary contradiction faced by this constituency: that these men were now unable to forge a heroic brotherhood in their work. Both

FIGURE 5-1

Budweiser Leverages Cultural and Political Authority to Reinvent Its Myth

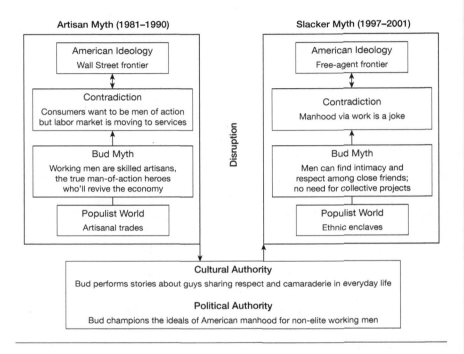

campaigns drew from an appropriate populist world—racial and ethnic subcultures of American men—to create a myth about the brotherly solidarity that comes from lifelong friendships (figure 5-1).

This genealogy begs a crucial question left unanswered in the previous chapters: Why are iconic brands able to reestablish such strong loyalty after cultural disruptions? And how is it that iconic brands can pull this off even when they've deviated badly from their myths for years? Iconic brands flagrantly violate how brand equity is supposed to work according to the mind-share model, which claims that brand's equity comes from the distinctiveness and strength of the brand essence and that equity is built by hammering home these associations consistently over time. Both "Lizards" and "Whassup?!" are antithetical to "This Bud's for You" and also seemingly unrelated to each other. To understand how this about-face worked, we need a new concept of brand equity, one appropriate for iconic brands. When disruptions occur, iconic brands don't go back to square one. While the brand's myth loses value, what remains intact is the collective memory of the brand's prior stories and what these stories accomplished for the people who used them. More formally, when identity brands are successful, they accrue two kinds of assets: *cultural authority* and *political authority*. These assets do not automatically convert to brand equity. Rather, managers must reinterpret the assets to align with important social changes to optimize the brand's equity.

Cultural Authority

Brands that author a successful myth earn the right to come back later with new myths that touch on the same cultural concerns. With "This Bud's for You," Budweiser took command of American stories about how men find respect and camaraderie. Consumers came to recognize Bud as an authority for this type of myth, regardless of the specific contents. Americans looked to Bud to tell new stories about how guys create fraternity and find respect. This is the brand's *cultural authority:* a brand asset based on the nation's collective expectations that the brand can and should author a particular kind of story.

Political Authority

In addition to cultural authority, the genealogy reveals the centrality of political authority in Bud's rebound. Budweiser's transformation—from the "This Bud's for You" era of blue-collar cheerleading to the cynical reflexivity of "Lizards" and the overt slacking of "Whassup?!"—is one of the most remarkable reinventions of a brand in recent business history. This repositioning is incomprehensible if interpreted using the conventional mindshare handbook. The protagonists of "Lizards" and "Whassup?!" were the antitheses of the heroic workers of "This Bud's for You." The Whassup guys seemed like losers, slackers who mostly hung out, drank beer, and watched television. Their ambitions apparently extend no farther than getting off the couch to get another round. Viewed through the lens of mind share, it looked as if Budweiser not only abandoned its hard-earned equity, but actually subverted its former self.

The transition worked because Budweiser has previously championed a world in which working men can be respected members of American

Rethinking Relevance

Building the equity of an identity brand is no easy task. In fact, even maintaining the equity of identity brands that have achieved iconic status has proven to be a considerable challenge, as the fates of Levi's, Pepsi, and Cadillac each attest.

Conventional branding models lack a coherent approach for managing brand equity in the face of cultural change. Advocates of mind share simply ignore the task and pass it off to their ad agencies, telling them to make the brand relevant while the brand managers control the DNA rudder, charting a path that ignores historical shifts. Viral branding takes just the opposite view: Managers virtually ignore the brand's past to gravitate to the next big thing. Culture, in this view, is reduced to trends: What's the latest music, fashion, or catchphrase? In both models, keeping the brand in tune with cultural change is reduced to the idea of relevance, which is understood to mean that the brand communications should fold in materials that have some currency in the popular culture of the moment.

This view of relevance is far too literal, however. It assumes that a brand's stories work as a mirror, that people simply want to see culture that they like reflected in the brand's communications. As long as the brand keeps up with fashion, pop culture, and catchphrases, consumers will find it relevant. But identity brands perform myths, not mirrors. They tell stories that are often far removed from anything currently in play in popular culture: an aging crooner taking a dive off a Las Vegas casino (Mountain Dew), a shabbily dressed guy throwing rocks at a tree (Volkswagen), two lizards commiserating in a swamp (Bud). Myths are relevant because, through simple metaphors, the stories address profound social tensions. It is the tension that is relevant, not how the characters

society and gather in solidarity around this status. Consequently, American society looked to Budweiser to create a new myth supporting the identities of these same constituents when the prior myth became obsolete. The problem was that for Bud to successfully deliver on this mission, the politics of its myth had to radically change when nonprofessional men's conception of work shifted beginning in the early 1990s.

are outfitted. Relevance is primarily about identity politics, not fashions or trends.

Iconic brands remain relevant when they adapt their myths to address the shifting contradictions that their constituents face. In the period stretching from World War II until Vietnam, Budweiser had allowed men who otherwise lacked the financial and cultural capacity to have a taste of the idealized suburban lifestyle that enchanted the United States. As this myth became politically untenable, Bud dramatically shifted its communications, championing not consumption but work. Men built intimacy and respect among each other through the heroic qualities of their artisan labor. And when this idea too lost credibility, Bud's myth was radically reinvented again to champion not a fancy lifestyle or heroic work, but the quotidian pleasures of hanging out with good friends.

Neither "Lizards" nor "Whassup?!" was based on anything trendy. In the case of "Lizards," one could argue that the campaign was the antithesis of conventional ideas of relevance—it didn't explicitly reference anything current in popular culture. The Whassup guys, though African American, bore little relation to the sizzling hot world of hip-hop culture found on MTV. Yet these campaigns proved to be extraordinarily relevant to Bud's constituency. Why? Because both campaigns touched a political nerve. Each addressed intense desires for a new mode of masculine brotherhood that was generated by the country's massive economic restructuring. For iconic brands, relevance is not about clothes or haircuts. It's about keeping up with changes in society. As their patrons' dreams and anxieties get pushed around by real changes in the economy and society, new kinds of myths are needed. Increasing brand equity is all about taking advantage of the brand's accrued cultural and political authority to create these new myths.

When the brand team understood Budweiser's equity as brand essence—timeless associations such as American, macho, and classic—they unknowingly abandoned Budweiser's most valued role for its constituents. These associations locked the brand team into an attenuated set of creative concepts that shirked the brand's responsibilities to its constituents.

Budweiser succeeded when its advertising finally delivered on its historic political commitments. This return to grace was the result of a daring political flip-flop. In order to side with working men, who were increasingly unable to use their work as a locus of self-respect, Bud advanced a new place for masculine camaraderie: a sanctuary rather than a competitive battlefield, a communal place rather than a heroic project. In *"Whassup?!"* the easy camaraderie that these guys formed became admirable because, like Frankie in the *"Lizards"* campaign, they had the self-confidence and force of will to remove themselves from the heat of insurmountable labor market competition. America responded in turn, treating the Whassup guys as heroes and celebrities. These campaigns violated the central pillars of conventional branding. But the brand had returned to the fold politically, reasserted its leadership role among the working men it had deserted in the early 1990s.[7]

Mountain Dew's Cultural and Political Authority

Brand equity also took the form of cultural and political authority for Mountain Dew. In its first two myth markets, Mountain Dew performed identity myths that borrowed from related rural backwoods figures (the hillbilly and the redneck) to celebrate the virility of guys weaned on America's traditional ideals of frontier masculinity. In the third myth market, Mountain Dew made a break from this rural heritage to create a slacker myth. Why did soda consumers immediately accept these new "Do the Dew" stories?

With its hillbilly and redneck myths, Mountain Dew established its cultural authority to author myths about men's daredevil escapades in the outdoors. Likewise, these previous myths earned Mountain Dew the political authority to champion for men with less-than-glamorous jobs the ideal that manhood is about virility, creativity, and daring-do rather than about how successful you are at work.

In terms of content, the "Do the Dew" campaign appeared to be worlds apart from these preceding hillbilly cartoons and rural watering hole spots. Yet the brand's missive was welcomed with open arms because it tapped this deep reservoir of cultural and political authority. Mountain Dew was, again, championing the id over careers for young men who felt excluded from the nation's definition of manhood. Iconic brands own an imaginative cultural and political space that can be reclaimed virtually at

FIGURE 5-2

Mountain Dew Leverages Cultural and Political Authority to Reinvent Its Myth

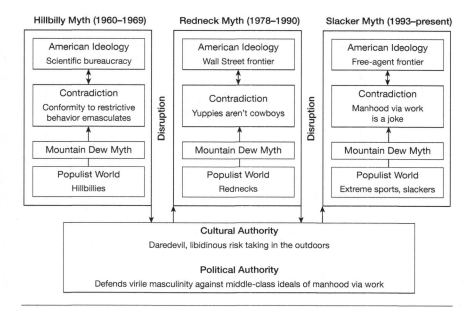

will even if the brand has fumbled or abandoned this commitment for years (figure 5-2).

Volkswagen's Cultural and Political Authority

The Volkswagen Beetle was one of the most influential iconic brands in the United States in 1970. Like Budweiser, Volkswagen abandoned its myth for mind-share advertising. More than twenty-five years after conventional advertising had buried Volkswagen's iconic value, Arnold Communications unearthed it, dusted it off, and found a way to recapture its tremendous strength. To yank the icon out of its slumber, Arnold had to reimagine the original myth so that it appropriately addressed a new social climate. To do so, Arnold leveraged the cultural and political authority Volkswagen had accumulated in the halcyon days of the Beetle. Volkswagen returned to form, speaking again to well-educated professionals about

FIGURE 5-3

Volkswagen Leverages Cultural and Political Authority to Reinvent Its Myth

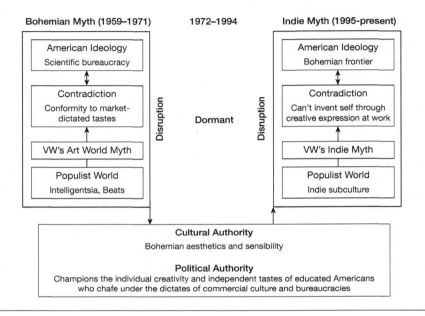

their desire to understand themselves as creative individuals in organizations that seldom allowed them such freedom (figure 5-3).

The specific content of Volkswagen's myth had to shift because the most acute contradiction facing educated professionals was no longer the specter of cultural conformity. Volkswagen instead addressed a poignant new contradiction: the rationalization of work, which impaired desires to act in the world creatively, like an artist. Because the brand could draw on its ancient cultural and political authority earned in the Beetle era, consumers quickly anointed Volkswagen the champion of these ideals.

CHAPTER 6

Managing Brand Loyalty as a Social Network

C USTOMERS OF ICONIC BRANDS VALUE THEM differently than the mind-share model predicts—as containers of identity myths that they experience through ritual action. Not surprisingly, brand loyalty works differently as well. To understand how loyalty is maintained for identity brands, we must look carefully at how customers use the brand in everyday life searching for the glue that creates allegiances over time.

In the following analysis, I draw on an ethnographic study of ESPN.[1] I found that this sports media company has three interdependent constituencies—customer segments that I call *followers*, *insiders*, and *feeders*. The key to how brand loyalty works for iconic brands like ESPN is found in the interactions between these three constituencies. To set up this customer analysis, we begin with an overview of ESPN's identity myth.

ESPN Genealogy

From its founding in 1979, ESPN quickly rose to become one of the most influential new cable channels. When the Walt Disney Company purchased ABC Capital Cities, Disney CEO Michael Eisner called the sports channel "the crown jewel" of the deal. ESPN has spawned a media empire, including ESPN2, ESPN News, ESPN Classics, ESPN Radio, ESPNZone sports bars, and the espn.com Web site. But the center of the empire remains *Sports Center*, the hour-long news and highlights program broadcast on ESPN seven times per day, 365 days per year.

For years, major media companies have tried to figure out how to tap into the business that ESPN created. CNN created CNN/si ("si" stands for Sports Illustrated), which combined the esteemed broadcast news entity with the most respected name in American sports journalism. Yet CNN/si failed to dent ESPN's armor. Similarly, the FOX network bought nine regional cable sports networks, unified them, and named the new entity FOX Sports Net. Its big-budget *National Sports Report* was designed to compete directly with *Sports Center*. FOX even hired ESPN's star anchor Keith Olbermann to lead the charge. Yet, after a few years of mediocre results and several program redesigns, FOX eventually moved the show to a time slot that didn't compete head-on with *Sports Center*.

ESPN's extraordinary hold on sports viewers is puzzling at first, because much of what the network does has been done before. For decades, television networks had devoted intensive coverage to the major team sports, especially football but also baseball, basketball, and hockey. Some programming, like ABC's *Wide World of Sports*, had treated sports with great devotion and enthusiasm. ESPN offers 24-7 coverage, but simply doing more of what other programs already do is not a formula for building a brand. Rather, ESPN's success stems from the same principles described in previous chapters.

ESPN's Man-of-Action Athlete Myth

It's no coincidence that ESPN began to exert enormous influence on American men's lives during the late 1980s and hit its stride beginning in the early 1990s, as the new free-agent frontier ideology and its man-of-action hero ideal took hold. As American men began to adjust to the new ultra-competitive labor market, they demanded new myths. Success no longer depended primarily on climbing the corporate hierarchy. No longer did men earn respect by contributing to collective projects. Rather, being a man now required winning difficult individual battles on a day-to-day basis, maximizing one's "human capital" potential, trying to "brand" oneself, and constantly honing one's mind and body for the intense competition now found in the labor market.

The escalating tensions in men's lives fueled the demands for new mythic sources of motivation and inspiration to sustain the new, hyperventilating work ethic. Along with Nike, ESPN was one of the most successful innovators in mining this new myth market. The brand performed a national myth based on a new kind of athletic achievement.

Team sports have long served as a potent populist world that has fed the creation of manhood myths. Sports teams were understood as analogues of the world of business, a training ground where boys learned to become men by following the rules and by collapsing personal interests into the interests of the team. Sports supplied the myth for modeling the desires and morals of adult men's work. The mass media, and the men who constituted their audience, celebrated dynastic teams like UCLA's basketball team under John Wooden and the Dallas Cowboys under Tom Landry. Authoritarian coaches like Vince Lombardi and quarterbacks with great leadership skills like Roger Staubach were revered.

In the emerging free-agent economy, however, stories about traditional authority figures and the troops who followed them became less relevant as resources for building and maintaining myths. Instead, individual athletic excellence was a better fit. American society demanded myths that made it desirable and intrinsically worthwhile to work in the intensive labor markets. Individual athletes who were successful in the most competitive sports were the perfect cultural source materials. Here were people who had enormous intrinsic motivation to do whatever it takes to win, to compete ferociously, to train their bodies relentlessly. Competitive athletes worked endlessly because they had a competitive drive that pushed them to train harder than their rivals. The best athletes were in sports because they loved the intensity of competition; they couldn't imagine doing anything else.

Supported by ESPN's broadcasts and Nike's famous advertising, the man-of-action athlete—the athlete who didn't abide by team norms but, as a result of this spirit, led the team to greater heights—became the new hero of sport and one of the central cast members for man-of-action myths.[2]

Sports Center's Myth Treatment

ESPN's *Sports Center* was certainly a well-produced sports program. But its iconic value stemmed from qualities beyond just good journalism and production values. Unlike any other sports news show, *Sports Center* provided its viewers—the vast majority of them men—with a new way of experiencing sport as myth.

Because ESPN is a television network, its iconic qualities evolved differently from those of Budweiser, Volkswagen, and Mountain Dew. Although advertising played a key supporting role, ESPN's storytelling happened primarily in its broadcasts rather than its ads.

ESPN's broadcast journalists lauded the *pure athlete:* the athlete who thrived on intensive competition, worked to develop superior skills, and exhibited the right attitude, the gumption, and the tenacity to keep fighting the toughest battles. Pure athletes possessed little interest in the commercial and celebrity side of sport. Instead, they lived to experience the ideals of athletic achievement and its correlates: aggression, danger, teamwork, determination, and domination.

Jocks had been celebrated before, but ESPN's treatment of them was special because the network so zealously scrutinized individual athletes. ESPN delivered to the audience the athletes' psyches laid bare—their personalities, their biographies, their difficulties, their character defects, warts and all—to spotlight how competitive athletes approach their lives. Through these psychologically penetrating interpretations of the day's sport stories, the *Sports Center* broadcasts invited their mostly male audience to try on the mind-set of the pure athletes, to identify with their tenacious habits and competitive drive and to join in berating their opposites.

One way ESPN enticed viewers—many of whom had rarely competed in team sports since adolescence—to identify with the pure athlete was to demonstrate the myth's expansive relevance. While ESPN's bread-and-butter offerings were the major team sports, the network continually showed that pure athletes could be found everywhere if only one looked hard enough. The channel enthusiastically showcased middle-aged guys competing on small motorcross bikes around a backyard track in Orange County using the same pure sport lens. Unlike any sports media before it, ESPN presented the case that both amateurs and armchair jocks could be pure sportsmen if only they adopted the right attitude.

Authentic Populist Voice: The Pure Athlete

Relying on the same principles that other iconic brands followed, *Sports Center* developed an authentic relationship with the populist world of competitive athletes by demonstrating its commitment to these athletes and its intimacy with them. For starters, unlike typical reporters of the day—who were usually talking heads reading from TelePrompTer material written by scriptwriters—ESPN reporters were hard-core sports fans who worked more like a beat sports reporter for a local newspaper. They knew their material cold and wrote all their own copy, often improvising on top of it. Their style grew from the network's early days, when the major broadcast networks viewed ESPN as a threat and wouldn't provide clips of game highlights as they did to the local affiliate television stations.

Lacking highlight videotape, improvisers like Chris Berman and Dick Vitale, and later the famous duo Keith Olbermann and Dan Patrick, learned to excel at describing action that the viewer couldn't see.

In *Sports Center*'s early years, an anchor often enthusiastically described, off the cuff and with impeccable insider knowledge, any game, either a contest still under way or one recently completed. At any moment, anchors would have to fill time by talking about their favorite players, statistics, or all-time great battles. To this day, audiences listen as much to the ESPN broadcaster's voice as they watch the highlights. Because television is essentially a visual medium, what was initially considered a constraint— limited highlight tape—helped *Sports Center* create an intimacy with the sport that the prior highlights programs had lacked.

ESPN's "This is *Sports Center*" ad campaign worked wonderfully to build claims to authenticity. The campaign was the first to rely on *mockumentaries*—parodies of documentary films—as exemplified by the widely adored heavy-metal film spoof, *Spinal Tap*. The campaign satired the true-to-life backstage activities of Sports Center's anchors (arguing over the wording in a report, putting on their own makeup in the restroom). The signature creative element of the campaign was to bring in famous athletes to play funny, self-deprecating roles, using insider sports humor to interact with ESPN's anchors backstage or off-camera in the plain-Jane ESPN newsroom in Bristol, Connecticut. Because the satires were so funny, especially for athletes, it soon became a badge of honor among star athletes to appear in a spot. As viewers came to understand that athletes wanted to appear in the ads and did so for free, the ads became less commercials than little time-out skits that celebrated the bond between great athletes and ESPN.

ESPN's less-than-polished anchors and its humble settings also worked to symbolize the network's commitment to athletes. Founded in Bristol, Connecticut, the network was never moved. The on-air personalities constantly made lighthearted jokes about the place, demonstrating that the network was a populist haunt, neither big-business nor Hollywood. The humble location of its headquarters allowed ESPN to be a populist champion amid the overcommercialized hype of professional sport.

Likewise, the well-known back stories of beloved personalities like Berman reinforced ESPN's credibility. Though many reporters and personalities were accomplished print journalists, others were simply sports junkies (a term supposedly coined by an early ESPN employee) who bull-rushed their way into the spotlight with knowledge, passion, and quirkiness. They embodied the antithesis of Hollywood polish. And, like the athletes they covered, their speech and manners exuded physicality, attitude, and grit.

Charismatic Aesthetic: The Locker Room

ESPN treated the viewer much as its early journalists treated each other, like athletes and rabid fans. Because they were so immersed in the athlete's world and so passionate about it, the ESPN journalists became proselytizers for the athletes' values. The network defined itself by imposing an occupational boundary: Only people who identified totally with athletes were allowed in the conversation. To enter the world of ESPN was to imagine oneself as a fellow insider. The network made room for the rotund, middle-aged sales manager who hadn't laced up athletic shoes since puberty as long as he came to the broadcast as a jock.

Because most brands embed myths into inert products, their charisma stems from marketing communications. Service offerings can also sometimes create myths with creative store design and service interactions. In contrast, ESPN's charisma sprang directly from its on-air personalities, especially Olbermann and Patrick's performances on *Sports Center*. ESPN personalities routinely offered aggressive opinions, which they passionately supported with evidence as if they were on a college debate team. The network taught fans how to watch sports as an athlete watches his peers, not as a spectator watches professionals.

The anchors routinely stood up against ESPN management as standard-bearers for pure sport. Sports reporting, like any other national reporting, was a dignified, professional field before ESPN anchors entered. While ESPN management tried to build professional style and credentials to match the broadcast networks, its reporters would have none of it. Instead, these Young Turks developed their own rambunctious, often potty-mouthed style that quickly won over men around the nation. For instance, Berman developed his "Bermanisms"—goofy nicknames for athletes whose play he found notable. When management forbade his unprofessional clowning, Berman responded creatively, with his own on-air protest. He began to identify highlighted players by their full names, as though he were reading from their drivers licenses, speaking each name with deadpan accuracy. The viewers, used to his playful, ridiculous nicknames, understood his sudden lack of emotion as an ironic checkmate, a rebellious shot at management. Fans jammed the network's phone lines and fax machines, telling ESPN that they missed Berman's quirky ad-libbing. Perhaps more embarrassing to management, the fans also made it clear that they understood Berman's insubordination and that they approved of it nearly as much as his nicknames. Management soon relented, and Berman returned to his improvisational form.

Before ESPN, the major networks treated their audiences as minimally knowledgeable spectators. They hired broadcasters to describe the action and to teach the audience how to appreciate what they were viewing. Sportscasters generally channeled the story "on the field" to the audience in a fawning tone, respectful of the heroes on the field.

ESPN upended this convention, treating athletes as peers. *Sports Center* journalists acted as if they were sitting in the locker room with fellow players. The commentators lauded the play of some who deserved it and berated others aggressively if they performed poorly or rejected the proper, pure athlete values. Consider one of the legendary *Sports Center* moments—an episode that ESPN devotees retell over and over, the way devotees of other brands describe breakthrough ads.

Sports Center showed videotape in which track star Carl Lewis sang the national anthem before a New Jersey Nets basketball game. Although Lewis was periodically the world's fastest sprinter, he was, unfortunately, one of its worst singers. *Sports Center*'s audience would have derived a good chuckle from a clip of Lewis singing. The *Sports Center* team, however, let the tape roll, showing the athlete in close-up as he maimed the entire song. As Lewis stumbled, the NBA fans in the arena began to boo, and the tape's audio track picked up their derision. The *Sports Center* anchors, Charley Steiner and Jack Edwards, could be heard trying, and failing, to suppress their laughter. When Lewis had finished butchering the anthem, Steiner and Edwards reappeared on screen, both completely overcome by hysterical laughter. Neither was capable of continuing the show. Steiner's face glowed crimson and tears streamed down his cheeks. He tried to speak, but could only stutter. Edwards cradled his face in his hands, unable even to look at the camera.

To understand how Lewis's bad singing—and the anchors' insolence—could have so moved *Sports Center* fans, it's important to understand that many fans viewed Lewis as a phenomenal, but self-absorbed athlete, a poster child for the antithesis of the pure sport ethos. As a college athlete,

Lewis was the world's top-ranked 100-meter sprinter and won three events at the U.S. nationals, an unheard-of feat. The following year, he won four gold medals at the 1984 Los Angeles Olympics. But one of his performances caused fans to wonder if he deserved their admiration. On his first attempt (competitors get six tries), he thought he'd jumped far enough in the long jump to win. To save his strength for his other races, he walked away from his other jumps, leaving others to try to beat his first. The fans who'd paid hundreds of dollars to get in the stadium weren't pleased and booed him. They wanted to see him try to break Bob Beamon's world record, which had stood since the 1968 Olympics.

After his incredible performance, Lewis made no secret about his desire to parlay his Olympic gold into endorsement loot. When the marketing offers failed to match his expectations, he was displeased and said so.

Although Lewis was audibly bitter about what he perceived to be his second-class fame, he continued to dominate competitors on the track. Nobody had ever defended 100-meter or long-jump Olympic gold medals, but Lewis did both.

Lewis regularly crowed about his own impressive feats. After winning the 100-meter race at the 1991 Tokyo World Championships, he congratulated himself, then condescended to those who may or may not have understood the depth of his accomplishment. "The best race of my life," Lewis said. "The best technique, the fastest. And I did it at thirty."

Sports fans devoted to the pure athlete ethos didn't care for Lewis. They thought he needed a good dose of comeuppance, and when *Sports Center* delivered the insult, fans loved it.

Olbermann and Steve Levy shared another of *Sports Center*'s most famous playtimes. ESPN's commentators were renowned for favoring scatological locker room banter, including one infamous incident in which an injury report about a player's bulging disk in his back was misspoken by a reporter as a "bulging dick." For the remainder of the show, the anchors riffed themselves to tears, using and reusing the silly miscue like a pair of high-school cutups. Fans not only loved their shtick, but also talked about the anchors' irreverence for years.

ESPN management occasionally suspended Olbermann and others for behavior deemed inappropriate or detrimental to the company's image. To fans, these punishments only enhanced the anchors' reputations. Once, after Olbermann spatted with management and served a suspension, coanchor Patrick surprised him on the air by saying, "Where the hell have you been?" Olbermann, a little surprised, nevertheless replied crisply, "I overslept." Viewers were well aware that the classroom brat Olbermann had landed in hot water and had been punished. Yet to fans, this was a wink and a nudge from their heroes, demonstrating to them that the clowns had to serve a little time-out now and then, but that the bad boys still ran the show.

Olbermann also showed fans that when it came to speaking his mind about celebrities whom he considered overrated, Steiner had nothing on him. One of Olbermann's more famous on-air comments was a gurgly, gagging sound, used to indicate an athlete's choking, or failure to perform under intense pressure. During a Bulls-versus-Sonics NBA finals game, when the highlights from the first game in Seattle showed the obligatory celebrities in the stands, the shots included pop saxophonist Kenny G, a Seattle native whose sentimental music many men found too syrupy. Where most sportscasters would have said, "There's Kenny G," Olbermann coughed up one of his signature "Gggggghh!" sounds, indicating his distaste for Kenny's music, not to mention his long, thin, somewhat effete curly hair. It's difficult to imagine another nationally known sportscaster, like ABC's *Monday Night Football* announcer Al Michaels, commenting with a gagging sound when his show's camera showed a celebrity.

ESPN was like a locker room full of athletes. As journalists, Olbermann and his comrades enacted the same man-of-action sensibilities as that of their favored athletes. The sportscasters, extremely accomplished and passionate guys, were not going to take orders from anyone when those directives violated first-order values. Rather than simply report sports, ESPN's anchors had picked up the ethos of the athletic community and brought it into the broadcast booth.

ESPN's Three Constituencies

Deciphering the drivers of ESPN's brand loyalty requires first specifying what customers find valuable about the brand and then identifying the mechanisms that maintain their loyalty over time. Iconic brands develop three interdependent constituencies: followers, insiders, and feeders. Because each constituency uses and values the brand's myth in different ways, the nature of each constituency's relationship to the brand varies as

FIGURE 6-1

Brand Loyalty Is a Product of the Social Network

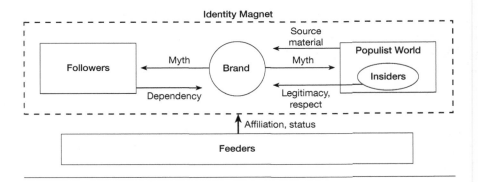

well. Furthermore, the overall loyalty to the brand is determined in large part by the relationships between these constituencies. Brand loyalty is a product of this social network (figure 6-1).

Followers: The Brand's Magnets

Followers, as the moniker suggests, are those customers who identify strongly with the brand's myth. They rely on the myth as a panacea for the desires and anxieties they experience in their everyday lives. As a result, followers become devoted to the performer of the myth—the brand—because it provides for their identity needs and acts as a moral compass. In previous chapters, to simplify the exposition, I've implied that all customers are followers. This is certainly not true. But followers do form the nucleus of the icon's customer base, for they find the greatest value in its myth.

ESPN's followers are mostly men, often fathers with children. Team sport is the primary domain of myth in their lives, the place where they go to get emotionally involved in heroic activities. Followers deeply personalize the pure-athlete ethos preached by ESPN. In their view, sport is a sacred world that should be cordoned off from the profanities of the marketplace. They look to sport to dramatize not just winning, but, as the old saying goes, "how you play the game." Followers build a moral hierarchy around sports and find almost as much value in losing as they do in winning, because losing provides powerful parables about manhood. This moral hierarchy shapes how followers experience sport. They greatly admire some players and teams and viciously scorn others. For instance, if an athlete is playing for statistics to enhance his market value—and by implication, places his team's interest second to his own—followers will loathe him. Followers admire overachievers, athletes who aren't necessarily the best but who are known for always playing hard, never quitting, and exceeding expectations. Showboaters, on the other hand—athletes who don't learn the game as apprentices and who don't respect the game's traditions—are booed mercilessly.

These tenets animate followers' game experiences and shape how they create pleasures in their spectating. Sports spectating is the glue that followers use in their social life at work, among friends, and, if they have kids, at home. Followers work mostly in organizational settings, mostly with other men, where sports talk is the lingua franca. They understand themselves as serious sports fans and find great joy in sharing their dedication with like-minded others. They take enormous pride in their teams' performances and feel strong solidarity with other fans of the home teams. Nonetheless, followers usually watch sports alone at home, or with their children if they have them. Only occasionally do followers congregate with other men, when they attend games in person or when they watch important games such as playoffs.

Spectator sports comprise an oral tradition. The value of sport resides in the lore of its stories that are passed around in everyday talk. Followers forge a personal connection to these stories primarily through their relationships with the local home teams and players. They build these relationships by weaving together their own autobiography with the team's biography over long periods. Being a fan is about developing an intimate and durable relationship with the team through its players, establishing a shared history. It's a badge of honor to have rooted for a hapless team over several struggling seasons. Followers view their loyalty as tangible proof of a genuine relationship. Relationships with teams and their players are measured by time and the accumulation of milestones that show the strength of the commitment: driving long distances to see games, sitting in bad weather until the last whistle, watching every game during a season even though it costs political points with the family.

Followers continually assert the quality of their relationships with teams through stories ("I remember when . . .") and intimate contacts ("I met so-and-so at a bar. . . ."). For example, one man's Chicago Cubs stories included his catching a ball in a fishnet in the bleachers at Wrigley Field, his memory of the horrors of the 1969 Cubs' choking against the New York Mets in September, and his drive in from the suburbs to join in the joyous postgame drinking festivities when the Cubs clinched the 1984 pennant. Followers also assert their relationship through the accumulation of memorabilia, often displayed in "shrine rooms." Usually in the basement den or study, the shrine room is a vast historical record documenting a man's relationship with teams and players.

Brand Loyalty as Fealty to Charismatic Authority. Followers view the ESPN journalists who anchor *Sports Center* as their fun-loving high priests and tour guides, leaders who create a moral universe by translating the day's sports into parables. This loyal constituency counts on the network to spin the day's sports events into poignant tales that reveal the core values of pure sport. By having an imaginary conversation with the anchors, followers test out their analyses and evaluations against their mentors' views. Since followers understand ESPN as the fount of sports wisdom and information, they, by paying close attention to ESPN and acting as the channel's acolytes, anoint themselves as serious fans. They learn from ESPN how to view sports from an athlete's point of view and use this vantage point to communicate with their friends. Ultimately, ESPN teaches followers how to be part of the rarefied world of pure sport, a place where previously only real athletes were allowed.

The relationships between followers and ESPN looks nothing like the brand relationships described by branding experts. Scholars who have advanced emotional branding emphasize the interpersonal qualities of brand-customer relationships. They argue that intimacy, reciprocity, and dependability drive loyalty.[3] Instead, ESPN's followers display a type of dependency that is characteristic of people who identify with charismatic leaders. ESPN's followers feel little reciprocity with the channel. The channel doesn't go out of its way to personalize the ESPN experience or build trust with its audience. Rather, the relationship is more paternalistic. Followers look up to ESPN as do followers of political leaders and celebrated artists. ESPN doesn't need to forge a personal connection with its core customers to earn their devotion. Followers have no problem personalizing their relationship with ESPN in do-it-yourself fashion. Rather, to earn devotion, ESPN must continue to exert credible cultural leadership.

Insiders: Populist Legitimacy

Insiders are the gatekeepers to the brand's claims on the populist world. Although usually much smaller in number than followers (survey data suggests that insiders constitute less than 10 percent of ESPN's audience), insiders have powerful influence. They often hold the brand in considerably less esteem than do followers, partly because the brand competes with them for leadership within the populist world. Nonetheless, insiders are a crucial constituency because they wield considerable influence on followers.

ESPN's insiders are guys who are often colloquially called jocks. While many of ESPN's other viewers may play sports casually, a small fraction of the audience are men who have a significant history in competitive sports and continue to self-identify as competitive athletes. They've played varsity sports through high school and often competed at the college level as well. As adults, they are driven to compete, and to the extent that they're able, they play in very competitive amateur leagues. Insiders see themselves as athletes and love to watch their fellow athletes perform. Whereas followers thrive on hanging out on the periphery of professional sport, assisted and encouraged by ESPN, insiders live within sport and watch sports as fellow athletes, not as spectators.

While other fans routinely miss most of their team's games, insiders take pains to avoid missing any action. Because it takes a huge commitment to experience sport through games alone, most fans bank on highlights and news media to keep up. But since insiders understand themselves as players, not spectators, they must be there for the team, night in and night out. One man I interviewed showed the extent of his commitment:

Joe: If I miss a [Lakers] game, I'm pissed off. If I don't go to twenty games a year, I get pissed off. If I miss an away game on TV, I get pissed off.

Q: If you miss one, do you tape it? Or watch the highlights?

Joe: No, I pout and wait for the next game.

Watching sporting events in this participatory style is a highly organized and ultimately exhausting activity. Watching requires advance preparation and concentration, so insiders watch mostly at home. They don't watch games in bars, because they want to control their viewing environment. Because insiders organize their lives around game broadcasts, work, family, friends, and lovers must adapt, or they are relegated to the sidelines. During the game, insiders become so absorbed in the contests that they lose track of time and then find it difficult to forget the game once it's over. They agonize over losses (what could we, the team, have done better?) and dissect wins to glean tendencies that can be applied in the next game.

Insiders voraciously gather fine-grained statistical and biographical information to enrich their game experiences. They track the entire league and all players to develop nuanced insights. Most use the Internet to go to team Web sites and other specialized resources. Many read sports books and specialty magazines to get inside the head of the players and coaches. Insiders expend so much effort in their spectating—the tracking of personnel moves in the off-season can be nearly as engrossing as league play—that they usually follow only one or two sports.

Just like the athletes themselves, insiders prepare for games and experience pregame jitters. With his brother and other friends, Justin, a Buffalo Bills fan who lives in Los Angeles, has developed a special ritual even though they are thousands of miles away from Buffalo. They have a closet stuffed full of Bills paraphernalia. On game day, they empty the closet, decorate the apartment so that it looks as if there is a party going on. Then they "prepare" for the game, meticulously reviewing detailed player-by-player information. They listen to a cable radio broadcast of the local Buffalo sports station to imbibe the home stadium atmosphere so that they can imaginatively transport themselves to the parking lot outside the stadium, where they used to tailgate as kids.

Similarly, George has a Los Angeles Lakers shrine next to his television, which is shrouded by a Lakers jersey given to him by the team's owner. Precisely thirty minutes before the start of the game, George removes the shroud and goes through a preparation sequence that he would not divulge to me. During the game, he sets up his notebook computer beside his television so that he can carefully track charts that illustrate the other team's shooting patterns, much as a coach would do.

When watching games with others, an insider prefers to watch with fellow insiders because they'll have the motivation and knowledge to participate properly. An insider will ban friends and family members, even though they're sports fans, if they haven't developed a fine enough appreciation for the game and background knowledge. The non-insiders' ill-conceived comments will ruin the insider's suspension of disbelief, dispelling his imaginative leap from living room sofa onto the players' bench.

Like their fellow athletes, insiders are singularly concerned with achievement and winning. And so they assign moral value to personality traits that correlate with winning. One of the toughest challenges for an insider is to continue to root for a home team when it fails to meet his achievement standards. Insiders understand professional sports as the ultimate proving ground: It's the place you go to compete, over and over, to show that you have what it takes to win against the best. George summarized this attitude:

> I don't deal with loss well, in business, personal life, and sports. When the Lakers lose, everyone out [of his apartment]. I don't like to lose. Don't like to beat other people, but like to lose less. It's unacceptable. I'm not comfortable with my team losing. You have a job to do, you do it and you win or lose. If you lose consistently you should find a different job. Play in a small media market and be mediocre. But don't come to L.A. I'm so frustrated how mediocre teams are in L.A. right now. It's ridiculous. If you're not coming to win, don't come to L.A.

Some insiders transfer this same intensity to business in their professional lives; others remain fixated solely on sport.

Insiders work extra hard at their mode of watching sports to build a boundary between themselves and mere spectators. They respect other cognoscenti who live for the subtle details that separate winning from mediocrity, and they dismiss the more casual rah-rah fans, who root for teams without understanding the game's intricacies.

Brand Loyalty as Institutional Legitimacy. Insiders watch ESPN more than most followers do. But, significantly, they don't value the channel nearly as much. Because insiders are game devotees who demand unmediated interaction with players, coaches, and games, the network cannot serve as a game substitute. Rather, ESPN is a good forum to appreciate the outstanding play of some of the best athletes in the game and one of many information sources that insiders rely on. They watch ESPN, but usually do so instrumentally, to gather information, rather than commune with the pure-athlete ethos. In other words, insiders view ESPN as a news program, just as it's billed.

Nor does this group look to ESPN to make sense of sport or to spin sport into myth. Rather, insiders respect ESPN reporters as fellow travelers who share their belief in the centrality of sport in life. They emphatically reject ESPN's guru role. Because they are self-provisioners in building the context and knowledge they need to experience sports, insiders find it a bit insulting that someone might think that they would need ESPN in this way. Insiders see ESPN as a crutch for mere spectators, consumers of sport who aren't devoted to the life of sport as they are.

To perhaps stretch a metaphor, insiders act like Protestants, asserting a direct and personal relationship with their god. They create myth experiences for themselves through their extraordinary dedication to continually updating massive amounts of facts, figures, and personal tidbits about sport and to continual interactions with teams, games, and athletes through watching games.

To insiders, ESPN seems like a theocracy, like the Catholic Church; the network asserts that the pure sport myth can only be accessed through the channel. They refuse to grant ESPN this standard-bearer role. Insiders aren't particularly enamored by ESPN, partly because the channel makes spectating too easy: ESPN has appropriated their nuanced and intensively engaged mode of consuming sports and repackaged it for less committed fans.

Populist worlds always have insiders: people who either inhabit the populist world or at least hang out on its periphery. For Harley-Davidson, it was the outlaw bikers and their hangers-on; for Volkswagen, it was the indie artists and their fellow bohemians who lived in gentrifying urban areas and gravitated to underground arts events. For Apple, it was the cyberpunks and commercial arts technicians who relied on Apple for their creative careers, and for Mountain Dew, it was the extreme-sports enthusiasts.

Because of their direct and intimate relationship with the populist world, insiders strongly resist its commercialization. They detest parasitic brands that treat the populist world as a semiotic mother lode to be mined. Insiders see themselves as fellow participants, rather than as consumers. They have a legitimate claim to the populist world. People who aren't willing to make the same commitment and, therefore, who rely on others (brands, critics, other insiders) to mediate their experiences—do not.

Because they have legitimate authority to speak for the populist world, insiders can bestow or rescind the brand's authenticity—its position as a credible actor speaking from within the populist world. Astute marketers of icons, including all the brands studied here, work to assure that insiders are at least tolerant of, if not fully supportive of, the brand's claims on the populist world.

If the brand is extremely persuasive in its populist mythmaking, insiders will adopt the brand to enhance their own identity projects. In this case, the icon becomes all the more valued in the eyes of its other constituencies. Conversely, if insiders trash the brand's claims—berating the brand for selling out or because its actions reveal ignorance—the brand loses considerable credibility. Depending on the size and authority of the insiders, they can destroy the icon when they withdraw their approval.[4]

We can now see why it's so critical for iconic brands to use literacy and fidelity to establish an authentic position in the populist world. If they don't, insiders will quickly turn on the brand as a traitor. On the other hand, when iconic brands are especially good in their populist expressions, they become recognized as a contributor to that world and insiders not only allow the brand inside, but also further legitimize it by becoming advocates. Apple and Nike are prime examples. The primary role of insiders is not to generate revenue but to bestow legitimacy. Insiders act as opinion leaders, positioned to make authoritative judgments as to whether the brand really has populist chops or is a mere dabbler faking it to make a buck.

Feeders: Cultural Parasites

Feeders are those customers of the iconic brand—often the majority—who thrive vicariously on the identity value that icons produce for their followers and (sometimes) insiders. Feeders have only a superficial connection to the values propagated by the icon through its myth. Attracted to the status and social ties that the brand produces, they use the brand as a vehicle to build social solidarity with friends and colleagues, as an interaction lubricant, and as a status symbol. If enough people register deeply with a brand's myth, their passionate use of the brand creates a magnet effect on others, who become the brand's feeders.

ESPN's feeders are people who are colloquially termed fair-weather fans: promiscuous fans who jump on the bandwagon of any winning team, accomplished athlete, or celebrated contest. They engage in opportunistic rooting—dedicating themselves to teams or athletes when either do well. For feeders, the pleasures of watching and talking spectator sports are shaped by their friends and, particularly, by the media. When friends' and colleagues' interest in a team heightens, they'll join in. Similarly, when the media constructs a player as a star, they will follow. Feeders don't follow teams or players; they follow trends. They take their cues from more informed fans and from the most respected media, especially ESPN. They're on the lookout for teams and players that are receiving particular admiration in the media and quickly orient their attention and affections in that direction.

Feeders make little attempt to build a long-term relationship with the home team or any other or to seek out contextual information to enhance their game viewing. But when a local team is playing well or an athlete's quest to break a record is drawing tremendous attention, feeders quickly absorb this passionate interest, as if by osmosis, and become highly involved fans, following closely and whooping and shouting as much as anyone else. Without this social context to create enthusiasm, feeders find little intrinsic pleasure in spectating. During seasons without a local winner, feeders rarely watch games, although they regularly watch championship matches.

Feeders understand that sport is the central pipeline for masculine mythmaking in everyday life. On a day-to-day basis, then, feeders take an instrumental approach, looking for the quick gloss that allows them to converse with friends and fellow workers as one of the guys.

Brand Loyalty: The Identity Magnet Effect. Feeders are heavy users of ESPN, but watch in an entirely different way and for different reasons. This group watches ESPN to watch sports. For them, ESPN is simply more enjoyable than most games because the program offers such an efficient distillation of what's worth seeing. Feeders view ESPN's capsule summaries of games as a fine substitute for the game itself, unless the game is "important." ESPN separates the wheat from the chaff. For feeders, games lack easily digestible interpretations that wrap the story into regurgitated video bites and catchphrases. Feeders consider ESPN the Mecca of men they perceive as hard-core sports fans (followers and insiders). As a result, feeders watch plenty of ESPN because they feel the need to be tapped into the network to garner legitimacy as a sports fan. The group nevertheless has little emotional attachment to the program through its journalists. Feeders take advantage of ESPN's high credibility among more dedicated fans and use it as a shortcut of sorts to becoming a fan. ESPN provides them with an efficient way to prep for socializing with their friends and colleagues. It represents what being a sports fan is about, providing feeders with language and attitude, which they are happy to pilfer and mimic. For them, ESPN condenses the world of sports into a usable form: a pocketful of catchphrases, a juvenile swagger, and a macho sense of humor.

Feeders are cultural parasites, feeding off the identity value that the brand delivers to followers. They aren't nearly as committed to the brand's myth as followers. Rather, the extraordinary devotion of followers and the credibility bestowed on the brand by insiders together create an easily accessible and effective identity currency that sustains feeders. Feeders don't imbibe much in the myth experience, but instead feed off the experiences of others to construct an identity for themselves. Feeders want to be part of the gang and use the brand as a shorthand currency to do so.

In the mind-share model, brand owners grow their brands by adding product designs that can fit under the brand's associations and by stretching the brand communications to appeal to a wider set of customers. Iconic brands don't work this way. They operate as identity magnets, delivering myths that are precisely focused to address an acute contradiction in society. If the myth resonates, the brand accumulates followers. And the passion and devotion unleashed among the followers (and sometimes insiders) acts like a magnet, pulling in a mass constituency of feeders.

The most effective way to expand the market power of an identity brand is to enhance the devotion of the core customers situated at the brand's nucleus. The more successfully a brand performs myths that feed the desires of the followers at its nucleus, the more customers in total the brand will attract.

Brand Loyalty as a Social Network

ESPN's three constituencies together form a social network around the brand. Brand loyalty is held together by the relationships between these different types of customers.

Brand loyalty is the customers' willingness to stay with the brand when competitors come knocking with offerings that would be considered equally attractive had not the customer and brand shared a history. The degee of customer stickiness is key to the brand's market power. There are multiple causes of brand loyalty, which vary across product categories. For instance, a prominent idea is that switching is costly to consumers. They've built up a level of trust in the brand, and searching for a new brand takes effort. This idea makes sense for more utilitarian products like Clorox bleach or a Sony television, but is less consequential for the sorts of products that compete to deliver identity value.

For iconic brands, the conventional argument comes from emotional branding: Loyalty is produced by the customer's relationship with the brand. As customers fall into a relationship—which often mimics interpersonal relationships with intimacy, reciprocity, loyalty, and so forth—they are less likely to switch, as doing so would violate the relationship.

But this atomistic concept of loyalty fails to capture the social mechanisms that create (and destroy) brand loyalty. Customers of iconic brands are loyal because they're locked into a social network. Much of the value of the brand is imparted by other constituents, not just the one-to-one relationship with the brand.

Once a brand has inserted itself as the performer of myths for a network of insiders, followers, and feeders, individual customers find it very difficult to walk away from the brand to competitive offerings because they lose the social effects of this network. To decommission an iconic brand is a collective decision. An icon's tenacious hold on its customers can be broken by two events: (1) A critical mass of followers abandons the brand because the brand's myth is not addressing their current anxieties, or (2) a critical mass of insiders rallies against the brand because it has denigrated the populist world in which they participate. Unless one of these two tipping points is reached, individual customers who leave the brand not only leave their individual relationship behind, but also lose the interactions facilitated with other like-minded consumers.

Consider the well-financed and sophisticated effort by FOX Sports Net to break ESPN's hold on the sports news market. Even if the product were superior, feeders weren't likely to switch, because their friends were still watching ESPN, as were insiders, whose opinions they valued. FOX's best hope was to lure insiders, who were looking for ways to signal their independence from ESPN. If it had attracted insiders in significant numbers, it could have damaged ESPN's credibility with followers and feeders. But FOX followed a conventional gap analysis—an analysis that looked for a spot in the market that the competition wasn't targeting—to produce entertainment programming targeted at feeders. FOX thought it was programming for a gap, but it was really challenging the entire social network that ESPN had constructed. Feeders would only switch over if followers did, and followers would move only if insiders switched in large numbers. Such a strategy was doomed to fail. Breaking up social networks that form around brands requires a detailed understanding of what holds the network together and a strategy that seeks to intervene in the network precisely where it is the most vulnerable.

Managing Across Constituencies

An iconic brand's three constituencies are interdependent. The value that each constituency finds in the brand partly depends on the other constituencies. Thus, managing such a brand requires managing relationships across the network. The value that followers find in the brand hinges on the institutional legitimacy bestowed by insiders. Likewise, the value that feeders experience is based on the extraordinary value of the brand's myth to followers. Even insiders need the other two groups, for their status as insiders requires the existence of less worthy "outsiders" who crave to get an authentic piece of their populist world.

For example, as we'll see in chapter 7, the explosion of interest by upscale professionals and managers in Harley-Davidson has had the unintended effect of alienating Harley's long-standing group of insiders—mostly working-class men who emulate and occasionally mingle with outlaw bikers. These insiders increasingly struggle to maintain their claim on Harley's myth against the new middle-class interlopers. They're disappointed that Harley is pandering to professionals who have lots of money but little time to become real enthusiasts. These long-standing bikers fend off the new bourgeois bikers—whom they call RUBs (rich urban bikers)—by denying them access to the Harley myth. "How to Spot a Biker Wannabe," a popular biker humor site on the Internet is telling. According to the Web site, wannabe Harley riders

- wear a Harley t-shirt with nothing on the back (real shirts have dealer artwork on the back and chronicle a biker's travels)

- know where to put the key and gas, anything else should be done by your authorized Harley dealer (wouldn't want to get those new Harley jeans dirty!)

- used to own a Harley, but can't remember which model (that's like saying you used to be married but you can't remember her name)

- [own] a "new" Harley but [have] never been further than a "three hour tour" (Ya, I own exercise equipment I never use. Never heard me call myself a body-builder!)

- own a new Harley, it's a first bike, and they're a total snob against "Jap riders" (I have more in common with someone who rides foreign iron than someone who profiles the latest from the Harley boutique. When all the hype moves on to some other thing like custom vans again or something, a lot of these bikes will be For Sale!)

- thinks a shooter does not involve tequila or Jack Daniels, just a lot of *crème de* this and that. (No, you definitely don't have to drink to be a biker, but if you do, have some class please!)

- have a new Harley tattoo, wearing at least 16 "official" HD items of attire ("biker boots," watch, hat, socks, etc.)

- have squeaky new leather in the spring, same squeaky new leather in the fall (wow, you must go through a lot of Mink Oil)[5]

And the list goes on. This checklist says to Harley's followers: You can't buy your way into the biker experience. Biking requires dedication, knowledge, and a certain spirit. It is part of a lifestyle. Hopping on a custom Harley with all the requisite gear does not make you a biker. (Like a status-conscious rookie at the office on the first day of work, middle-class bikers tend to overdress for the part so that they appear suitable for the role.) As Harley management has succeeded in making the Harley mystique more accessible to its most valuable customers, working-class riders increasingly feel slighted and are attempting to sabotage the company's efforts by denigrating the recipe for being a biker, a recipe cultivated by Harley management. If Harley's insiders are successful, the company will have to reengineer how it stages biking activities, or it risks having its middle-class clientele believe that they are participating in a superficial, weak imitation of the real thing.

Managing an iconic brand, then, is a juggling act. Managers must construct myths that draw from a populist world in a way that rings true with followers. At the same time, they must also converse credibly with insiders. This juggling act is difficult because insiders and followers don't always get along, and the brand is usually caught in the middle of flare-ups between the two constituencies. Insiders can become aggravated by the brand if they feel that it is "stealing" their special relationship with the populist world that they've cultivated over many years of dedicated participation.

CHAPTER 7

Coauthoring the Myth

T HE HARLEY-DAVIDSON COMPANY (HDC) is nearly everyone's favorite corporate turnaround story.[1] It goes something like this: HDC, which once competed with several dozen domestic motorcycle companies, became the sole American motorcycle manufacturer in 1953 when Indian, its only serious competitor, folded. HDC struggled in the 1960s as new Japanese competitors like Honda and Kawasaki entered the market and quickly dominated the smaller bike sizes. In an ill-fated attempt to expand into other motorized products, HDC failed to extend its business to snowmobiles and golf carts.

As the motorcycle market took off in the late 1960s, the recreational products company American Machine & Foundry Co. (AMF) bought HDC. The quality of Harley motorcycles deteriorated as a result of overly aggressive expansion plans and lackluster, arms-length management. Meanwhile, Japanese bikes made successful inroads into HDC's core business, big bikes. By the early 1980s, HDC was on the verge of bankruptcy. Senior managers, including the founder's grandson, Willie Davidson, led a leveraged buyout and took over the company. The new owner-managers turned the company around.

The turnaround was centered on two changes: restoring product quality and getting close to the customer. HDC finally fixed its notoriously leaky engines. But the crux of the comeback was that, instead of snubbing the customers, executives rode bikes with them and fed this learning back into relationship-building efforts, particularly centered on organizing activities through H.O.G. (Harley Owners Group), Harley's brand community.

Managers love this story and repeat it to each other as a mantra because it celebrates marketing's "truth." Harley suffered under the guidance of a conglomerate that ignored the product and the customers. Managers who believed in marketing came to the rescue. They listened carefully to customer wants and, lo and behold, consumer praise and corporate profits followed.

HDC managers approve of this story, also. They also like to say that the brand's value can't be analyzed, because it's magical: There is a Harley mystique that simply can't be explained rationally. Harley is a quintessential American product that embodies what the nation stands for in an especially pure and profound way.[2]

Why repeat this story one more time? Harley's transformation has become one of the world's most influential branding stories. Managers have spent the 1990s trying to replicate Harley's path to success. But the Harley story—the official explanation that circulates in the management community as part of business folklore—is wrong.[3] So managers and management writers have been drawing the wrong lessons from Harley.

I will demonstrate that the vaunted Harley mystique is nothing other than the brand's identity myth, embodied in the bikes, which works according to the same principles guiding other iconic brands. In the cases discussed in previous chapters, the company did most of the myth-building legwork. In Harley's case, however, the company did none of the important storytelling.[4] Other authors—the populist world of the outlaw bikers and the culture industries—turned Harley into an icon. Cultural texts—films, newspaper and magazine articles, political speeches, newsworthy events—produced by the culture industries were the key to building Harley's myth.

Contrary to the advice proffered by countless consultants and gurus, directly imitating Harley is a pointless exercise. Rather, Harley offers an exemplary case to learn about the role of the occasional coauthors of iconic brands—the culture industries and populist worlds.

Harley-Davidson Genealogy

Why did American men who had scorned Harley bikers for decades suddenly, in the early 1990s, desire so intensely to ride a Harley that they willingly sat on waiting lists for a year just to make a $20,000 purchase? And then outfit themselves and their bike with another $5,000 worth of accessories? Harley-Davidson stock began to dramatically outpace the market indices as revenues and profits shot through the roof. The company's astounding performance was driven largely because the company had increased its prices to levels previously unimaginable in the category.

Harley's identity value comes from its myth. This myth has moved through three distinct stages. The source material for the brand's myth—the populist world of the outlaw biker—was created by motorcycle clubs that formed on the West Coast after World War II. The culture industries produced an initial wave of cultural texts, from the early 1950s until the mid 1960s that glamorized the biker's outlaw ethos and stitched their story to the Harley bikes. From the late 1960s to the late 1970s, influential cultural texts repackaged the myth, transforming the outlaw into a reactionary gunfighter. As a result, Harley became iconic for lower-class, white, male customers, as this gunfighter myth addressed their identity anxieties. Beginning in the late 1970s, a third wave of very different cultural texts once again revised Harley's myth—heroizing the rough-and-tumble gunfighters as men-of-action who can single-handedly save the country. This man-of-action gunfighter myth took off in the early 1990s, but this time connecting with the older and wealthier middle-class male customers who have made Harley such a venerable economic asset today. The culture industry's impact in stitching the myth to Harley and then repackaging the myth led to Harley's extraordinary financial success in the 1990s.

Motorcycle Clubs Invent the Outlaw Ethos

After World War II, veterans joined with lower-class city kids, primarily in California and other warm-climate states, to form a countercultural scene centered on biking. These motorcycle clubs were a tightly bound community of men who created an alternative social world. Harley was just one brand of large bikes—Indian and Triumph were others—favored by these motorcycle enthusiasts. Any bike that was big and loud would do.

Modifications to the bike were much more important than the brand. To convert these motorcycles from their gentlemanly touring dispositions into bikes fit for outlaws, bikers removed "ornamental" features such as fenders and trim, installed smaller gas tanks, and modified engines to increase performance and provide a sleeker look. These customizations eventually led to new frame designs, the most famous of which became the extended front fork, the "chopper." In local shops across the United States, an informal economy developed for customizing large bikes.

Ethos of the "Outlaw" Motorcycle Clubs

The following principles constitute the ethos of the outlaw motorcycle clubs, as distilled from ethnographic studies of these groups.[5]

Libertarian life: Outlaws are nomads, always on the move. They're not tied down by jobs or restrictive relationships. A primary expression of freedom for these bikers is the ability to take off and go anywhere at any time. While rallies draw attention, the ideal is to ride without a destination. More than merely supporting libertarian views, outlaw bikers seek a life in which institutions of any kind—the state, the courts, the media, corporations, marriage—are held at bay. All institutions are emasculating because they steal the ability to act autonomously.

Bikers speak condescendingly of middle-class men, those successful in business and respected in society, as "citizens"—conformists who adhere too closely to society's rules. Outlaw bikers invert the typically positive connotations of the term *citizen* to reveal its dark side: the loss of individuality that accompanies participating in society, the need to conform to institutional norms, the lack of soul. The citizen's world of masculinity is hypocritical. It pays tribute to freedom and individuality, but adheres to strict conventions and willingly accepts limits on individual freedom.

Physical domination: Manhood is about domination, that is, toughness, aggression, and the ability to confront danger with confidence. Bikers ritualize fighting. Club brothers often fight violently with other clubs' members. Outlaws brandish an intimidating, interpersonal style. They enjoy placing a little terror in the minds of other men in their presence. Outlaws ride "hogs": big, loud, aggressive, basic primal machines. Outlaws further modify Harleys to accentuate the bike's expression of domination. They remove the muffler to make the bike louder and faster.

Tribal territories: Outlaw bikers see life as a territorial battle, fought against peoples of other nations and races, in which manhood comes with successfully defending the territory one shares with other like-minded men.

Danger: On the frontier, manhood was earned through surviving dangerous risky encounters with Native Americans and nature. Outlaws ride motorcycles. Every time he rides a motorcycle, the outlaw biker depends on his skill and bravery to stay alive, a fundamental aspect of being a man. Outlaws refuse to wear helmets, or they wear helmets that provide little protection. Bikers think that citizens do whatever they can to rid their life of risks. To outlaws, cars are *cages*, biker slang for an auto, with as many safety features as possible to protect the passengers from harm.

The wild life: Outlaw bikers pursue a life of pleasures, avoiding civilization's constraints. Bikers are happy to trade off the security of a settled lifestyle for the pursuit of the wild life—a life governed by thrill-seeking, intense pleasures, and the unknown. Citizens' actions are governed by instrumental goals, how one has to behave to be successful. Citizens are always planning for the future and living for the job, the family, and taxes. A biker carouses with his brothers; looks for excuses to get high, find a little bit of trouble, and exercise his hog on sun-bleached country roads. If a biker inadequately demonstrates his commitment to the wild life by succumbing to job or family pressures, his brothers harass and scold him. If the wayward brother continues to behave too much like a citizen, he is excommunicated from the club.

Nature: Outlaw bikers think of themselves as living in the grip of nature, and their lifestyle makes this point over and over. They live with nature, which is signified by dirt and odors. Outlaws wear dirty clothes, have beards and long dirty hair, and bathe infrequently. And while citizens travel in heated, air-conditioned automobiles, outlaws express their organic nature by riding motorcycles, fully exposed to rain, cold, and the sun's searing heat.

Misogyny: Outlaws create a patriarchal world, demanding that their women be docile, obedient, and subservient to their sexual needs. Bikers ritualize their dominance over women in many ways. Women are not allowed to join the clubs and cannot be in the clubhouse without escorts. Women are allowed to participate in the club only if they assume the appropriate role. Domination is at its extreme in sexual relations, in which women are expected to serve the members' sexual demands, whatever they may be. Sharing partners is commonplace. A clear sign of the dominance over women is the woman as passenger on the back of a hog. In the bikers' world, women never drive. Women are dangerous because they represent the settled world of families and commitments; they have the power to "lure" men away from their commitment to the club's ethos and back into the world of the citizen.

Know-how: Frontiersmen weren't able to rely on the specialized skills of other men, as one would do in modern society. They had to know how to make do, how to repair everything they owned, and how to improvise to get by. Outlaw bikers take perverse pride in the frequent breakdowns of older Harleys. Since outlaw bikers view a man's mechanical competence as evidence of his masculinity, a sick hog is nothing more than an opportunity to demonstrate that one has the know-how to live in a world free of dependency. Outlaw bikers build their bikes to suit their tastes. Citizens live in a world in which men need technology and the specialized expertise of others. Because they have no idea how their autos and bikes work, they must rely on others; their vehicles are an umbilical cord to dependency rather than an escape to freedom.

Men in motorcycle clubs were inspired by the outlaws of the American West, like Jessie James, and viewed their bikes as their mechanized horses. In their clubs, they invented a modern outlaw life. On the Western frontier, men were bound by few laws. Every man had to learn how to fend for himself in a Hobbesian world wherein the toughest man—often the most violent man—prevailed. While many nineteenth-century pioneers may have viewed the West as the land of opportunity, a place to achieve the American Dream, outlaws found in the West a place to escape modern society. Post–World War II bikers' imagined their own version of the outlaw ethos, which has remained more or less consistent ever since.

From the 1950s onward, these motorcycle clubs lived and honored the outlaw life, keeping alive these ideals at a time when American ideology lauded exactly their opposite: scientific expertise, rational administration, and the planned nuclear-suburban life. These motorcycle clubs soon became a potent populist world, standing alongside the cowboy, the hillbilly, the urban African American, and the beatnik as the most resonant populist figures able to challenge America's dominant postwar ideals. As the bikers were transformed from their isolated existence on the West Coast to nationwide media darlings, a significant biker myth market emerged for which Harleys eventually became the central prop.

This ethos would have remained stuck within the circle of motorcycle clubs and their hangers-on had it not been for the culture industries, which quickly realized that the bikers made a great story. When these industries propagated the outlaw biker story, they converted the biker into a mythic figure for their mass audience, and attached this myth to the Harley brand.

Stage 1: Cultural Texts Stitch the Outlaw Myth to Harley

Three key cultural texts harvested the outlaw biker clubs as source material: a *Life* magazine exposé, the film *The Wild One*, and the various journalist reports and film renderings of the escapades of the Hell's Angels, (figure 7-1). In their function, these three cultural texts operated no differently than the thirty-second ads described in prior chapters. The texts coauthored an identity myth, located in the populist world of the bikers. The key difference is that, at the beginning, the stories focused on the bikers rather than their brand of bike. So, initially, the iconic figure was the actor in the story (Marlon Brando, the Hell's Angels). But, as Harleys became an increasingly central figure in these stories, the biker myth gradually transferred to the Harley as well.

FIGURE 7-1

Time Line of Key Culture Industry Texts

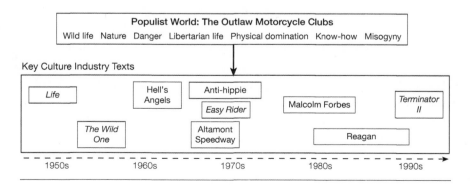

Life *Magazine*

As the Cold War paranoia of McCarthyism frightened the nation into nervously enforcing nuclear family norms, the motorcycle clubs proved to be perfect fodder. Over a Fourth of July weekend in 1947, a motorcycle club drank, caroused, and toyed with the locals on the streets of Hollister, California. *Life* magazine ran a "morning after" photo of a drunken man, his eyes glazed, his bulging stomach popping out of his shirt, swilling a beer while leaning back on a Harley. Dozens of empty bottles lay underneath the cycle. *Life* ran the photo to dramatize the magazine's description of a biker riot disrupting a small, defenseless town. The image sent a shock wave through respectable America. Suddenly, parents had to worry about debauched sexual predators on the loose—bikers—who obeyed no law and whose only objective was to cause trouble to decent, law-abiding citizens.

Though the photo was staged by the photojournalist, its cultural effects were pronounced.[6] The bikers provided a threatening counterpoint that gave meaning and motivation to the nation's ideological agenda. Bikers were hooligans on the loose, men who refused society's discipline and who had to be suppressed. To protect itself, American society had to rally against these barbarians.

The Wild One

While the *Life* incident created bikers as threatening hooligans, it was *The Wild One,* Hollywood's take on the Hollister spectacle, that provided the philosophical underpinnings of their way of life, giving purpose to their fighting and drinking and antisocial behavior. In the movie, Marlon Brando starred as the leader of a hooligan biker club looking for trouble. His gang passed through a small Norman Rockwell–esque town. For Brando, everything in the town reeked of *square*— a term, borrowed from the Beats, meaning dull conformity—a direct jab at the American ideology. Brando's merry band of bikers turned the town into a raucous party, overrunning the bar, harassing the women, and instigating fights. Lee Marvin, playing the macho leader of a rival gang, rode into town with his gang, got drunk, and picked a fight with Brando. They bloodied each other and tensions rose as the party surged out of control. Later, Brando took a waitress from the bar on his bike for a supposedly romantic interlude in the countryside. Aloof and worried that he lacked the proper civilities to impress, however, Brando rejected her before she could do likewise. Near the film's end, the town fathers, mobilized into a vigilante squad, trapping Brando and badly mauling him. As he fled on his cycle, one townsman heaved a tire iron into his wheel spokes, which threw Brando from his bike.[7] As the cycle spun out of control, it collided with an innocent man, killing him. Brando eventually beat the ensuing homicide charge. Along the way, though, the waitress fell in love with him. But Brando's troops were calling. So, as a true biker, he passed on the girl and rode into the countryside with his biker brothers.

The Wild One portrayed motorcycle clubs much as the members imagined themselves—as frontier outlaws. Like other men, bikers felt emasculated by the new technocratic U.S. ideology, but they possessed the courage to reject society and live out man's animal nature, much as did men in the Wild West, where no regulating bureaucracies governed men's actions. These men relied on physical dominance and staying on the move to avoid coercive commitments. Providing a mythic resolution to the nation's anxieties with the regimen of organization men and suburbia, Brando and Marvin were received as sexy rebel heroes. Along with James Dean, Brando became an icon of youth rebellion. He allowed men to dream of escaping the feminizing conformity of society using simple tools: black leather, denim, and a loud motorcycle.

Media Portrayals of the Hell's Angels

In 1964, bikers from a little-known motorcycle club were accused of raping a girl in a small town. The story broke in all news outlets, reviving the idea that bikers were barbarians. This time, however, the outlaw bikers had a name to match their dangerous reputation—the Hell's Angels.

Until the rape story broke, the Hell's Angels were a small gang of a few dozen men in northern California. Although they had attracted police attention for years, they had hardly struck fear into law enforcement. Soon after the incident, though, the bikers became media darlings, providing a voyeur's delight of sex, violence, crime, and filth all rolled into a single photogenic package. Again the nation was on the lookout for these thuggish barbarians, sexual predators who hunted society's daughters. The media frenzy transformed Hell's Angels into an explosive cultural force.

The B-movie impresario Roger Corman knew incendiary plot material when he saw it. Corman oversaw production on several biker films, including the box office smash *Wild Angels*. He encouraged his screenwriters to embellish the bikers' deviance to exploit nearly every perversion and aberration: "devil worship, sadomasochism, necrophilia, monsters, space aliens, Nazis, the Mafia, and every aspect of the occult, even bikers as transvestites."[8] Psychopathic cult leader and murderer Charles Manson, one the era's most disturbing cultural figures, apparently was inspired by Corman's films. Manson announced that he would lead his revolutionary charge riding on Harleys.

For boys growing up in the 1960s, the repulsive and ominous Harley riders exuded an irresistible attraction. The Harley was to a teen coming of age in 1965 what a punk's safety pin through the cheek was for a lad in England circa 1979 and what falling-off-the-butt, baggy jeans were to boys entranced by "gangsta" culture, beginning in the late 1980s. All these images were extraordinarily enticing to youths because they threatened bourgeois adults. The problem for Harley was that while a teenager had no trouble scoring a safety pin from mother's sewing kit, a $3,000 bike was another matter. Instead, Levi's and black leather jackets became choice gear for teen biker wannabes.

Hunter S. Thompson, the hip and influential gonzo journalist of the counterculture, trumpeted the inside story of the Hell's Angels in widely read exposés in *Rolling Stone* and *The Nation* and then in a documentary-style book in which he described his escapades as an Angels hanger-on. While the Angels that Thompson described were too violent and too misogynist for hippie tastes, they nevertheless commanded great respect because the bikers were "the real deal." These guys, more than any hippie, were rejecting everything to do with American society. They possessed authenticity in spades. They said "fuck you" to everything.

Stage 2: Repackaging the Outlaw as a Reactionary Gunfighter

In the late 1960s, two important cultural texts shifted Americans' understanding of the bikers from lawless and amoral outlaws to still dangerous but now nationalist gunfighters. Historically, American gunfighters were mercenary outsiders—Daniel Boone was the first popular version—who faced down savages (Native Americans) with the professional skills of a warrior. Gunfighters were uncivilized, but necessarily so because it gave them the toughness to take on the enemy.[9]

The roots of Harley's gunfighter myth were established during World War II, when various newsreels, newspaper photos, and stories depicted soldiers riding Harleys on the front much like a cavalry of old. Harley had become the new horse of the U.S. military. Soldiers cherished Harleys, along with Jeeps and Zippo lighters, as a trusty tool of battle. But this idea that men astride motorcycles were soldiers doing battle for the country was pushed aside by the domination of the outlaw myth.[10] Two key cultural texts—Altamont and *Easy Rider*—revived the idea that Harleys were the trusty steeds of the gunfighter.

Altamont

In December 1969, the Rolling Stones, on their *Let It Bleed* tour, performed at northern California's Altamont Speedway. Inexplicably, the Hell's Angels were hired to protect the Stones from the huge crowd. They pulled their choppers between the stage and 300,000 Stones fans, who were impatient from a several-hour delay past the concert's advertised start time. The crowd became aggressive as the Stones finally took the stage and pressed against the Angels' bikes. Fighting broke out. A man pulled a gun on an Angel, and the bikers responded by knifing the guy to death. A media feeding frenzy ensued. The impression given by media coverage was that the Angels were willing to fight the hippies to maintain order and defend their honor.

Altamont was a decisive break between the hippies and the motorcycle clubs. The Angels' actions against the hippies came at a time when a reactionary appeal for law and order was being made by President Richard Nixon and Vice President Spiro Agnew. And more conservative-minded citizens, particularly the white working class, were also taking up the cry. The Angels' stabbing was a poignant metaphor for these people's desire to squelch the political instability spawned by the civil rights and the peace movements. In the conservatives' minds, the hippies symbolized this instability: the country's sons and daughters who were led astray by distorted ideas. So those who sided with law and order took away from Altamont a different impression of the Hell's Angels: bikers may be violent, but they were also patriotic and conservative in a way, because they were more than willing to defend the nation's historic values.

The impact of Altamont was seconded by widely reported news stories covering the anti-peace-movement antics staged by the increasingly media-savvy Hell's Angels. The peace movement was beginning to have an impact, and Nixon and Agnew implored the "silent majority"—predominantly white, working-class men who lived in the interior of the United States and who supported the war effort—to voice their support for the war. Although the Angels had little admiration for politicians, including the Nixon administration, they deplored the hippies' apparent lack of respect for their brethren, the soldiers fighting in Vietnam. The Hell's Angels staged counterprotests at antiwar rallies, taunting peace protesters and occasionally inciting violence. The Angels' head honcho, Sonny Barger—no fan of the government—even sent a letter to Nixon volunteering the entire Hell's Angels membership to enlist as soldiers in Southeast Asia.

The American flag became the sign around which this contest was waged. While protesters burned flags, the bikers proudly waved them and placed flags on their bikes. The Harley-Davidson Company finally followed the bikers' lead and introduced a new chopper model that mimicked the bikers' modifications. Moreover, the company changed the Harley logo to incorporate the stars and stripes.

Easy Rider

Peter Fonda's and Dennis Hopper's 1969 film, *Easy Rider,* was one of the defining films of the Vietnam era. Consciously made in the style of a Western, *Easy Rider*'s impact resulted from its mix-and-match pastiche: Like *The Wild One*, the film celebrated masculine autonomy, but instead of a biker gang, we get solo motorcycle riders moving through a frontier setting in the American West, burnished with plenty of hippie dress, drugs, and lingo. Like the Westerns of the 1950s and 1960s, Fonda and Hopper used their movie to confront a society they viewed as sickly because it stole men's autonomy. They cast themselves as hippie drug dealers who financed their escape from society with the proceeds from dealing large quantities of cocaine. With soundtrack accompaniment by the rock band Steppenwolf's "Born to Be Wild," *Easy Rider*'s protagonists rode through the desert transporting the drugs in the gas tank of Fonda's chopped Harley, which had been painted like an American flag.

In a nod to *The Wild One*, Fonda and Hopper pull into a small town and ride their bikes in a town parade as a joke. They're thrown in jail, where they meet an alcoholic ACLU lawyer played by Jack Nicholson. In a role that helped make him a star, Nicholson plays a liminal figure. Dressed in fine white linen, he clearly lives a comfortable life in bourgeois society.

But, unable to resist his desire for the uninhibited life, he decides to join Fonda and Hopper on their ride. Explaining why the two were run out of town by the law-and-order town fathers, Nicholson lectures Hopper:

> This used to be a hell of a good country. They're not scared of you. They're scared of what you represent. What you represent to them is freedom. But talking about it and being it are two different things. It's real hard to be free when they're bought and sold in the marketplace.[11]

Easy Rider redirected young American men, then enamored by hippie ideals, toward the frontier values found in the period's Western films. The film told young men that the pursuit of freedom was about recovering the individual freedom promised by America's frontier, not about debating existential philosophy or communal living. Aside from a hallucinogenic visit to New Orleans, most of the film unfolds in the rural West. The men ride bikes and camp out, running into ranchers and hippies along the way.

Fonda, Hopper, and Nicholson push the idea that American manhood rests on a libertarian world of pure autonomy that men once found in the West. Fonda and Hopper eat lunch with a ranch family that is seemingly conservative in its way of life, exact opposites of the hippies. Yet Fonda praises the rancher's life: "It's not every man who can live off the land, do your own thing in your own time. You should be proud." Later, in a stoned soliloquy around the campfire, Nicholson describes a higher-order species from another planet: "Each man is a leader. There is no government. No monetary system."

Easy Rider portrayed bikers as lay philosophers of the frontier. The country's large institutions drained men of their masculinity because it forced them to conform to "unnatural" roles and norms. So to recover one's manhood—one's freedom—one must reject city life for the rugged and in-dependent life only to be found in the country, riding a Harley, of course. Freedom wasn't to be had in a Sartre reading group, a folk concert, or hanging out with a barefoot and braless hippie girl. True freedom was something that men pursued on their own, jettisoning dependencies on the government and large companies.

Altamont and *Easy Rider* worked together to repackage Harley's prior outlaw myth. Now Harley's myth showcased that these dangerous and he-donistic men were also stewards of the country's traditional masculinity and libertarian values. Harley bikers played the role of America's historic gunfighters: dangerous tough guys who would do whatever it took to restore the country's historic rugged individualism, a country that would once again celebrate white men's autonomy and power.

Harley's myth of the reactionary gunfighter found a waiting audience. Working-class white men who were disturbed by middle-class men's experiments with a kinder, gentler masculinity proved to be a perfect fit. Many of these men became rabid Harley enthusiasts, a counterculture formed as a reaction to the progressive zeitgeist of the day.

Harley Becomes an Icon

Harley became an icon for working-class white men well beyond the smallish circle of outlaw bikers. These men were facing an emasculation crisis of sorts as production jobs started to disappear and the United States entered a painful era of deindustrialization. Japanese companies began to dominate markets in consumer electronics, transportation, industrial machinery, and steel. At the same time, middle-class Americans began to experiment with a progressive ideology that envisioned a new future premised on ecology, feminism, civil rights, and the existential cultural experiments of the hippies. Alan Alda, not John Wayne, was the new role male model.

For young working-class white men, this was an anxiety-ridden time. Their economic futures were threatened at the same time that the nation was abandoning the patriarchal model of manhood that they believed in. These men were drawn to the story of the Hell's Angels as holdouts who still revered manhood as practiced in America's frontier past. They liked the idea that the outlaw bikers stood firm against the middle-class hippies, whom they viewed as overprivileged sissies. The idea of riding a Harley in a motorcycle gang became the last bastion of manhood, defending America's frontier values against the alien ideals proposed by the middle-class people living on the coasts. These men were easily able to displace wartime aggressions toward the Viet Cong to the new enemy—the "gook junk" Japanese motorcycles that had invaded the American marketplace. Epithets easily blended as the Vietnamese peasant and the Japanese motorcycle were re-imagined as having sprung from the same totalitarian, feminizing, un-American well. Years before Michigan auto workers began ritually smashing Hondas and Datsuns with Louisville Sluggers, Harley bikers proudly wore t-shirts printed with slogans that savagely attacked Japanese motorcycles. As a rallying point for this reactionary movement, riding Harleys became a circle-the-wagons exercise, a way for similarly disaffected men to gather in common cause against the evil forces of liberalism lurking everywhere in contemporary America and against the foreigners who were stealing their jobs.

An informal network of Harley riders grew into an extensive national Harley biker organization—the Modified Motorcycle Association—which sponsored rides and rallies. *Easyriders* magazine, these bikers' favorite read, began a political action group called ABATE. Originally, ABATE stood for A Brotherhood Against Totalitarian Enactments, but was eventually changed to the more politically acceptable A Brotherhood Aimed Toward Education. ABATE opposed helmet laws that were then being introduced state by state. These laws operated as a potent symbol for the encroachment of wrongheaded, liberal government ideas into the personal lives of American men.

With its glossy spreads of Harley after-market customization jobs, biker rally candid photos, and bare-breasted "Harley women," *Easyriders* celebrated the outlaw biker lifestyle. The publication's editorial direction gives us a flavor of Harley's followers at the time. The magazine explicitly promoted an ethos that aligned exactly with the outlaw biker clubs: anti-authoritarian, anti-elite, and against social norms of any kind. It celebrated what mainstream society would consider the most vulgar and offensive ideas and acts. "Fuck the world" ("FTW" appeared on the masthead) was the dominant motif. "In the Wind," a section of the magazine that published photos sent in by readers, almost always featured subjects giving the finger. Occasionally, a small child was encouraged to pose on a chopper and flip off the photographer. Women, usually with their shirts pulled up to expose their breasts, often gave the bird. Flipping the middle finger did not mean that the subjects could not smile. They often did.

The FTW aesthetic was central not only to the monthly columns, but also to most fiction published in the magazine. Stories often included what might be considered nonconsensual heterosexual sex, and at least one story was told from the viewpoint of the rapist, who was the hero. The rape theme was pervasive in the jokes, pictorials, and readers' letters as well. In a 1977 photo feature, a naked woman is shooting pool and she's held down onto the pool table, clearly struggling against a half-dozen bikers, and the rest is up to the readers' imaginations.

Easyriders was so successful that imitators (e.g., *In the Wind, Outlaw Biker,* and *Runnin' Free*) sprung up. By the late 1970s, combined circulation of the top five publications reached over one million readers. Harley had become an iconic brand for white guys on the lowest socioeconomic rung of American society, serving as a powerful container celebrating the reactionary gunfighter ethos. These men were bound in a fraternity that celebrated a virile, patriarchal, misogynist manhood that they vaguely imagined to have existed in preindustrial America.

As a result, in 1970s United States, Harleys were decidedly unacceptable among middle-class men, a sign of backwardness that pushed against the grain of the progressive zeitgeist of the day. For the Harley-Davidson Company, then owned by AMF, this iconic status was hardly a victory. These working-class customers picked up their tastes directly from the outlaw bikers and loved working on used bikes, modifying them with their own customized designs. Old, pre-AMF bikes were favored as the more authentic species. These preferences aligned well with working-class pocketbooks; many men couldn't afford a new machine, anyway.

Stage 3: Repackaging Gunfighters as Men of Action

While Harleys were immensely valued among young down-and-out white men who valued the patriarchal ideals that had become imbued in the bikes, they were anything but desirable among the middle-class, middle-aged white men who would become Harley's acolytes in the 1990s. How could Harley's thuggish gunfighter myth be revamped in a way that appealed to men with desk jobs earning $100,000 a year? Ronald Reagan and his gunfighter celebrity friends repackaged the Harley myth in the 1980s, preparing the ground for the anti-PC (anti–politically-correct) myth market that blossomed in the early 1990s.

Reagan Promotes Gunfighters as Men of Action

The rise of Reagan as the most influential American cultural icon and his strategic use of Harley was the single most important cause of Harley's resurgence. As a way to jump-start U.S. economic and political might, Reagan revived Teddy Roosevelt's turn-of-the-century gunfighter myth.

Reagan used his cultural authority as a star in the B Westerns of the 1940s and 1950s to reinvent the myth.[12] He spun a populist myth about a reawakening of the American spirit and delivered magnetic sermons on what made America great. He believed that the United States had a destiny divined from God, replaying John Winthrop's claim that the nation was a land of chosen people, "a city on a hill." As he pronounced a boyish faith in American goodness, he expressed disdain for government bureaucracy and elite expertise, and most important, he vowed to stand up to U.S. enemies. His capitalist take on the frontiersman painted the entrepreneur and small business as the engines of American success. To make his critique of bureaucracies and elite insiders stick, Reagan transformed America's historic gunfighter character into a man of action: a heroic figure who could single-handedly take on corrupt institutions in order to salvage the country's traditional values.

Roosevelt had used the figure of the gunfighter as the symbol of U.S. ambitions as an emerging global power after the Spanish-American War. Reagan called for the revival of Roosevelt's gunfighter ideals to overturn what he viewed as sickly institutions and a weak national spirit. He used Sylvester Stallone's Rambo character—a renegade Green Beret from Vietnam—as the quintessential gunfighter figure. And he routinely invoked the most prominent gunfighter actors—John Wayne and Clint Eastwood in particular—as symbols of his ideological revolution. Just as Reagan encouraged Americans to revel in these figures as heroes, he acted as a man-of-action gunfighter himself, taking on Noriega in Panama and Gadhafi in Libya, renewing a hard line with the Soviet Union and Iran, and supporting the contras as freedom fighters against the Sandinistas in Nicaragua.

Reagan's charismatic call to resurrect a nation of gunfighters galvanized men across the class spectrum. By his reelection in 1984, previous party allegiances had broken down. Instead of the class- and ethnicity-based alliances that had held since Franklin Roosevelt's New Deal, Reagan organized a new alignment that was strongly influenced by his ideals of manhood.

On the economic front, Reagan picked up on the working-class backlash, treating the Japanese like the American Indians of the day. The Japanese had "attacked" the United States, so it had no recourse but to fight back. The administration painted the Japanese as public enemy number one, an economic threat to American power and prestige. While the

United States seemed able to win the Cold War against the Soviet Union, Japan—with its superior business practices and long-term determination to penetrate export markets—appeared economically unstoppable. In the early 1980s, protests against Japanese capital investments in U.S. real estate such as Manhattan's Rockefeller Center and in American culture such as film and music companies became common.

On the cultural front, Reagan honed the rhetoric developed by neo-conservative intellectuals in the 1970s, excoriating "liberal elites" who'd corrupted the nation by dethroning American heroes and forcing anti-American ideas into the educational curricula and the media. He attacked the social agenda that emerged from the 1960s, calling it antireligious and unpatriotic and claiming it favored socialist ideas over morally superior laissez-faire individualism. Reagan found cultural elites to be wimpy, and mainstream America agreed.

Three key cultural texts repackaged Harley to evoke these man-of-action gunfighter ideals. These texts transformed the brand's unvarnished reactionary version of the gunfighter. The new gunfighter was still violent and patriarchal, but he was also a heroic man of action who had the power to save the country. This revival of the man of action proved to be exceedingly attractive to conservative middle-class men.

Malcolm Forbes's Capitalist Tools

While Reagan was building his political base in the late 1970s, one of his key allies, Malcolm Forbes, was already touting Harley's effectiveness as a symbol of the gunfighter myth. Forbes, publisher of his namesake *Forbes* magazine and renowned right-wing ideologue, was a publicity-seeking celebrity in his own right. He arranged adventurous trips on Harleys, which were widely reported in the press. He and his "Capitalist Tool" riders would fly their Harleys to exotic and often politically sensitive "frontiers" like Afghanistan, take a ride, and then present the local authority with a gift, a Harley. He also led "freedom rides" for libertarian causes on his Harley. Forbes applied his famous name to the Harley dealership he owned. Behind a limo that broke the Manhattan wind for him, Forbes often cycled to work on one of his Harleys.

Forbes crafted the Harley gunfighter as a distinctly capitalist figure. Harley riders were warriors championing capitalism and liberty in the face of socialist threats. These men had the virility to reinvigorate society with libertarian values. For Forbes, unlike the working-class riders who preceded him, Harleys symbolized a potent type of masculinity *within* the world of business. Being a man meant pursuing the life of a rugged individualist manager, as an entrepreneur willing to take death-defying risks both professionally and personally. It meant being manly in demeanor and conservative in politics and social mores. In Forbes's view, real capitalist men were defiant entrepreneurs who thrived in a world of competition.

Reagan Anoints Harley as Man of Action

In the early 1980s, Harley was still suffering from mismanagement (AMF had expanded too rapidly and with poor quality controls), a recession, and the debt taken on by a management-led leveraged buyout. The Reagan administration was well aware of Harley's precarious financial position and was worried about the political fallout if it allowed a company with the heritage and symbolism of Harley to slide into bankruptcy. In April 1983, Reagan came to Harley's rescue. He imposed a huge tariff increase against imported heavyweight motorcycles and power-train subassemblies (from 4.4 percent to 49.4 percent) to protect Harley's business. The political task was to spin the bailout to make an overtly protectionist policy align with the administration's laissez-faire rhetoric.

Again proving his rhetorical wizardry, Reagan skillfully wove Harley into his efforts to revive the gunfighter myth. He told Americans that because HDC had been wronged by America's economic foes (the Japanese), the nation must rally around Harley, especially since it was the last American motorcycle company.

Although Reagan had effectively enlisted Harley into his vision of the frontier, alongside the mythical gunfighters friends Stallone, Wayne, and Eastwood, the brand received little benefit from these ideological coattails at first. First of all, the real capitalist gunfighters were to be found predominantly on Wall Street, working as investment bankers and corporate raiders. Harley's ties to rural working-class guys didn't make sense in this environment. Second, the story was all wrong. The nation was hungry for strong men who could effectively topple the old model of capitalism and, then, conquer America's aggressive new rivals. Wall Street bankers fit the mold; the Harley-Davidson Company did not. Harley seemed to be a fumbling old-economy company, beaten up badly by the Japanese, and with a history of attacking rather than backing bikers. Not exactly the heroic frontiersman that American society wanted to rally around. Rambo worked much better.

But as the five-year tariff protection approached expiration in 1987, the Reagan administration schemed with Harley management to pull off an extraordinary public relations coup. On March 19, Harley CEO Vaughn Beals asked the International Trade Commission to cancel its tariff protection—a purely symbolic move as Honda and Kawasaki had moved production to the United States to avoid the tariff. What's more, the tariff, which started at 45 percent of wholesale prices, was to be only 10 percent in the last year. On May 6, Reagan gave a speech from the factory floor of Harley's York, Pennsylvania, plant, proclaiming, "American workers don't need to hide from anyone." The event was covered in major newspapers across the United States. *USA Today* and other major newspapers even ran a photo of Reagan revving up a hog.[13] On July 1, Beals and Forbes led twenty Harleys on a ride, which had been scripted by their ad agency, from the American Stock Exchange to the New York Stock Exchange, where a bike was parked on the trading floor for the day. On October 9—six months before the tariff was set to expire—President Reagan canceled the tariff. Reagan praised Harley's recovery as a victory over the Japanese, further attributing the recovery to the spirit of the frontier West that his presidency was championing. Harley symbolized the revitalization of U.S. economic power that was possible through the Reagan-styled capitalist gunfighter myth.

The rhetorical impact of the event was stunning. The media jumped on Reagan's performance, for it was perfectly scripted as a classic American comeback story: A company whose customers were the quintessential American frontier warriors had lost its way when bought up by a statist conglomerate. The company was salvaged by real gunfighter-cum-entrepreneurs who understood the ethos. With help from an insurgent gunfighter-friendly president, the company was turned around and was again a proud and profitable company.

With this story line in place, Harley quickly became a central prop in Reagan's storytelling. Harley's consecration was made all the more meaningful by events that transpired after Reagan's New York speech. The stock market crash of October 1987 signaled the end of the Wall Street financiers' run as the nation's gunfighter heroes. Wall Street's version was untenable not only because of the outlandish corruption but also because the symbolism wasn't entirely coherent. The new entrepreneurial spirit could not be centered in the heart of the "city"—in the midst of large, capitalist, bureaucratic institutions. To be truly effective, the new myth needed to incorporate some sort of frontier.

The Harley-Davidson Company, a Milwaukee concern with a heritage tied to the heartland and the West, was untainted by the crash. The company earned gunfighter credibility because it had somehow survived in the decimated Northern industrial region that had become known as the rust belt. As Wall Street and its yuppies were on their way out, and with them such symbols as BMWs and Rolexes, Harley was left standing as the most credible branded symbol for those wedded to Reagan's ideology.

America's Man-of-Action Stars Sign On

Following the Wall Street crash, Harley became the favored ride of Reagan's Hollywood cronies. Not only Stallone and Eastwood, but also fellow men of action Arnold Schwarzenegger and Bruce Willis were featured in entertainment magazines on their hogs. These celebrity endorsements closed the circle that Forbes had initiated in the late 1970s, fixing Harley as the most potent symbol for Reagan's gunfighter through its associations with these charismatic actors and their gunfighter films.

But the ultimate consecration of Harley as the favored ride of America's new breed of men-of-action gunfighters came with the release of 1991's hugely popular *Terminator 2: Judgment Day* (T2). Arnold Schwarzenegger (switching sides from his villain's role in the prior film) plays the quintessential man-of-action gunfighter. He's a machine, just like his molten metal enemy that has been sent back in time to terminate John Conner (the boy who would grow up years later to lead the resistance to save humankind). Yet he's one of the good guys; he uses his violent powers toward just ends.

In the opening scene, Arnold does in some Hell's Angels-styled outlaw bikers with paunches that signal they're well past their prime. He steals one of their Harleys and rides off as a new-and-improved biker: a brutal and talented assassin whose violence is necessary to save Americans from totalitarian technologies. T2 was one of the most potent masculine myths of the era, and it all took place on a Harley!

These texts combined to reinvent Harley's gunfighter into a new breed of man necessary to revive America. From a transgressive myth for men on the margins, Harley now carried a myth that helped men forge a connection with Reagan's frontier call to revive American power. In so doing, these texts had separated the Harley bike from its old moorings in the outlaw biker world. Not only had the outlaw bikers all but disappeared, but so had the undesirable aspects of their ethos—the overt misogyny and in-your-face antisocial behavior and antibourgeois rhetoric. Harley's new myth paid out handsomely as the United States hit a major cultural disruption in the early 1990s. When demand swelled for myths that imagined the revived authority of middle-class white men, Harley was perfectly positioned to respond.

Harley Becomes an Icon, Again

The new Wall Street–driven U.S. economy created extraordinary pressures and incentives that pushed corporate managers to expand markets, lower costs, and innovate better than competitors. By the early 1990s, as these financial pressures had spread around the globe, they carved out a new marketplace organized around the flexible networked organization, the knowledge-driven, winner-take-all labor market, and the aggressive re-engineering of the firm.

Reagan had unleashed a juggernaut when he revitalized America's frontier ideology. However, this next stage of American capitalism proved a poor fit with certain parts of his mythic construction. Reagan had vowed to advance a social conservative agenda aligned with the Christian right. In his vision, American ideology was to consecrate Christian ideals of morality, communicated through such touchstone issues as antiabortion and prayers in public schools. But Christian conservatism and the gunfighter myth were strange bedfellows, for gunfighters were not beholden to Christian morals—not in the American West of the nineteenth century, nor, as it turned out, in the "turbo-capitalism" at the end of the twentieth. Aside from a few highly publicized skirmishes—such as when Tipper Gore's Parent's Musical Resource Center lobbied the government to regulate lewd lyrics on heavy metal and rap albums—these issues fizzled.

Rather, an ideology that took up the first part of Reagan's agenda—the free-agent frontier—proved to be the most functional and became favored by the majority of both political parties. The new economy required an ideology that sanctified dynamism, meritocratic competition, and absolute commitment to economic goals above all. Companies embraced cultural diversity to pursue global agendas, and they sought out the most talented and motivated employees, regardless of creed, gender, or ethnicity. The old idea of hierarchical command gave way to flatter structures and more flexible teams and alliances. Moreover, the new global free market was structured to court and amplify every consumer desire, be it for tabloid television, hip-hop couture, or even pornography. The neoconservatives in the Republican Party combined with Bill Clinton's "New Democrats" to embrace the free movement of capital and labor, cultural diversity, feminism, meritocracy, and economic goals over military conquest.

The Anti-PC Myth Market

As this free-agent networked economy took hold, economic insecurity, mostly a blue-collar problem for the previous two decades, extended into the rest of the labor market. This economy created highly competitive labor markets and downward pressure on salaries for virtually every occupational category except for senior executives and highly specialized knowledge worker positions. The middle-class jobs on which men had previously depended for authority and prestige became unstable, subject to the same cost-benefit knife that had slashed so many blue-collar jobs during the 1970s and 1980s. And, like the economic dislocations in blue-collar work before, these shifts threatened men's identities.

The result was a populist backlash led by men of European descent who had lived in the United States for several generations—a group whom the media came to call "angry white men." These men had had their economic security and masculine status yanked from them. The most visible expressions were the explosion of shock radio, the paramilitary survivalist groups that together formed the militia or patriot movement, John Bly's runaway best-selling book *Iron John,* and the Million Man March.

Populist observers pushed theories to explain these troubles, as well as myths to assuage these angry men's pain. A cohort of social conservatives, led by Rush Limbaugh, used the economic turmoil of the day to paint a theory of cultural decay. Limbaugh was far and away the most influential cultural leader of the day, holding millions of self-proclaimed "dittoheads" under his sway in his role as a demagogue-like pundit on talk radio. He was eventually joined by fellow shock jocks such as Oliver North and G. Gordon Liddy. Limbaugh's radio show climbed to number one in the

United States, reaching more than 20 million listeners every week. A mostly male audience listened for hours at a time, much as people used to do in the pretelevision era. Limbaugh had to hire 140 people just to respond to the bagfuls of mail he received each day. His book *The Way Things Ought to Be* hit number one and spent many months on the *New York Times* best-seller list.

Limbaugh and his brethren effectively wove the shifting economic realities—the network economy, the free-agent winner-take-all job market, the increasing power of highly educated knowledge workers who were often immigrants and ethnic Americans—into a story that captivated those men dethroned by the new economy. Limbaugh argued that this devastating emasculation was caused by the "socialist-slash-communist" ideology of the liberal elites who controlled the federal government, the media, and Hollywood. In particular, Limbaugh singled out "whiners," who selfishly berated how the country had wronged them rather than celebrate the nation's inherent goodness: feminists (or "femiNazis" in Limbaugh's memorable phrasing, signatures of which were Hillary Clinton and Anita Hill), civil rights activists (whose signatures were affirmative action, the Rodney King beating, and the O. J. Simpson trial), and environmentalists (the "tree-hugging" hypocrites who refused to acknowledge that they enjoyed the bounties that natural resources provided). In Limbaugh's influential view, the success of 1960s agitators caused the anxieties felt by disgruntled American men.

Limbaugh advocated a return to patriotic values, which he located in post–World War II United States, when the nation was at its apex of power and prior to the 1960s upheaval. Limbaugh held up Reagan as a deity, one of America's greatest leaders, because the president had fought against the 1960s culprits to rekindle America's "traditional" values.

Part and parcel of this reactionary backlash was the spread of a nationalist fervor against the globalized competition for jobs. Americans, particularly the angry-white-men contingent, wanted to seal off the borders of the nation. Politicians as different as Jerry Brown, Pat Buchanan, and Ross Perot championed protectionist and isolationist "fortress America" policies.

The 1992 election of Bill Clinton (and his wife, Hillary) to the presidency set off a shock wave among these men. Clinton's economic policies continued to push the market liberalization policies of the Reagan and Bush administrations. And to make matters worse, he, unlike his predecessors, didn't cloak these policies in cultural conservatism. Clinton's ideological agenda flaunted new-economy values—the antithesis of what the angry-white-men contingent desired. To these men, Clinton was one of Limbaugh's liberal elites in good standing with his Yale law degree, a guy who not only enjoyed talking with blacks but also played a passable rhythm-and-blues saxophone. He came packaged with an assertive, liberal elite wife (also with a Yale law degree) who was determined to influence major policy initiatives rather than dabble in polite but tangential causes, as first ladies were supposed to do. Clinton began his presidency by pushing a "don't ask, don't tell" policy for gays in the military, searching for a "politics of meaning" with Jewish leaders, and holding national debates on racism, meanwhile acting as international statesman, a reverse of Reagan's antagonistic swagger toward political foes.

Clinton's election galvanized the opposition that Limbaugh and other social conservatives were stirring up. Consequently, Reagan's call for men to stand up, like gunfighters, to Washington bureaucrats and the liberal media became all the more compelling. The gunfighter myth engulfed the periphery of American mass culture: in fundamentalist religion, in community organizations, in AM radio. Harley, with its well-established gunfighter credentials and ties to Reagan, was perfectly situated to become a central icon for this constituency.

Harley's gunfighter myth, constructed with Reagan's blessing, was ideally suited to work as a salve for these tensions. Harley served as the nucleus of a brotherhood of men joined to a conservative vision to restore "traditional" conservative masculinity (i.e., white, patriarchal, Christian, American) over the cultural free-for-all of the new global networked economy.

Men who could afford it flocked to Harley, seemingly overnight. The bike's popularity soared among politically conservative, white, middle-aged, middle-class men—a group that had never before yearned for a Harley. The waiting list to buy a bike grew to a year or more, the prices of Harley bikes climbed to nearly $20,000, and the average Harley buyer soon earned around $80,000 in yearly income and was more likely to be in his forties than his twenties. The Harley-Davidson Company began to significantly outpace the Standard & Poor's 500 in 1991 and hasn't looked back since, achieving tremendous financial success as the central icon of the anti-PC myth market throughout the 1990s.

Harley-Davidson Learns to Coauthor the Myth

For decades, Harley-Davidson had studiously ignored its core customers. But, starting in the late 1970s, the company finally did an "if you can't beat 'em, join 'em" flip-flop. Harley began to run ads that it hoped would mirror the brand as seen through the eyes of its core constituents—at the time the working-class white guys who identified so strongly with the outlaw bikers. In other words, while Reagan and his comrades were busy repackaging the Harley myth for a much more lucrative clientele, the company was still playing to its lower-class constituency.

Harley finally began advertising in *Easyriders,* and soon featured outlaw bikers in its mainstream print ads. In April 1980, Harley placed a five-page ad in *Easyriders*. The first page appeared on the right-hand page and functioned as an introduction, so that you'd have to turn the page to see the two-page spreads that followed. The first page was mostly black and white, except that on the top, giant red characters occupied a quarter of the page. Who knows if they actually said something in Japanese. Under these characters, in businesslike serif type about an eighth the size of the red characters, ran this copy: "They talk low. They talk custom." The bottom half of the page shows the shadow of an eagle's head, its carnivorous hooked beak a little open and ready for action. The print on the page bottom read, "Now, maybe they'll stop talking." The two gatefold photos that follow show a couple of new Harleys. The purpose of the ad was clearly to bait the vicious anti-Asian complex nurtured at the time among Harley's working-class male constituents. Harley advertising continued to hold up a mirror to its patrons, doing its best to parrot their views. But since the semiotic stars aligned for Harley in the early 1990s, the Harley-Davidson Company has become much more adept at contributing to the brand's myth.

The Anti-PC Poet. Harley understood that, in the minds of its constituents, the Harley myth was firmly lodged in the 1950s. Within the frame of the Harley mythology, the 1950s was the golden era of the United States. It was when the nation was at its most dominant, when men had secure jobs and were the unchallenged heads of nuclear families, and when the population was unthreatened by immigrants and women entering the work force. And this period predated the reviled 1960s social movements championed by the so-called liberal elites. It is certainly ironic, but also a demonstration of the power of myth to rewrite history, that a bike that supposedly represents libertarian ideals would locate its halcyon years in an era when the nation was the most conscripted to conventions!

Because Harley's myth is about a brotherhood of gunfighters, much Harley mythmaking goes on at group events, especially the big rallies such as those held each year in places like Sturgis, South Dakota; Daytona Beach, Florida; and Laconia, New Hampshire. The company does its best to contribute to a richly evocative, revisionist history that places Harley at the center of the story.

A prime example of HDC's creative branding efforts is the hiring of Martin Jack Rosenblum, "the Holy Ranger," a folk musician and longtime Harley buff who holds a Ph.D. in English. Under his pseudonym, Rosenblum had published a book of poems that became popular among Harley enthusiasts. The Holy Ranger's poetry provided Harley customers with a direct pipeline from bike to gunfighter ideals of manhood:

> PRAISE OUR LADIES
> *These Harley women*
> *straddle their choppers*
> *with lustrous precision*
> *& when packing behind you*
> *with hands tucked under the*
> *belt buckle at your waist a*
> *man rides amidst powers of*
> *awesome potential & the*
> *bike actually lathers*
> *like a stallion*
> *bulging at the*
> *barndoor.*[14]

Sensing a potent marketing opportunity, Harley-Davidson quickly hired Rosenblum as the official Harley historian and poet laureate. Then the company encouraged him to rekindle his musical interests. Rosenblum subsequently released several CDs of music filled with lyrics like the above. Rather than folk music—which for Harley possessed all the wrong hippie/Beat connotations—Rosenblum abruptly switched to American "roots" music. Rosenblum's cultural assignment was to build for Harley a musical genre that fit the 1950s focus of the mythology. He concocted an amalgam of electric blues and rockabilly-influenced rock of the 1950s and billed these styles as the "true American musical genres." He has performed regularly at Harley functions, playing from these styles and using lyrics that he's written as the poet of the Harley tribe.

Militia as Metaphor. In addition, Harley has become much more adept in its advertising, taking advantage of the political currents that influence their constituents. In place of its pedantic advertising of the past, the company began to draw on symbols that resonated with the anti-PC movement.

For Harley's constituency, some of the most effective raw materials of the early 1990s came from another populist world that often intersected with the outlaw motorcycle clubs—the militia/patriot movement, a right-wing counterculture that had grown to sizable numbers mostly in the Pacific Northwest. These libertarian "patriots" argued against paying taxes and refused to obey national institutions unless they were in the Constitution. Members of patriot groups organized militias for projected future armed struggles to "save" the nation. They often took racist stands, spinning idiosyncratic readings of the Bible to support their views.

To tap into this symbolism, Harley produced a memorable print ad that depicted a lone cabin in the mountains of the West, with a Harley parked outside. The mountain cabin had become an icon of the militia movement, thanks to the Unabomber and Ruby Ridge incidents, both of which involved patriots holed up in mountain cabins. In fact, the Unibomber's cabin had become a major tourist attraction. The Harley ad signaled the brand's alignment with the values of the patriot movement, even if the company and its constituents refused to condone the patriots' tactics.

Unveiling the Harley Mystique

Harley's astounding rise in identity value in the early 1990s followed the same path as other iconic brands. Harley-Davidson motorcycles became a convincing symbol for a myth about manhood, a contemporary reinterpretation of America's gunfighter. The brand gained iconic status because its myth anticipated the extraordinary anxieties experienced by a particular class of men who faced the American economic restructuring of the early 1990s.

The Harley myth felt authentic because it was so firmly grounded in the most credible populist world for championing gunfighter values—the outlaw motorcycle clubs. And because it was communicated with such charisma by film characters, actors, and an actor-turned-politician, the myth was particularly compelling. Harley had the right myth, with the requisite authenticity and charisma, and at the right time to lead culture.

The Harley mystique stemmed from the fact that its myth seemed to emanate organically from the bike. Its authors could not be sourced because they were too diffuse and because the usual suspect—the manufacturer—was only peripherally involved. Rather, the Harley myth was built over many decades by numerous authors. Initially, the mystique was the cumulative and unintended consequence of the motorcycle's use by biker clubs as an emblem of their outlaw values. Later, filmmakers, journalists, and politicians picked up these bikers as raw cultural materials for their own varied agendas. In particular, Harley's success hinged on the contributions by Malcolm Forbes, Ronald Reagan, and Reagan's pantheon of gunfighter friends from the film industry. Without this helping hand from coauthors, Harley management would still be struggling to sell bikes to working-class guys.

Coauthoring an Iconic Brand

Iconic brands are usually built with advertisements: films produced by the brand owner. But two other potential coauthors—culture industries and populist worlds—can also contribute significantly to the brand's myth. Harley is the most important American case of this sort of coauthorship. What can we learn from Harley's success? The brand cannot be copied directly, but we can draw broader inferences about how coauthoring works.

Don't Imitate Harley

Branding gurus continually praise Harley's H.O.G. initiatives and advocate that companies should imitate Harley by building a brand community. All for naught. Followers form communities around icons (brands and otherwise) because the icons contribute to their identities, providing myths that resolve acute tensions. Followers sometimes gather together because doing so heightens the ritual power of the myth. "Community" isn't an end in itself, one that brand managers can program by themselves. Rather, brand communities form when a brand provides a myth that is compelling enough to draw people together, on their own, so that they can amplify the myth through their interactions.

Harley's customer group was organized by Harley enthusiasts in the 1970s, not by HDC in the 1980s. The company forcibly took over the riders' organization—leading to considerable resentment among members at the time—because the group was hugely successful and the company recognized that it could be a tremendous marketing tool. Similarly, customer groups centered on Volkswagen and Apple—the other two poster children of brand community—were organized by enthusiasts who were so taken by the brand's myth that they wanted to weave it more intensively into their lives. Brand communities never exist as ends in themselves. No amount of marketing attention to building a brand community will compensate for lack of a resonant identity myth.

Harley's path to iconic status cannot be copied. While most iconic brands develop their myths via breakthrough advertising, Harley is a rare example of a different and rare evolution: a brand built autonomously by the culture industries and a populist world. Harley's path cannot be replicated because Harley's iconic power was never managed. The irresistible authenticity is a product of its ghost authors. Instead of imitation, we must push for broader lessons.

How Cultural Texts Affect Brand Myths

As consumers have become increasingly cynical about firm-sponsored communications, senior managers have eagerly shifted their attention to the other engines of identity value: the culture industries (via product placements) and populist worlds (via viral branding efforts). This shift makes sense. Society's best mythmaking engines are found in these two locations, not in advertising.

But marketing has yet to crack the code on how to develop branded cultural texts, largely because the discipline continues to apply conventional branding models to the cultural terrain. When cultural texts are viewed as mere entertainment, rather than as myths, their potent identity value remains hidden.

The mind-share model treats cultural texts as a means to build up the brand's DNA. Managers seek to align their brand's associations with the right text to maximize fit and exposure. The viral model offers little strategic direction other than the old public relations saw to cause a stir, to get people talking. Pursuing the texts they believe will be the most popular— the most cool— managers try to get their brands into the mix.

These perspectives ignore that what consumers value most about these texts is the identity-buttressing myths that they perform. When cultural texts include a brand as a central prop, they can dramatically amplify and alter the brand's myth. The Harley genealogy reveals two processes through which these texts can affect the brand's myth: stitching and repackaging.

Stitching Texts. Cultural texts can draw a brand into an existing myth. The outlaw myth was not originally owned by Harley. It was developed by outlaw motorcycle club members, who sometimes rode Harleys as one of several acceptable big bikes. In the era of the *Life* magazine exposé and *The Wild One,* this myth was anchored to images of the scraggly bikers and their gear: leather, jeans, and big bikes. Not necessarily Harley. It was the Hell's Angels news stories, Hunter S. Thompson's articles and book, and in particular the film *Easy Rider* that stitched the outlaw myth to Harley.

Repackaging Texts. The culture industries can also reinvent the brand myth. The most important strategic question that one must answer to explain Harley's success is one that the many management book treatises on Harley have never asked: How is it that a brand that provided extraordinary identity value to young working-class men by championing values that the middle-class found offensive could, a decade later, become one of the most prized possessions of middle-class executives?

Reagan and his comrades converted the rebellious gunfighter favored by down-and-out guys in the 1970s into a mythical hero: the man-of-action gunfighter whose violent bravado would save the country. Historical characters drawn into myth are malleable. Good storytellers can shape these characters to suit the story that needs to be told. Reagan grabbed the gunfighter and recast it to suit his political purposes. Harley, because of its gunfighter credentials and comeback story, proved to be the most useful symbol for Reagan to tell this story. The collective effect of Forbes's freedom rides, Reagan's "rescue" of the company, and the man-of-action celebrities who began to ride Harleys was to reinterpret Harley riders as heroic men-of-action—patriotic gunfighters committed to renewing the

FIGURE 7-2

Culture Industry Texts Repackage the Harley Myth

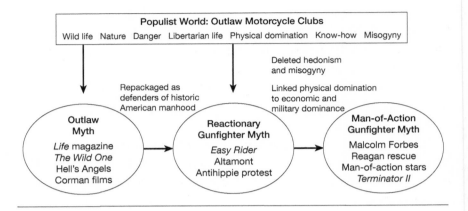

nation's economic and political dominance by recharging its lapsing values (figure 7-2).

To accomplish this alchemy, these new texts usefully "forgot" key elements of Harley's outlaw ethos that conflicted with the new myth: the misogyny, the violence, the willful sloth, and the vitriolic dislike of authoritarian institutions. Moreover, the texts built up and reinterpreted other elements of the ethos. The libertarian politics, physical domination, and patriarchy were all kept and expansively reinterpreted to include economic and political dominance as well.

Repackaging texts don't just disseminate the myth. They reinvent it by spotlighting and reinterpreting certain features of the myth while hiding others. Ad campaigns that have refurbished a fading brand myth to address a new contradiction—recall BBDO's "Do the Dew," Arnold's "Drivers Wanted," and Goodby Silverstein & Partners' "Lizards" campaigns—work in much the same way. By tracing the path of the brand's repackaging texts (culture industry and ads), we can explain how the brand's myth gets transformed over time.

Collaborating with Coauthors

The source material for Harley's initial outlaw myth was created by the outlaw motorcycle clubs that sprung up in the 1950s.[15] Despite the high hopes of viral branding, however, populist worlds alone cannot create a brand myth. If the culture industries had not grabbed the bikers as source material for mythmaking texts, Harley would never have become an icon. The key question, then, is how should firms manage the brand when culture industries, outside the firm's control, take control of the brand's myth?

In the twenty-year period following Word War II, HDC offered an object lesson in how not to manage this collaboration. The Davidson family did its best to distance the brand from the outlaw bikers and their cronies. It was disturbed by the brand's outlaw stories and wanted nothing to do with them. The family viewed the Harley as a grand touring bike for gentlemen and adventurous racers and was proud of the bike's role in the war effort. To the owners' mind, the media attention paid to outlaw bikers soiled Harley's image. So Harley ads featured nuclear-suburban settings, and new Harley products like golf carts and three-wheeler bikes were geared to respectable, middle-class families. Harley even attacked the bikers' use of "unauthorized" customized parts in their ads. These misguided efforts resulted in Harley's missing a golden cultural branding opportunity in the 1960s. If properly managed, Harley could have easily joined Levi's and Volkswagen as an iconic brand with wide appeal extending into the middle class.

When the Harley-Davidson Company finally decided to play along, it offered unimaginative and meek efforts to parrot the myth that the culture industries had produced. Such a policy basically ceded control of the brand to the culture industries. Harley was very fortunate that relinquishing control turned out so well, but this was pure luck. The culture industries could just as easily have lost interest or spun stories that worked against the brand's myth.

In the 1990s, however, HDC became much more sophisticated at cultural branding. Instead of fighting against or parroting the influential cultural texts, the company began to elaborate on and tweak these texts to shape the myth to best suit its customers. For instance, the lone-cabin advertisement stitched relevant current events to the Harley myth in a way that a photojournalist's shot in the newspapers was unlikely to capture. Similarly, the use of the Holy Ranger at Harley events extended the idea that Harleys are fighting actively for the rejuvenation of a "traditional" America, not just mimicking the culture industries (e.g., a screening of *Easy Rider* for the festival goers).

CHAPTER 8

Advancing the Myth

A FTER A BRAND'S MYTH IS ESTABLISHED, usually with breakthrough advertising, what happens next? If myth markets can last a
decade or longer, how does a brand sustain its iconic status over such a
long period? How can managers keep the brand's myth relevant, provocative, and inspiring? While originating a potent myth is no easy feat, managing it so that it remains vital for many years is often just as difficult. Even
the most successful iconic brands routinely stumble. Mountain Dew,
Volkswagen, and Budweiser, for instance, each have struggled to extend
their myths.

To extend a powerful myth, the brand's communications must steer a
path between two traps: milking the myth to capitalize on its popularity,
and abandoning the myth entirely to pursue the next big trend. Let's examine these traps first. Then we'll take a look at the principles that allow
the most successful iconic brands to steer a fruitful course.

Milking the Myth's Popularity

An icon must possess integrity, demonstrating its commitment to advancing the values espoused by its myth. When a brand appears to be taking advantage of its followers' allegiance to the myth for quick commercial gain,
the brand hemorrhages credibility and loses its effectiveness. Consequently, a sure way for a brand to destroy its myth is to milk it, to behave
like a shill, much as Hollywood studios treat a hit movie. Companies milk
myths in two ways: formulaic repetition and pursuing buzz.

Plug-in-the-Formula Copies

When Mountain Dew's "Done That" ad became a blockbuster, the brand
team quickly produced three cookie-cutter sequels that leveraged the

original's most compelling elements. Each spot was structured like "Done That," with the Dew dudes commenting on impossibly outrageous stunts in their implacable manner, only to be overwhelmed by the power of Dew at the end. The spots tendered more fantastic and absurd stunts—water skiing behind a helicopter past icebergs in the North Pole, in-line skating off the Sphinx in Egypt, wrestling an alligator in the Amazon, taking a platform jump off London's Big Ben clock tower—but the rest of the shtick remained essentially the same.

To maintain its charisma, a brand must continually prod the imagination of its followers with distinctive and original communiqués. Instead, the brand team tried to wring every drop of popularity from its original hit. Consequently, consumers grew tired of Dew's formulaic ads. These repetitive spots ran for over a year and nearly killed the campaign.

Pushing Buzz

Another good way to kill off a myth is to pull another Hollywood trick—to promote the most memorable aspects of a myth to develop buzz. Anheuser-Busch pursued this strategy with its "Whassup?!" campaign when, after a year and a half of successful extensions, Bud's brand team altered its extension strategy.[1]

The brand team produced "Come Home" for the 2001 Super Bowl telecast. The sci-fi spoof began with a golden retriever exiting a house at night and getting "beamed up" to a spaceship. Inside what looked like a football stadium filled with alien creatures, the critter pressed a button on its collar and stepped out of what turns out to be its dog costume. The boss—seated on a throne and wearing a crown—then asked the remotely humanoid spy who had just emerged from the dog suit what it had learned on Earth. After a pregnant pause, the little creature did its best tongue-waggling "Whassup?!" imitation. After another pause, the thousands of aliens in the spaceship joined in. The ad then switched back from the computer-animated spaceship to a live-action milieu, and the picture showed a giant radio telescope. Inside the astronomic facility, a young man wearing headphones and apparently monitoring heavenly radiation with his ears, leaned back in his chair and declared, "We are not alone," as his fellow scientists looked on.

The production values of "Come Home" lived up to the Super Bowl's hype and glamour, and the well-crafted spot scored well in USA Today's

Admeter poll. The ad was great entertainment. Advertising critics lined up to praise the ad as well. But the pursuit of short-term applause sacrificed the myth that the original "Whassup?!" ads had created because the ad yanked the Whassup?! ritual out of its original context, thereby eviscerating its potent meaning. The ad celebrated Whassup?! as a hollow catchphrase.

In chapter 6, we saw that when a brand like ESPN delivers a great myth, it attracts followers like a magnet, drawing in a large constituency of consumers (feeders) who find value in the brand's popularity. Concerned primarily with fashion, the feeder consumers don't particularly identify with the myth. Rather, they consume the icon because other people are doing it. Likewise, part of the popularity of "Whassup?!" was that millions of fashion-following guys across the United States were greeting each other with a resounding "Whassssuppp?!" They were participating in what was in at the time, even though many of these guys didn't resonate with the "Whassup?!" myth. To them, it was just a faddish phrase to use until it was no longer popular with their friends.

To avoid allowing a myth to be overrun by faddish popularity, the brand team has to discipline itself to do something counterintuitive. It must resist the urge to communicate in a conspicuously instrumental or self-congratulatory way. Icons must ignore the attention of fad seekers and, instead, continue to champion new and creative variants of the myth.

By treating "Whassup?!" as a mere fad, these later ads actually belittled the values that the campaign had advanced. Although such ads will momentarily excite feeders, they have exactly the opposite effect on the core constituents of Bud's myth—its followers and insiders. For consumers at the brand's nucleus, actions that seek to take commercial advantage of a myth's popularity convey the notion that the brand is more interested in money than it is in its values. Such a lack of fidelity strips the brand of credibility. Ads like "Come Home" accelerated the demise of Bud's myth, which likely could have been extended for years.

Chasing Trends

Alternatively, in the juggling act to extend an effective myth, a brand team can make a wholly different mistake. Too often, potential icons desert their myth to chase trends in popular culture.

Since the early 1980s, the Mountain Dew brand team has been seduced three times by the extraordinary popularity of the populist world of hip-hop. By the mid-1980s, African American urban culture was on a path to become the most powerful cultural epicenter for American youths. Mountain Dew's managers thought that the brand had to be integrated with hip-hop for the brand to grow in metropolitan areas. Each time, the team made a huge bet and shifted the brand's strategy in an effort to move Mountain Dew into the 'hood. And each time it failed.

Act 1: Dew Does MTV

Rolling Stone and a few other music magazines aside, before 1981, the culture industries lacked an institution that could organize a national youth culture. By creating a single, national vehicle for promoting music and lifestyles, MTV changed the way companies marketed to youth. PepsiCo understood the power of the network as early as anyone and signed one of MTV's first superstars, Michael Jackson, to headline the company's blockbuster ads for its Pepsi brand. With this success under its belt, PepsiCo management believed that MTV had built the road that could finally take Mountain Dew from the NASCAR Belt into the country's cities. The company scrapped its very successful redneck myth advertising to take a crack at reinventing Dew within the world of urban culture that MTV was then creating.

The new campaign centered on break dancing and freestyle BMX bike riding, the leading edge of a growing teen interest in creative individual athletic performances instead of organized team sports. These activities flowed from the emerging culture of poor, urban African American and Hispanic neighborhoods that would soon be called hip-hop. Soon after its arrival, MTV began to integrate many aspects of hip-hop subculture, including fashion and music influences, into its overall look, sound, and feel. A number of MTV's first stars, like Madonna and Billy Idol, used fashions from hip-hop.

Mountain Dew's first MTV-influenced ad, "Breakdance," featured an integrated cast performing acrobatic dance maneuvers in a park. The dancing youths showed off for each other; one bounced gymnastlike off a picnic table and another somersaulted backward off a tree trunk. "Breakdance" clearly referenced the fashion that the brand team knew the nation's youths were gobbling up when they watched MTV, or for that matter, when they bought tickets to see Hollywood movies like *Breakin'* or *Breakin' II.*

In 1985, Mountain Dew produced "Bikedance," which was stylistically similar to "Breakdance," but included BMX bicycle stunts. The kids wore new-wave clothing, like black-and-white checked sneakers, appropriated from the U.K.'s punk and ska scenes. The ad began with a teen boy spinning his BMX bike in circles, hopping from front wheel to back as he zipped past a crowd of cheering classmates. In the next shot, another young man twirled on the handlebars as though they were a pommel horse. A few shots later, a trick rider emerged from behind the crowd and vaulted his bike over the boy's outstretched legs as the others cheered. The kids grabbed iced cans of Mountain Dew and chugged them. The flow of quickly edited bike stunts and Dew-chugging was interrupted by a shot of a small, wooden pier jutting into a rural pond. With forested hills as a backdrop, a boy zoomed his bike through a crowd of his friends and launched his bike off of a ramp that rested at the dock's end. Airborne, he twisted a full-circle spin and plunged into the pond.

While we can question the creative choices in these spots—for example, the intended synthesis of "urban plus rural equals a suburban park," with a splash in the pond at the end is certainly stilted—the big problem here is the strategic intent, not the creative execution. With a history spanning several decades in which it used the hillbilly and redneck populist worlds admired by rural working-class guys, Mountain Dew simply didn't belong performing stories using hip-hop materials and MTV outfits.

In the wake of these ads, Mountain Dew sales declined significantly. The suburban teens that the brand team was targeting couldn't make sense of the spots, and Dew's core rural constituency felt violated. The brand they depended on had abandoned them for the city. On the heels of the sales nosedive, the brand team ditched its MTV strategy after two years of sales declines and beat a path back to the NASCAR Belt with more redneck myth spots. Sales quickly recovered and began to climb again.

Act 2: Dew Does Nike

When the transitional Wall Street frontier ideology fell apart in the late 1980s, Mountain Dew's redneck myth ads suffered and the brand team began experimenting with new communications. The team had found some traction with fast-paced rock-and-roll ads that displayed radical outdoor sports—introducing some of the key elements of the later "Do the Dew" campaign. But PepsiCo management still yearned to broaden Mountain Dew's primarily rural sales. Scanning the pop terrain, the team again spotted an obvious host that they could use to deliver their brand to a broader pool of youthful consumers: the populist world of hip-hop was now in full bloom.

In the early 1990s, rap music had become the rebellious music of choice for suburban white male teens. NWA and 2 Live Crew, so-called gangsta rap artists, were selling as many records to kids in Westchester County and Iowa as they sold to inner-city kids. By 1992, a lighter version of rap, appropriately called gangsta lite, had emerged, and these next-generation rap performers helped rap infiltrate deeper into suburban, middle-class homes. Likewise, professional athletes brought a dose of urban hip-hop to the middle class. NBA players wore their uniform trunks so long and baggy—just like the rappers—that it was suddenly nearly impossible to remember the tight trunks that African American heroes like Magic Johnson had sported just a few years earlier.

Similarly, the era's most salient image of hypermasculinity—the celebratory slam dunk—had been derived from a hip-hop-influenced NBA. Although a slam dunk produced the same two points that any other shot garnered, the gesture delivered a message to the opponent and audience: domination. Whereas players had used the dunk for decades, they had not previously paused afterward to taunt an opponent or preen for the crowd. In the past, fans and opponents considered such behavior unsportsman-like. On the rare occasion that a player engaged in such a spectacle, it often incited his opponent to attack him and the crowd to boo angrily.

Yet, in the early 1990s, many players had absorbed rap's braggadocio and were routinely using the dunk as a curtain call for celebrating their temporary dominion over another player. Moreover, one of the era's most popular vernacular expressions—*in your face*—stems directly from this virile showmanship. Cultural causes and effects became entangled, and it became difficult to separate the players from the singers. Rappers wore basketball jerseys, and NBA players recorded their own rap albums. Basketball performances and virile gangsta rap performances became tied together into a knot, expressing a new kind of masculinity, the no-holds-barred, ultracompetitive warrior.

Mountain Dew managers were certainly influenced by their branding peers in their bid to tie the brand to urban culture. Nike was in the midst of a brilliant five-year run of ads that mythologized Nike's philosophy of sport by commingling the populist world of the African American ghetto with the NBA. Mountain Dew's arch rival Sprite had just signed on to sponsor the NBA. The 'hood's hip-hop/NBA nexus was prime cultural territory, and after Nike struck gold there, an urban-culture land grab ensued.

Unfortunately, the Mountain Dew brand team again found its trip through urban streets to be riddled with land mines. The team grabbed the inner city's most salient artifacts, the NBA and rap music, and constructed communications that tried to place the brand in this milieu. Unfortunately, like earlier efforts, the subsequent spots proved to be a jumble of cultural references and appropriations that sat awkwardly in relation to Mountain Dew's prior myths.

In 1993, the brand team unveiled "Super Dewd," the first Dew spot to star an African American, although significantly, "the Dewd" was a cartoon figure. The ad mixed the Dewd's animated world with live-action shots into a sort of hyperpaced cinematic collage. The whole affair was set to an equally hyperactive soundtrack that mimicked the Red Hot Chili Peppers.

The Dewd appeared as an intimidating figure, a comic-book cipher of steroid-extended masculinity. A familiar Mountain Dew object, the sun, appeared behind his head as a gigantic pulsing, black-and-white blob that imitated the sunshine halo that had appeared so frequently in past Dew ads. The Dewd wore his red baseball cap backward, just like the rappers. With a monstrous lion's roar, he crushed the empty Dew can, jumped on his skateboard, and rode into the animated urban jungle. The edit then moved to live-action shots, such as a skateboarder performing a somersault against the distant Manhattan skyline and another skater charging through an enormous spray, like one from a fire hydrant. From an extremely low angle, the spot's first real black person threw back his head and chugged a Dew. In a boxing gym, a dark-skinned woman punched a heavy bag.

The spot then interspersed rapidly edited images—both live and animated—of African Americans aggressively weightlifting, playing basketball, and boxing. White kids performed more stunts on BMX bikes and skateboards. Many characters chugged Dews before the Dewd returned to chug his last Dew and crush the can in his mighty fist.

Perhaps inspired by cartoons like *He-Man, Master of the Universe,* the Dewd seemed to approximate the most glaring media-fed stereotype of the young urban black male. He was a virtual superpredator. Not only was he literally and figuratively a cartoon, he in no way appeared capable of being credibly linked to the live-action stunts that peppered the spot. Upon closer inspection, none of the twisting and turning stunt athletes in the spot were African American. The ad's only black people either dunked a basketball, fought, or, in a single shot, pumped iron. In the context of so much stereotypical imagery rolled into a single half-minute, the ad tread dangerously close to bigoted turf.

Like PepsiCo's excursion into MTV, the brand team had bet the brand on the Dewd campaign. The company planned to devote the brand's 1993 and 1994 ad budgets to the series. And, like the earlier MTV-inspired spots, these ads failed miserably. By its second year, the campaign was yanked off the air and replaced with odes to a populist world that Dew could credibly inhabit—extreme sports and the slacker ethos of "Do the Dew."

Act 3: Dew Goes Native

By 1998, the world of hip-hop had become even more vital for American youth while the extreme-sports world that Mountain Dew had been using for its populist voice had lost currency. Like Nike, The Coca-Cola Company's Sprite had experienced great success with the hip-hop/NBA nexus. In 1996, Sprite had a career year, gaining nearly a whole share point, an unheard-of move in a category in which a successful trajectory is usually measured in tenths of a percentage point.

Once again, the brand team attempted to venture into urban culture. This time, the marketers pulled out all the stops, launching one of the more sophisticated guerrilla marketing efforts of recent years. And rather than simply borrowing urban cultural cues to build ads for white, urban metro audiences, this time the brand team also created advertising for African Americans.

To get the insider credibility they felt the brand needed, PepsiCo brand managers hired the editors of *The Source*—one of the two most influential national magazines that covered and promoted hip-hop as a countercultural lifestyle—as key informants. In addition to advising on Mountain

Dew's ad and promotion activities, *The Source*'s managers also brought the brand into hip-hop's inner circle. The magazine helped plant Dew on the inside, and guided the brand into sponsoring the right underground parties and events that held currency in African American entertainment culture. In addition, the team executed on-the-ground sampling operations, dispatching young promotional reps in neon green Hummers to inner-city neighborhoods to spin music and dish out Mountain Dew samples.

In their boldest move, the brand team sponsored Wu-Tang Clan—one of the 1990s' edgiest gangsta rap acts. The Clan was known not only as performers, but also as radicals who lived a committed life and routinely got themselves into trouble with establishment authorities. After their first hit, the Clan took four years to deliver their sophomore record, which quickly hit number one on the charts. Mountain Dew seemed to be standing in just the right spot, as the brand had previously agreed to sponsor Wu-Tang Clan's triumphant tour.

Despite the group's hit music and attention-attracting ability, Mountain Dew didn't catch on in urban turf. Fearing that the Clan's extracurricular activities could blow up into a publicity nightmare, PepsiCo replaced them with a more mainstream rap artist, Busta Rhymes. Rhymes may have possessed less swagger than Wu-Tang Clan, but he maintained broad appeal among African Americans and was, for the most part, still tied to rap music and hip-hop culture.

BBDO produced an initial ad with Rhymes placed, incongruously, within Dew's extreme-sports world. The spot showed the rapper ice-picking his way up a mountain, dreadlocks and all. Like the MTV ads fifteen years before, the ad tried to blend Dew's familiar populist world—now slackers and extreme sports—to urban hip-hop culture. The ad seemed to make fun of Dew's existing cultural home while failing to do justice to the hip-hop nation, an unfortunate and unintended effect.

Recognizing the ad's creative limitations, PepsiCo hired Uniworld, the largest African American agency in the United States. Uniworld subsequently made a number of ads that could easily have been rap videos for Rhymes, except for their promotional content: a lime-green painted Hummer that Busta drove, crushing other cars as he sang a Dew-inspired rap and chugged on his Dew.

While Uniworld's ads weren't particularly innovative, they were at least credible advertising within the then-current conventions of rap videos. But in so doing, the ads had ditched the Dew myth. Uniworld's spots showed no evidence of an effort to reimagine Dew's wild man within the hip-hop environs.

Again, a major effort to wedge Mountain Dew into urban culture bore little fruit. Dew's dismal brand development metrics in urban metro areas only inched up slightly. Sales remained disproportionately skewed toward nonurban, white, working-class consumers.

Three times, the team radically revamped Mountain Dew's branding strategy in an effort to take advantage of the enormous cultural draw of the hip-hop populist world. And each time, the temptations of this cultural gold caused the brand's managers to ditch Mountain Dew's valuable cultural authority earned over several decades. At first glance, Mountain Dew's stance in support of the wild man against American ideals seems to have parallels in the 'hood. But Mountain Dew had always located its wild-man myths in the populist worlds of the white non-professionals—hillbillies, rednecks, and slackers. Because the cultural equity was located in rural and white figures, the brand lacked the credibility to use hip-hop. Mountain Dew had a big authenticity problem that even the most aggressive grassroots campaign couldn't fix.

When a brand chases after populist worlds that are incongruous relative to its cultural and political authority, the brand comes off as an opportunistic cultural parasite. Inevitably, in its stretch to fit in the new populist world, the brand comes off as stilted, even foolish.

Advancing the Myth: Four Principles

Despite its early missteps, Mountain Dew recovered quickly from its overly formulaic "Done That" sequels to produce many successful ads that have extended the "Do the Dew" campaign for over a decade. And Mountain Dew is not alone, as other brands, like Nike and Volkswagen, have also been able to extend their myths for many years. These brands follow four principles that keep their myths vital throughout the tenure of a myth market.

Develop Plot and Characters

A myth is a kind of story, one that serves an important cultural function in the society. Just like the stories found in other media like television, film, and novels, myths concocted through advertising rely on the development of plots and characters.[2] For an icon to sustain its myth, it must apply the art of storytelling to the commercial format of advertising.

Ad agency creatives have a better sense of how to extend a myth than do most brand managers. Unlike creatives, who often come from liberal arts backgrounds, managers tend to be trained in pragmatic business skills. While future copywriters and art directors are reading Don DeLillo, admiring De Kooning paintings, and listening to obscure indie rock, future managers are learning how to use spreadsheets, calculate debt ratios, and conduct a regression analysis. M.B.A. programs teach managers to think of advertising in mechanical terms, not in storytelling terms. The result is that while storytelling may appear as a lively tool to creatives, managers often find narrative construction to be an opaque process. Iconic brands rely on two general approaches to develop myths as stories: a serial mode and a short film mode.

Extending the Myth as a Serial. Brand managers can extend myths by treating the story as a serial, like a television program or a serialized book, sticking with the initial characters and plotting, but extending them in each performance. Budweiser's "Lizards" campaign is a seminal example of this technique. The first ad introduced the Frankie and Louie characters (Frankie as the world-weary cynic and Louie as the ambitious, whiny schlep who can't get a break), the setting (the swamp with its various other animals, and the log cabin bar featuring Budweiser), and the initial story line (Louie wants to become famous by getting featured on Bud ads and will do whatever it takes; he's intensely jealous of the frogs). Each subsequent ad built from this base, developing the characters and extending the plot. Louie showed more tragicomic yearnings, and Frankie's deadpan worldview became more obvious. The spots also introduced new characters, like the weasel and the turtle. The creatives freely substituted plot lines and situations, such as Louie's assassination attempt on the frog and the lizard's run for the presidency of the swamp. Likewise, the characters adapted to these new situations, as when the frogs suddenly began to talk back to Louie and lashed at him with their tongues, and when Louie's detective work revealed that the weasel was living a clandestine life of lusty pleasures. Budweiser's constituents eagerly anticipated each new installment, treating the campaign as they would a favorite television program.

Extending the Myth as a Set of Auteur Films. Alternatively, a myth can be explored through a more loosely linked group of "films" that are held together by a set of themes and communication codes that the brand, as performer, is exploring. This cinematic method of myth extension was made famous initially by DDB's Volkswagen work in the 1960s. The method was then later extended by Wieden and Kennedy's work on Nike in the 1980s, Goodby Silverstein's "Got Milk?" campaign, and Arnold's "Drivers Wanted" campaign in the 1990s.

In this approach, the brand—like a writer or filmmaker—explores the myth by changing the cast and plot. What coheres, in addition to the myth itself, is a set of distinctive communication codes invoked differently in each spot. Over time, the audience learns to recognize a Nike spot or a Volkswagen spot by how the ad is composed.

Building a campaign around autonomous auteur ads is more challenging than the serial approach, since each spot requires entirely original creative. But when done well, this approach succeeds like no other because it is such a persuasive demonstration of the brand's cultural leadership.

Sample New Popular Culture

An iconic brand can't behave like a cultural parasite, as Mountain Dew did when it chased after hip-hop culture. On the other hand, since iconic brands must speak to contemporary issues faced by their constituencies and because popular culture provides many of the raw ingredients with which myths are made, these brands must engage new popular culture as it unfolds. The key to success is for the brand team to carefully select new culture that can be credibly brought into the brand's milieu, and then give these artifacts a new spin, inflecting them with the brand's point of view in a way that advances the brand's myth. For example, consider how Mountain Dew recovered from the overly formulaic sequels to "Done That."

"Mel Torme" featured the aging crooner hanging out with the Dew dudes at a Las Vegas casino, belting out a lounge classic. Standing in a black tie and tux in front of a brightly lit Vegas casino, he sings next to the piano while the Dew dudes act almost as backup singers. He updates the lyrics to "Don't Get No Thrill" to reflect the dudes' seen-it-all cynicism. Torme sings, "A thousand foot fall doesn't faze them at all, so tell me why should it be true? That they get a *kick* out of Dew, dewdadeww!" The dudes wave off the accomplishments dismissively. Torme then suddenly appears on the casino's roof and takes a twelve-story dive to land on his back on an enormous movie-stunt air mattress. The dudes, the ultimate tough crowd, are finally impressed. "All right, Mel!" they shout.

This bit of cultural sampling was just the right move to bring the brand out of the dead end it had hit. By 1995, a countercultural lounge scene had emerged among slackers, who used the swinger and its attendant artifacts to create an ironically charged atmosphere. Urban club owners decorated their establishments with discarded furniture from the 1950s and 1960s. Cocktails replaced beer, and the martini was recast in a thousand flavors to suit younger tastes. The original era's surviving singers, like Tony Bennett, Frank Sinatra, and Mel Torme, enjoyed the renewed interest in their work.

To use the aged Torme—of all the swinging singers, the only one firmly rooted in jazz, not pop—displayed considerable confidence. Most advertisers are nervous about properly tailoring the communication to the audience, and they obsess over capturing their target's lifestyles and tastes. Although Dew targeted teens and young adults, most of them had probably never heard of Torme. Yet in this instance, Dew relied on a guy who, superficially, seemed to be the antithesis of Dew. He was old and could in no way be tied to alternative rock music and extreme sports. Moreover, in contrast with the Dew dudes, Torme was justifiably out of shape, and although he was no James Bond, he was dressed in a tux.

Through silly parody, the Torme ad argued that this seeming outlier actually was an exemplary if unexpected Dew dude. By making such an unexpected claim, and one that drew from the popular culture of the moment, Mountain Dew asserted itself as a cultural innovator, one in touch with what many consumers considered the cutting edge of urban youth culture. As a bonus, the Torme ad freed the Dew myth from its sole dependency on the declining grunge rock scene and alternative sports, which by then had been thoroughly commercialized.

The brand team repeated this success two years later with a spot featuring Jackie Chan, whose comic martial arts movies had become quite popular. The Hong Kong filmmaker had blended Buster Keaton's offbeat and warmly human physical humor with an unlikely counterpoint, Bruce Lee's kung-fu fighting. Since Lee's death in the 1970s, his star had simmered in various subcultures, and when his son emerged as an action star— and was then killed in an on-set accident—martial arts was again all the rage. Youths were attracted to Chan's self-aware movies, because in addition to the films' obvious irony, the fighting stunts were incredibly inventive. Chan's signature elements—the improvised macho stunts overlaid with a bit of tongue-in-cheek irony—suited Dew ideally.

Both ads worked by sampling appropriate yet unexpected artifacts from emerging popular culture and then reframing them to creatively retell the Mountain Dew myth. Ads like these reinvigorate the myth by injecting it into emerging pop culture.

Speak from New Populist Worlds

Iconic brands rely on populist worlds as source material. But these worlds can rise and fall, gaining and losing cultural potency. Managers can revive a brand's myth by engaging a new populist world appropriate for the brand. But for this strategy to work, managers must find a good fit, rather than simply jumping on the world with the most currency, as Mountain Dew did with hip-hop.

Mountain Dew established a beachhead in extreme sports by committing early and earnestly to the most radical versions of these new sports and, in so doing, built credibility for itself among the elite athletes of these sports. Importantly, the brand did not simply throw sponsorship money at the fledgling sports.

By the late 1980s, snowboarders and skateboarders had their own heroes and stars, underground performer/athletes whom ordinary shredders idolized. Within the respective subcultures, these popular athletes' celebrity status was based as much on their credibility as their athletic ability. Like other populist worlds, the stars were expected to be committed to their sport and maintain loyalty to its noncommercial ethos. Thus, when these prominent athletes weighed whether to accept complimentary equipment from manufacturers—in effect, endorsing the snowboards or skateboard wheels—they concerned themselves not only with the equipment's quality but also with the company's commitment to the sport.

So to accept equipment or a stipend from a firm rooted in the sport's genesis, like Burton Snowboards, was perfectly OK. On the other hand, to accept anything from K2, a major multinational corporation that owned numerous brands of ski and snowboard gear, was to sell out, to go corporate. To endorse a commercial interloper was to betray the independent and autonomous values held so dear by those within the populist world.

The celebrity athletes' reputations were spread via an unusual medium. Snowboarders and skaters shared with one another homemade videotapes that exhibited incredible stunts, tricks, and mountainside runs. The most prized of these movies was a new genre that most shredders considered to be their own, which mixed documentary and music video styles, intricately edited to rock music. These movies and the accompanying music were, like the equipment and apparel, important pieces of the subculture. Shredders idolized the filmmakers and musicians just as they idolized the athletes. So, by hiring these filmmakers and the real athletes who performed the tricks and then designing stunts that pushed the envelope of danger and creativity, Mountain Dew earned considerable credibility with the fickle alternative sports insiders.

But, like so many youth subcultures, alternative sports were destined to either wither or enter the mainstream. By the mid-1990s, the outsider athletes had become stars. Alternative sports had grown into a commercially viable product with professional sanctioning bodies, event tours, ESPN coverage, and myriad sponsorships. In the computer age's most obvious signal that an artifact is no longer underground, alternative sports became franchises within the video game industry.

Most successful icons must eventually defend themselves against imitation. When Nike showed how to stitch the NBA and inner-city hip-hop culture together, dozens of other marketers chased after the same bandwagon. When Volkswagen demonstrated that quirky creativity and indie rock could build an auto brand, KIA, Mitsubishi, and Ford quickly tried the same tack. Similarly, Mountain Dew's slacker myth provoked a variety of copycats, including Coca-Cola's ill-fated me-too brand, Surge.

But the horde of commercial sponsors that jumped into extreme sports was perhaps Mountain Dew's most formidable problem. Together, not only did these marketers crowd the field, but the cumulative effect of their presence was to make the erstwhile subculture look exceedingly colonized by corporate interests. Not content to allow ESPN to control a portion of the youth market with its X Games, NBC had followed suit with its own Gravity Games. In addition, top alternative athletes became well-paid stars who endorsed an array of products, from antiperspirants to automobiles. By the late 1990s, alternative sports were about as alternative as the Rolling Stones. Mountain Dew needed a new populist world.

While the brand team's next ad to hit pay dirt may have initially seemed like just another spot built on snowboarders' backs, "Thank Heaven" proved to be a useful evolutionary move.[3] The spot was directed by Sam Bayer, who had also directed Nirvana's *Smells Like Teen Spirit* video. "Thank Heaven" featured Leslie Rankine, the female lead singer from an obscure Seattle indie band, Ruby.

The ad began with close-ups of alpinists clinging to storm-battered vertical ice with their ice axes. As the soundtrack kicked in, the climbers—women—looked up through their mirrored snow goggles and watched a snowboarder shred her way through a drift. As she approached the cornice above the climbers, the snowboarder unleashed an extreme-sports scream (in close-up, so that no viewer could continue to mistake her sex), launched her board off the cornice, and dropped past the climbers.

On an urban rooftop, Ruby's singer appeared in close-up, snarling from between her plush, rust-colored overcoat lapels, which she pulled to her cheeks like Joan Crawford on amphetamines. She sang the popular standard that Maurice Chevalier sang in the 1961 film *Gigi*, "Thank Heaven for Little Girls." The song, traditionally sung by fathers to their daughters when they married, was completely transformed, the meaning inverted by her snarling delivery.

> *Thank heaven for little girls, for little girls get bigger every day!*
> *Thank heaven for little girls, they grow up in the most*
>   *delightful way!*
> *Those little eyes so helpless and appealing,*
> *one day will flash and send you crashin' thru the ceilin'.*

Rankine's velvety alto growl underscored her audacious style. She looks like Bjork, but, in the ad, exhibited an in-your-face presence that referenced some of the then-emerging woman rock insurgents like Courtney Love, P. J. Harvey, and Liz Phair.

After a few quick, wide shots of the snowboarder flying through the steep couloir, four girls—the Dew dudes' female analogues—leaned into the camera and sneered, just like the dudes. There were then close-ups of a woman's mouth and her hands releasing a white dove—a symbol of peace and, presumably, femininity. She screamed a Dew scream and jumped from a tall antenna tower. The singer and Dew girls appeared in rapid succession, their aggressive physical posturing stating flatly that they approved of the female athletes' fearlessness. The picture then cut to a woman—thin as a fashion model and wearing black leotards, in-line skates, and protective gear—being towed across an urban rooftop by a rope attached to a helicopter. Clutching the rope like a water skier, she hit a ramp at the parapet and flew across the street to the top of another building, where she executed a skidding stop that shot sparks from her skates.

The four Dew girls, also trim enough to audition for *Beverly Hills 90210,* caught flying cans of Dew, screamed into the camera, and slammed their drinks in Dew fashion. Then, in a move unimaginable for a Dew dude, one of the girls planted a kiss on the camera lens, leaving behind lipstick traces that read, "Do the Dew." The spot ended with the Dew dudes themselves, atypically speechless, dumbfounded by what they've just witnessed. One of them leaned into the camera and sputtered, "I think I'm in love."

"Thank Heaven" celebrated a new populist world, what became known as "riot grrl" and "girl power," the youth culture version of third-wave feminism. Where previous feminism had largely rejected the sexual appeal of male-centric images, riot grrl's politics (and also its charm to both young women and young men) explicitly purported to invert the images' power. Riot grrl expressed its politics through classic boy's activities: rock music and alternative sports.

Until the 1990s, women rarely performed in the libidinal style found in hard rock's guitar wails, sexual innuendo, on-stage posturing, and anthemic singing. Women musicians were either steamy sexpots or mother figures who cooed to the audience while the men thrashed about. Taking cues from the handful of exceptions—Janice Joplin, Patti Smith, Chrissie Hynde, and Joan Jett—young women in the 1990s jumped feet first into rock's deep end. Building on punk rock's do-it-yourself spirit, riot grrl cobbled together a new feminist sensibility in which women—instead of rejecting masculine sexuality—asserted an equally narcissistic sexual prowess. P. J. Harvey, the Breeders, Liz Phair, Courtney Love, Garbage, and Alanis Morrisette asserted aggressive yet distinctly feminine personae. They sang explicitly about sex and sexual politics in a fashion that for the previous few decades had remained mostly male propositions.

By the mid-1990s, this new feminist chorus had coalesced into a countercultural scene, brimming with rock bands, fan-zines, and independent record labels. To a significant degree, riot grrl was punk rock's niece, and the apple did not fall far from the tree. One of the most popular riot grrl artists, Sleater-

Kinney, screamed, "I Wanna Be Like Joey Ramone." When they performed, they flailed their guitars and bodies across the stage, just like the punk boys.

"Thank Heaven" captured the riot grrl spirit in an authentic yet Dew-biased way. Once more, the brand brought the populist world into the Dew orbit, demonstrating that Dew girls could be every bit as daring, creative, and sexy as Dew boys.

Push the Myth's Boundaries

As a myth market matures, the brand's myth will become more predictable and less engaging, no matter how creatively the brand team tuck-points the story. As Mountain Dew's brand team pushed hard on the communication codes it discovered with the Torme ad, they produced parodies featuring James Bond, the punk band the Sex Pistols, tennis star Andre Agassi, the rock band Queen, and the film *Crouching Tiger, Hidden Dragon*. By the end of this run, the parodies had hardened into a formula. The audience knew what to expect from the ads before they began. If the brand was going to avoid killing the myth, it had to find new creative ideas.

At this point in a myth's life cycle, the brand team can use the audience's familiarity as a foundation to allow for more inventive explorations of plot and characters. Ads that would have been incoherent early in the campaign are perceived, later in the campaign, as welcome evidence that the brand is still a compelling performer.

The brand team began to experiment with more liberal reinterpretations of "Do the Dew," pushing beyond simple character and plot progression. In the several dozen previous spots, some variety of extreme sport—BASE jumping, daredevil mountain biking, diving out of planes, land luges—had served as the action around which the ad was built. Beginning in 2000, the brand team stripped alternative sport down to its bare bones. What remained were daredevil activities of any kind that allowed guys to express their masculine ids. (Nike has done the same thing with sport in its advertising since the mid-1990s, broadly interpreting any quasi-athletic activity to fit in the universe of its myth.) The Mountain Dew team located two new daredevil activities—man-versus-beasts and auto stunts—both of which have proved to be fertile material for Dew's slacker wild man.

"Cheetah" began with a color-saturated view of a vast African plain, the kind of picture familiar to anyone who'd watched nature programming. In a slightly tighter shot, an animal raced across the plain, its presence betrayed by the dust plume billowing behind it. A closer shot revealed a cheetah on the run. In a sequence of quickly edited, shaky action shots, a mountain bike rider hotly pursued the cheetah. The rider pedaled madly, his face a sweaty knot of cop-on-the-chase determination. The animal tried a few futile, evasive moves before the cyclist locked his brakes, vaulted over the handlebars, and wrestled the animal to the ground. The rider re-leased the bewildered beast, circled it like a kung-fu fighter, then lunged to pry open the cheetah's jaws. Jamming his arm elbow-deep down the cat's throat, he fished about to some sticky, gooey soundtrack noises. The guy located what he was after and pulled it from the cat's gut. The cat shook off the intrusion with another disturbing noise. The rider held up a Dew can, which was empty and punctured by teeth marks, and shook it. "Bad chee-tah!" he scolded the cat. The cheetah licked its chops, like a dog's mock sorrow after it's had its way with the birthday cake.

On a distant mesa, three other riders looked at each other in dismay. One said to the others, "That's why I'm not a cat person." In alternating close-ups, they all poured Dew into their mouths in the hot sun. The money shot: Through a telephoto lens, the cheetah strutted in the sun, its own spots rearranged on its side to spell out, "Do the Dew."

In "Ram," one of the dudes got in a territorial skirmish with a male bighorn sheep over a bottle of Dew. High in the mountains, the bighorn guarded the Dew as he would a young female. The Dew dude traded snorts with the ram as they squared to butt heads. After two rounds of skull-crunching head slams, the ram retreated. The three other dudes asked their friend how he felt, to which he responded, "Not ba-a-a-ad."

These man-versus-beasts spoofs provided effective new fodder for Dew. The primal drama of men squaring off with animals in the wild proved to be an apt and creative extension of the adrenaline-pumping, high-risk dramas that Dew celebrated in its wild-man myth. Not only was the spot on-strategy in terms of its mythmaking, the story was also located in a populist world—hunting and fishing—which was a bull's-eye for Dew's historic position in rural working-class culture.

Branding as Storytelling

Advocates of mind share are obsessed with copy points, not stories. They examine the list of key words in their brand bibles and watch proposed ads to make sure that the two align. In the world of mind share, there is no notion of developing plot and characters. Rather, stories are superfluous creative material, great as long as they get people to remember the brand's DNA, but traded out on a dime when they don't. The purpose of an ad is to get people to pay attention to the list of concepts in the positioning statement.

For iconic brands, this approach is exactly wrong. The "Do the Dew" campaign continued for a decade, something of a record also shared by Nike, Bud Light, and few others. The brand team kept the Mountain Dew myth vital by applying four principles for extending myths. To maintain the myth's vitality, brand managers must continually extend its performance and also allow the brand to respond creatively to new popular culture.

CHAPTER 9

Branding as Cultural Activism

ICONIC BRANDS ARE BUILT by cultural activists. Yet, while many companies would love to create a Nike, a Budweiser, or a Mountain Dew, most are organized to act as cultural reactionaries, whose practices are the opposite of the activism that is required. Managers typically view identity brands through the prism of the mind-share model. Mind share constructs a present-tense snapshot view of the brand, which blinds managers to emerging cultural opportunities. And mind share's impulse to abstract—to yank the brand out of its cultural context—leaves managers arguing over adjectives that are largely devoid of strategic consequences. Managers routinely ignore the cultural content of the brand's myth, treating this content as a tactical "executional" issue. As a result, they outsource the most critical strategic decisions on the brand to creatives at ad agencies, public relations firms, and design shops.

To systematically build iconic brands, companies must reinvent their marketing function. They must assemble cultural knowledge, rather than knowledge about individual consumers. They must strategize according to cultural branding principles, rather than apply the abstracted and present-tense mind-share model. And they must hire and train cultural activists, rather than stewards of brand essence.

Four Kinds of Cultural Knowledge

Managers require knowledge about their brands and their consumers to develop strategy. For cultural branding, this knowledge differs dramatically from the standard kinds of brand and consumer knowledge that managers now rely on to guide their branding efforts.

- Cultural knowledge focuses on the major social changes impacting the nation, rather than on clusters of individuals.

FIGURE 9-1

The Cultural Brand Management Process

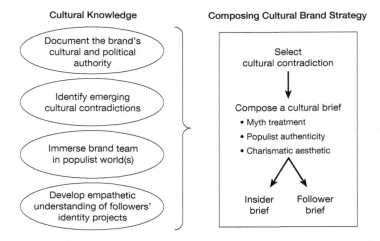

- Cultural knowledge examines the role of major social categories of class, gender, and ethnicity in identity construction rather than obscuring these categories by sorting people into "psychographic" groups.

- Cultural knowledge views the brand as a historical actor in society.

- Cultural knowledge views people holistically, seeking to understand what gives their lives meaning, rather than as customers of category benefits.

- Cultural knowledge seeks to understand the identity value of mass culture texts, rather than treating mass culture simply as trends and entertainment.

Specifically, to build an iconic brand, managers must assemble four kinds of cultural knowledge (figure 9-1).

Inventory the Brand's Cultural and Political Authority

Identity brands are malleable assets. Their growth depends in large part on whether managers understand the brand's historic equities well enough to direct the brand toward the most advantageous future position. In the mind-share model the brand is understood as a set of timeless concepts. So the interpretation of its past efforts and direction into the future is a simple matter. Once the brand has earned valuable associations—the brand essence—don't change anything! Consistency is the watchword, and brand stewardship is the mode of management.

For identity brands, the approach is different. We need to ask: What assets has the brand accrued through its historic activities that enhance (and also constrain) its future mythmaking ability?

Iconic brands build reputations, but not in the typical economic sense. Rather, successful brands develop reputations for telling a certain kind of story that addresses the identity desires of a particular constituency. In other words, iconic brands accrue two complementary assets: cultural authority and political authority. When a brand authors myths that people find valuable, it earns the authority to tell similar kinds of myths (cultural authority) to address the identity desires of a similar constituency (political authority) in the future.

Specifying the brand's cultural and political authority provides managers direction to develop appropriate myths for the brand, and allows them to rule out myths that are a poor fit. If Volkswagen's managers in the 1990s had understood that the brand had earned significant cultural authority in the 1960s to perform myths about individual creativity, and political authority to assuage a cultural contradiction that particularly afflicted the well-educated, urban, middle class, they could have directed creative partners toward the types of myths that would appeal to the new identity desires of the Bobos.

Develop Empathic Understanding of Followers' Identity Projects

In conventional branding models, consumer research seeks to unearth deep insights into how customers think and behave. Researchers watch people in the act of consumption and interview them intensively to dig out tacit thoughts and feelings, all in the quest to reveal "consumer truths" that the brand can hang its hat on. Given the enormous attention paid to this kind of research in branding, it is noteworthy that I was unable to find a single example in which conventional consumer research contributed to the building of an iconic brand.

Because iconic brands create value differently than mind-share brands, they require a different kind of customer understanding. Great myths are grounded in an empathic understanding of people's most acute desires and anxieties that, because they are generated by social forces, touch the lives of a broad swath of society. Resonant myths spring from an understanding of people's ambitions at work, their dreams for their children, their fears of technology, their difficulties in building friendships, and so on. Notice that we are not talking about consumer behavior "truths" or emotional hot buttons—the usual language of consumer research. Indeed, the kind of understanding necessary for building identity value rejects thinking of the brand's customers as merely consumers. Iconic brands address existential issues far beyond the usual benefits and behaviors associated with a product category. So consumer research must seek out the most significant identity projects of existing and prospective customers, and identify the most acute tensions that inflict these projects.

Further, this mode of understanding goes well beyond documenting people's attitudes and emotions to acquire an embedded sense of what life really feels like if one were in their shoes. The kind of knowledge required to build an iconic brand is more like what an author requires to write a great novel or screenplay. Great authors are highly attuned to the world around them so that they see the world through the eyes of the other. The best ethnographies in anthropology and sociology achieve a similar result. Likewise, the most successful authors of icons have empathic antennae that connect with the critical identity issues that animate the lives of people they encounter. As a result, these authors create cultural texts that embody the society's particular existential concerns.

Empathic understanding like this can't be distilled and formalized into a research document. Nor can a manager gain this understanding indirectly. It cannot be outsourced to a research firm or brand consultancy, transferred to a research department, and finally distilled for those who are writing a strategy or creating brand materials. Icon builders reject conventional market research, and rightly so, for it lacks both the breadth and the depth of understanding required. Either managers must acquire this understanding firsthand, or they must gather and live with research that presents rich portraits of their customers' lives, not glance through a Powerpoint summary of key findings.

For brands with an effective myth, managers need to cultivate empathic understanding of the identity projects of their followers and insiders. For brands in search of a new myth, managers should dig into the identity projects of prospects who best align with the brand's cultural and political authority.

And ignore the brand's feeders! Most customers of iconic brands are neither dedicated followers of the brand's myth nor insiders tapped into the brand's populist world. Rather, they are feeders: cultural parasites who use the brand for fashion, status, and community by feeding off the customers at the nucleus of the brand. Because their preferences are directly influenced by the desirability of the brand generated in the nucleus of followers and insiders, their preferences are of little use in guiding the brand strategy. Moreover, since feeders usually maintain a vague and idiosyncratic understanding of the brand, research that includes them will badly distort strategy. Nevertheless, because feeders often dominate sales, managers tend to build strategies from research heavily weighted toward how feeders understand and value the brand. Managers of iconic brands like ESPN, Nike, and Patagonia, never aim their strategies at these peripheral customers. Rather, they work to create the most desirable myth for their nucleus of followers and insiders and use this desirability as a magnet to attract others to the brand.

Immerse the Brand Team into the Populist World

Iconic brands rely on populist worlds as source materials for their myths. Populist worlds are typically far removed from the life experiences of the majority of the brand's customers. Consequently, brand strategies guided only by a customer worldview can never make the necessary creative leap from identity desires to identity myth.

Iconic brands are usually built by people deeply immersed in the populist worlds that they draw from. At Nike and their agency Wieden and Kennedy, you'll find inveterate jocks who live and breathe sport. In its halcyon days of Volkswagen Beetle advertising, DDB creatives drew from the New York City intelligentsia with whom they circulated. Thirty years later, the lead creative on "Drivers Wanted," Lance Jensen, drew inspiration from his lifelong experiences inhabiting the indie bohemia. Mountain Dew's lead creative Bill Bruce was a proto-slacker who worked in a record store before turning to advertising.

Similarly, Anheuser-Busch and DDB–Chicago have had great success with Bud Light, in no small part because both sides of the account are stocked with mostly Midwestern guys who share their target's sense of humor because they've grown up in a similar cultural climate. "Whassup?!" on the other hand was outsourced to an African American director from Brooklyn. So, when DDB tried to take over the creative content, the campaign lost its verve.

Identify Emerging Cultural Contradictions

Cultural activism centers on identifying and responding to emerging cultural contradictions and the myth markets that form around these contradictions. Managers of incumbent brands must monitor how their brand's myth works in the culture, tracking how changes in society influence the effectiveness of their brand's myth. Likewise, managers seeking to develop new iconic brands must pinpoint emerging cultural opportunities.

To spot contradictions in society and isolate how these contradictions are addressed by myth markets, managers need to adopt a genealogical approach to the marketplace. Genealogical research documents emerging socio-economic contradictions, and then examines how the texts of the culture industry (films, ads, books, television programs, and so on) respond to these contradictions with new myths. Rather than static, microscopic research that delivers a snapshot of individual consumers, genealogy is macroscopic and dialectical.

Because most brand managers today rely on present-tense models of branding, they have little guidance in pushing the brand into the future other than keeping up with trends and trying to predict the next big thing. The false assumption here, which stems from the popularity of viral branding, is that brands must be first in the race to commodify new culture before it becomes hot. In the cases that I've studied, this assumption rarely holds. Rather, iconic brands play off cultural texts that the other culture industries have already put into play. In other words, iconic brands usually borrow from existing myth markets rather than create new myth markets themselves.

Brand Manager as Genealogist

In the mind-share model, the manager is anointed the steward of the brand's timeless identity. The manager's role is to identify the transcendental core of the brand and then maintain this core in the face of organizational pressures to try something new. In the cultural-branding model, the manager becomes a genealogist. Managers must be able to spot emergent cultural opportunities and understand their subtle characteristics. To do so, managers must hone their ability to see the brand as a cultural artifact moving through history. They must develop sensitive antennae to pick up tectonic shifts in society that create new identity desires. And they must view their brands as a cultural platform—just like a Hollywood film or a new social movement—to respond to these desires with effective myths.

Cultural knowledge is critical for building iconic brands, yet is sorely lacking in most managers' arsenals. This knowledge doesn't simply appear in focus group reports, ethnographies, or trend reports, the marketer's usual means for getting close to the customer. Rather, such knowledge requires that managers develop new skills. They need a cultural historian's understanding of ideology as it waxes and wanes, a sociologist's charting of the topography of social contradictions, and a literary expedition into the popular culture that engages these contradictions. To create new myths, managers must get close to *the nation*—the social and cultural shifts and the desires and anxieties that result. This means looking far beyond consumers as they are known today.

Cultural Branding Strategy

Cultural branding strategy is a plan that directs the brand toward a particular kind of myth and also specifies how the myth should be composed. A cultural strategy is, necessarily, quite different from conventional branding strategies, which are full of rational and emotional benefits, brand personalities, and the like. Let's return briefly to two iconic brands examined earlier—Volkswagen and Mountain Dew—to find out why.

Volkswagen Branding Strategy

In the early 1990s, as the company struggled to survive in the U.S. market, Volkswagen North America gave its longtime ad agency, DDB, one last chance to revive the brand's once potent equity. DDB research identified that Volkswagen had carved out a distinctive mind-share position in the auto market as a brand engineered for great driving at a value price. In the 1980s, Volkswagen had developed new models—the Golf, Jetta, and especially the GTI—that performed more like their German brethren (BMW, Mercedes, and Audi) than the squishy handling of a Toyota or Ford. Since the mid-1980s, advertising had emphasized the excellent engineering and developed the tag line "the German Engineered Volkswagen."

The new strategy pushed the communications from product features (e.g., tight turning radius) to benefits (Volkswagens provided a great driving experience for people who really enjoyed driving and appreciated the feel of the car on the road). After many months of deliberation to concoct the strategy and then to develop the best creative idea based on the strategy, Volkswagen and DDB produced the aforementioned disastrous *"Fahrvergnugen"* campaign. The campaign delivered precisely on Volkswagen's strategy, communicating very clearly that Volkswagen built cars for people who really enjoyed driving and appreciated performance. Yet, while these odd ads made good on the mind-share strategy, the campaign managed to communicate an approach to life—sensory-deprived, mechanical, and isolated—that was virtually the inverse of what Volkswagen had historically championed in its myth.

After DDB was fired, a new marketing team at Volkswagen asked Arnold Communications to pitch the account. Like DDB, Arnold spent months doing research to devise a strategy. Arnold's strategy was spurred by a J. D. Power survey, no doubt similar to what DDB drew from, describing Volkswagen owners as people who viewed driving as an experience rather than as a utilitarian means to get from A to B. According to the survey, Volkswagen customers liked to drive fast and appreciated the finer points of how the car performed. Hence, the agency developed an advertising strategy to communicate that Volkswagen is a car for people who love to drive. After months of debate, Arnold arrived at a mind-share strategy nearly identical to that used by DDB to produce *"Fahrvergnugen."*

From this strategy, however, Arnold crafted an entirely different campaign, "Drivers Wanted," which evolved into a huge and enduring success. Like the *"Fahrvergnugen"* campaign, "Drivers Wanted" also communicated the drivability benefits of Volkswagen. But the campaign was different in every other way. On the same product-benefit platform, Arnold built a myth about iconoclasts who are able to find ways to be creative and spontaneous in everyday life. What made the myth successful was that Arnold had located a way to update DDB's Beetle myth about creativity in a way that worked in the social milieu of the United States of the late 1990s.

Mountain Dew Branding Strategy

Consider also PepsiCo's strategy for Mountain Dew in 1993. The strategy emphasized the experiential qualities of consuming the brand, exhilaration and excitement, which were delivered by its sugary, caffeinated buzz: "You can have the most thrilling, exciting, daring experience but it will never compete with the exhilarating experience of a Mountain Dew."

Guided by this strategy, PepsiCo and BBDO bet the brand on the disastrous "Super Dewd" campaign, in which a cliché African American cartoon character stomps around the inner city, chugging Mountain Dew while skateboarders and bikers scoot by. The action was exhilarating, to be sure. But the story didn't fit at all with Mountain Dew's cultural and political authority, which was the championing of wild-man ideals for nonprofessional rural white guys.

At the same time, the marketers created a side campaign for Diet Mountain Dew—a campaign that later became "Do the Dew"—from the same strategy, with the additional directive to encourage trial of the diet drink. Unlike "Super Dewd," the "Do the Dew" campaign tapped the most viable cultural opportunity for Mountain Dew in the early 1990s: a new wild-man myth that combined the cultural raw materials from the emerging extreme sports populist world with ideas borrowed from Hollywood's slacker myths.

Like Volkswagen, identical strategies produced very different campaigns with diametrically opposite results. Mountain Dew's strategy failed to rule out a grossly ineffective campaign and, likewise, provided no direction to BBDO creatives in devising a winning campaign. In 1993, there were literally hundreds of expressions of "thrilling, exciting, daring experience" available in American culture. BBDO creatives might have drawn on any of these expressions to craft Mountain Dew ads. The strategy document gave no clues as to which were better expressions.

PepsiCo and Volkswagen spent many months with their agencies debating the proper adjectives to attach to their brands, adjectives that would distinguish the brands from their soft drink and auto competitors. Yet, in the end, the selected concepts provided guidelines so vague and imprecise that campaigns from the most brilliant to the most mediocre could be evaluated as on-strategy. What marketers have been calling a brand strategy for decades is not doing the work that strategy is supposed to do: forcing tough decisions by specifying criteria that distinguish better choices from worse ones.

The single most debilitating mistake that managers can make in regard to the long-term health of an identity brand is to develop a strategy so abstract that it yanks the brand out of its social and cultural context. Product design and benefits are the platform on which myths are built. A wide variety of myths can be built atop any product-benefit platform, and most of them are worth little to consumers.

What, then, is a strategy for an identity brand? Cultural brand strategy must identify the most valuable type of myth for the brand to perform at a particular historical juncture, and then provide specific direction to creative partners on how to compose the myth. Drawing from the cultural knowledge described above, a cultural branding strategy should include the following components:

> *Target the most appropriate myth market.* With knowledge of the country's most important existing and emerging myth markets and the brand's cultural and political authority, managers look for the best fit. The most opportune myth market is the one that the brand has the most authority to address. Mountain Dew's equity made the slacker myth market a perfect choice, while the Indie myth market was a natural fit for Volkswagen given its cultural and political authority.[1]

> *Compose the identity myth.* Managers shouldn't usurp the role of their creatives, but they must give specific direction on creative content if they are to play a significant strategic role. The first step in composing the myth is to prepare a *myth treatment:* a synopsis of the myth that describes the identity anxieties the myth should address and the way in which the myth will resolve these anxieties. Next, managers must describe the populist world in which the myth will be located, and the strategy for the brand to develop an authentic voice within this world. To maintain legitimacy, the executions of the myth must aim in part at the insiders who control the populist world that the brand inhabits. Brands win this authenticity with performances that express the brand's populist world literacy and its fidelity to the world's values. Finally, managers need to work with their creative partners to develop the brand's *charismatic aesthetic,*

namely, an original communication code that is organic to the populist world.

Extend the identity myth. When a brand performs the right myth targeted at the right myth market, consumers jump on board, using the product to sate their identity desires. They come to depend on the brand as an icon and remain fiercely loyal, but only as long as the brand keeps the myth fresh and historically relevant. Once established, myths must evolve creatively and also weave in new popular culture in order to remain vital.

Reinvent the identity myth. Even the most compelling identity myths will eventually falter, not because competitors attack, but because societal changes drain their value. The seemingly rock-solid value of a brand's myth in one year can come unglued the next. Socio-economic and ideological shifts reconfigure the identity desires of the nation's citizens, sending them searching for new myths. These cultural disruptions create extraordinary opportunities for innovative new identity brands while also presenting treacherous hazards for incumbents.

Even the most successful brands routinely struggle to understand the cultural disruptions that send their brands into tailspins. Witness Volkswagen's two-decade-long struggle to regain its iconic stature and Budweiser's dead-end experiments that stalled the brand for most of the 1990s. Other brands, like Miller, Levi's, and Cadillac, have yet to recover.

Brand Manager as Composer

Brand managers must act as composers of the brand's myth. Too often, the job of the brand manager is reduced to adjective selection—the management of meaningless abstractions. As cultural activists, managers treat their brands as a medium—no different than a novel or a film—to deliver provocative creative materials that respond to society's new cultural needs. While they must leave the actual construction of the myth and its charismatic voicing to creative talent, managers must become directly involved in the composition of the myth, or else they give away the strategic direction of the brand.[2]

The Cultural Activist Organization

Marketing organizations are today dominated by spreadsheets, income statements, reams of market data, and feasibility reports. The rationality and pragmatism of the everyday business of marketing smothers cultural activism. Moreover, the breeding ground for brand managers—M.B.A. programs in business schools—conscientiously socializes managers into a psycho-economic worldview that runs directly counter to the cultural point of view needed for identity brands. Many business schools marginalize social issues as the domain of not-for-profit ventures and treat the texts of the culture industries superficially, if at all. Most M.B.A.'s leave their programs without even a rudimentary ability to evaluate an ad from a cultural perspective.

Iconic brands have broken out of this rationalized mind-set to make contact with the nation's culture. They are exceptions to the rule, led by the intuitions of ad agency creatives and the occasional marketing iconoclast. Because companies have not nurtured a cultural perspective and the talent that goes with it, the primary architects of iconic brands have been copywriters and art directors. Not surprisingly, the members of the brand team with the greatest cultural competencies take the lead. As a result, cultural strategies have evolved haphazardly by the chance engagement of talented creatives, rather than through the consistent deployment of a brand strategy.

For brand owners that seek to build iconic brands, the challenge is to develop a *cultural activist organization:* a company organized around developing identity myths that address emerging contradictions in society; a company organized to collaborate with creative partners to perform myths that have the charisma and authenticity necessary to attract followers; a company that is organized to understand society and culture, not just consumers; and a company that is staffed with managers who have ability and training in these areas.

Mind-share branding is today slipping out of favor even among its most loyal stalwarts. And commingling brands with culture seems to be in. Procter & Gamble, The Coca-Cola Company, and Unilever all have made significant gestures of late to move in new directions, often mentioning Hollywood as the most likely destination.

In a speech to the Publicity Club of London, Niall Fitzgerald, then chairman of Unilever, proclaimed that the "interrupt and repeat" model of advertising is in decline, and so marketers can no longer push "messages and memorability into the skulls of the audience."[3] In place of mind share, Fitzgerald sees advertising moving into the space occupied by other culture industry products like film: "Today we should conceive and evaluate our brand communication as though it were content—because today, in effect, that is what it is. We are in the branded content business."

Fitzgerald is certainly right. Marketing companies can no longer ignore that consumers have become tremendously cynical about advertising and can now act on this cynicism with technologies like TiVo, which allows them to edit out ad exposures. Instead, advertising is looking more and more like entertainment. Madison Avenue and Hollywood are becoming incestuous partners.

But how should companies, long enamored by mind share, proceed? Fitzgerald seems to suggest that branded content is a new-to-the-world proposition. But, as this book makes clear, the most successful identity brands have long focused on delivering branded content, at least since the beginning of the television age in the mid-1950s. The extraordinary successes of Marlboro and Volkswagen in the 1960s; Coke and McDonald's in the 1970s; Nike, Budweiser, and Absolut in the 1980s; and Mountain Dew and Snapple in the 1990s were all the result of branded content. So managers interested in new branding models would do well to glean some lessons from their predecessors rather than try to reinvent the wheel.

Fitzgerald's provocations beg the question: What branded content? If brands merely deliver entertainment like most culture-industry products, they will be handicapped from the start. We live in a world oversaturated with cultural content, which is delivered not just by the traditional culture industries (film, television, magazines, books, and so on) but also increasingly by video games and the Internet. How can a thirty-second ad compete with a film or rock concert in terms of entertainment value? Or, alternatively, why would customers seek out a film when the plot is stilted by commercial sponsorship?

The greatest opportunity for brands today is to deliver not entertainment, but rather myths that their customers can use to manage the exigencies of a world that increasingly threatens their identities. To do so, companies would do well to follow the lead of the most successful brands of the past half-century rather than throw their marketing budgets at Hollywood. Brands become cultural icons by performing myths that address society's most vexing contradictions.

APPENDIX

Methods

Building Theory with Cases

Theory is sometimes a dirty word in management circles, associated with arcane abstractions that are irrelevant to real business decisions. But managers do require theories—simplified models that guide decisions—to manage. The challenge is to build theories that speak directly to management issues rather than tangential abstractions of only academic concern. In this book, my goal is to build a theory that explains how brands become icons, a central concern of many brand managers. To this end, I followed the time-tested approach used often in organizational studies and other social sciences: building theory with cases. I began by drawing on existing theories in the culture-focused academic disciplines to specify the general contours of iconic brands. I then selected cases of iconic brands that would allow me to build a new brand strategy model. I found it necessary to devise a new empirical method for studying these brands—what I call a brand genealogy—because previous research has not examined brands from a cultural perspective.

Building a new theory requires many iterations of tacking between the cases and the general cultural theories that informed the research to search for patterns. Through this comparative process, I built a new model that I call cultural branding strategy. Along the way, I threw out several dozen tentative models that I rejected either because they didn't quite map onto the case data or because they didn't make sense in relation to existing cultural theory. The details of this process follow.

Case Selection: American Iconic Brands

I developed the theory through case studies of some of the most successful identity brands of the last half century. These are the iconic brands, or

223

brands whose identity value is so powerful that they become accepted as consensus symbols in American culture.

I first identified those brands whose value stems primarily from story-telling rather than how well the product works. I eliminated from the sample universe those composite brands whose value is strongly driven both by storytelling and by other factors, such as superior product performance, innovative product designs, advanced technologies, or a superior business model. Apple, Polo, and BMW are examples of the types of brands that I eliminated. To isolate how cultural branding works, it was important to study brands for which cultural branding is the predominant branding tool and, thus, for which it is difficult to construct alternative explanations for the brand's success.

I was particularly interested in studying brands whose value waxed and waned over time. This kind of variance gave me more interesting and difficult data to explain and required that I pay close attention to historical changes. The brands I worked with most extensively—Mountain Dew, Volkswagen, Budweiser, Harley, ESPN, and Nike (I don't report on Nike in the book, because of space limitations)—are from six industries, with very different histories, competitive situations, and consumer bases. The historical investigation nevertheless revealed that the brands have defini-tive commonalities that led to their success. These commonalities, their implicit cultural branding strategy, form the core of this book.

While the principles of cultural branding apply widely (with some necessary adjustments for cultural differences across countries), I chose to focus on American brands for two reasons. First, from a research perspec-tive, the brand genealogy method requires an intensive immersion into so-cial and cultural history. Including brands from other countries would have lengthened the project by years. Second, from an expository perspec-tive, it's much easier for me to orient the reader to the cultural branding principles using similar historical material in each case. This redundancy allows me to show patterns across these brands, as each brand engaged the same historical forces in different ways to create valuable myths.

Data: Films

Cultural branding works when the brand's stories connect powerfully with particular contradictions in American society. Consequently, the only way to study cultural branding is to study the stories that the brand performs over time.[1] For reasons described earlier, television ads provided the core empirical data for this book, dominating four of the six brands that I analyzed extensively. At first glance, this emphasis may seem myopic. After all, most firms execute their branding strategies comprehensively across product, customer service, distribution, and more. It's never just ads. But this choice makes sense, because my focus is on identity value. And identity value is created primarily through storytelling.

Sponsored films—advertisements broadcast on television, in theaters, and, more recently, via the Internet—have been far and away the most effective means for building iconic brands. For the cultural branding process to work, the brand must perform stories. And for fifty years, television advertising has been the best storytelling vehicle available. There are exceptions, to be sure. Service providers and retailers, like Starbucks, for example, can effectively use their store space and customer interactions for storytelling purposes. But, for all the cultural brands I've studied, the point of difference—what made the brand so desirable—was film, usually in the form of television advertising. Identity brands must be very good at product quality, distribution, promotion, pricing, and customer service. But these attributes are simply the ante that marketers must pony up to be competitive. They aren't drivers of business success. Identity brands live or die on the quality of their communications.

This argument runs against the grain of the current marketing zeitgeist, which has again forecasted the death of advertising. Certainly, conventional advertising—ads that seek to persuade people to think differently about product benefits—are becoming less effective as media get more fragmented and as audiences become more cynical about marketer's claims.

But cultural branding is different. Iconic brands perform ads that people love to watch. With the advent of the Web, customers search out these ads on Web sites, download them, and e-mail them around the world, watching them over and over. These ads don't wear out, at least not easily. Some companies I've studied have even relaunched favorite ads, much as a well-liked film can be re-released.

Further, advertisers are now aggressively developing alternative media for their films: in theaters, on the Internet, in dedicated cable channels, and in retail spaces. Even if network television fades under the effects of media fragmentation and TiVo, iconic brands will simply find other venues to tell their stories through film. Media may shift, but the principles for constructing valued myths are enduring.

For the six brands I studied, I gathered historical reels of brand advertising extending back decades. These were comprehensive reels, not highlights. The number of ads I analyzed ranged from sixty to several hundred for each brand. I developed detailed narratives that explained the cultural fit (or lack thereof) between the ads and American culture and society, pushing to explain the major ups and downs of the brand throughout its history. Although I present an edited, highlights version of the analyses in the chapters for the readers to follow, each brand genealogy required much more detailed analysis. The complete analysis included most of the ads produced rather than just the most influential. This kind of attention to detail allows the researcher to plumb the nuances of strategy that explain success versus mediocrity. With more superficial data, these nuances would be invisible.[2]

Method: Brand Genealogy

I developed a new method for studying brands by adapting the most influential analyses of mass-culture products found in the various cultural disciplines.[3] By tracing the fit between the text and changes in American society and culture and by following how these resonances ebb and flow over time, these analyses explain why important cultural products (e.g., Western films, romance novels, Elvis Presley, and Oprah Winfrey) resonate in the culture at a particular historical juncture.

The brand genealogy method begins by assembling a close chronological interpretation of the content of the brand's advertisements. I paid particular attention to ads that managers (and occasionally the trade press) have told me were particularly successful or, alternatively, were tragically flawed. Most of the time, however, I had to infer what elements made the ads successful. To do so, I looked at the patterning of different elements in the ads over time. Successful elements of the ads are those that the creators keep in the mix and try to elaborate on over time. Unimportant or weak elements are eventually tossed out as the campaign develops.[4]

I overlaid this chronology with changes in the identity value of the brand, which I estimated from archival reports and managers' recollections of sales, share, and price premiums (figure A-1). This is the history

FIGURE A-1

Data to Be Explained: Why Ads Resonate or Disconnect

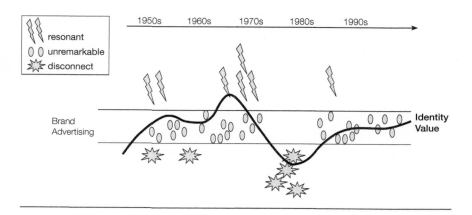

that I want to explain with my analysis: Why did particular advertisements resonate perfectly in American culture, leading to great increases in brand equity, whereas others sent the brand into a tailspin?

Alongside the patterns of advertising, I traced the history of the most influential mass-culture products relevant to the brand's communications. I also looked at the relevant social, political, and economic history that might affect how the brand's stories resonated (figure A-2).

The brand genealogy method consists in moving back and forth between these three levels of analysis: a close textual analysis of the brand's ads over time, a discourse analysis of other related mass culture products as they change over time, and a socioeconomic tracking of the major shifts in American society. The goal is to explain why particular stories generate extraordinary resonance whereas the vast majority fall flat and some are veritable disasters. For each important ad, or set of related ads, I tacked back and forth between the ads, popular culture, and society to construct an interpretation that describes the fit. I continued with this process until I had constructed an explanation that made sense of all the data.

Systematic Comparison

Robust theories are built through systematic comparison of cases to identify patterns. Any individual case can be explained in several ways, each of

FIGURE A-2

Linking Advertisements to Mass Culture and Societal Change

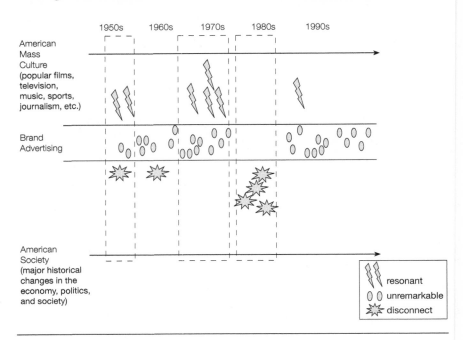

which makes equally convincing sense, given the available data. On the other hand, it's much harder to construct an explanation that works equally well across several cases. As a result, the analyst can more readily rule out alternative explanations. In management studies, the comparative case method has produced some of the most influential books in recent years, including *Built to Last* and *The Innovator's Dilemma*. There's no reason that brand theories cannot be similarly rigorous in their construction.

A second problem with anchoring on celebrated individual cases is that any given case always has some idiosyncratic qualities that can only be identified through comparison. Take Harley-Davidson, a cause célèbre used in a raft of books. My research reveals that previous analyses have badly misinterpreted why Harley was successful. I have discovered that the pervasive emulation of Harley is unwarranted because the Harley brand evolved like no other and is virtually impossible to imitate. When viewed with the benefit of comparison to other cases, Harley is clearly one of the worst brands for managers to use as a model (see chapter 7).

The Theory-Building Process

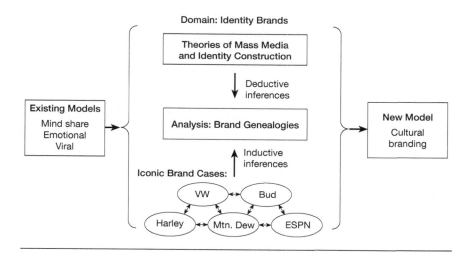

Academic theory building is based on systematic skepticism. A researcher challenges conclusions with data until the theory proves that it can handle all comers. Rather than selling a favored theory, he or she seeks out strong challengers and subjects these theories to an empirical test with sufficiently detailed data. The best theory wins. Throughout this book, I compare cultural strategy to the two most important challengers, mindshare and viral models, to demonstrate that my theory provides a superior explanation for the success of the iconic brands that I study. I began with Nike, Mountain Dew, Volkswagen, and Budweiser. And then, to push the boundaries of the theory, I added two cases (Harley and ESPN) in which the brand was built without much help from advertising. The ability of the cultural branding model to explain how these brands became so desirable increases confidence that the model is robust. Figure A-3 shows a simplified version of the theory-building process.

Deductions from General Cultural Theories

As an applied discipline, marketing works under the umbrella of the great intellectual traditions of the past century—from economics and psychology to sociology, anthropology, and, more recently, the humanities—adapting knowledge of these fields to the peculiar tasks of marketing. Good applied theories are rarely inducted out of the blue. Rather, they are informed by the more general theories in the fields from which the discipline draws. These general theories are used as a flexible tool kit, pulling out the appropriate ideas, amending them, and combining them to fit the problem at hand.

To build a theory of cultural branding, I drew selectively from a variety of fields that specialize in cultural analysis: cultural sociology, cultural anthropology, cultural history, and various other humanities disciplines that are often called cultural studies. These disciplines have developed powerful conceptual tools that, with some modifications, usefully inform how cultural branding works. I have placed this paper trail in the endnotes so that the book is easier to read.

Notes

CHAPTER ONE

1. The idea of a cultural icon differs from the way that the term icon is used in semiotics. In Piercian semiotics, an icon specifies a particular kind of symbol, the meaning of which is implied by its sensorial relationship (usually visual) to that for which it stands. For instance, the Pillsbury Dough Boy is an icon because he is a character made of dough and represents a product that is raw dough in a tube. Alternatively, a cultural icon is related to the conventional use of the term icon in art and design (e.g., the Eames LCW chair is an icon of mid-twentieth-century modern design). In this usage, a particular design is iconic when it becomes conventionally understood as a quintessential or exemplary design of a period or a style. So, like a cultural icon, the design serves as a metonym representing a broader set of ideas. Some design icons are also cultural icons (the Eames chair or the Volkswagen Beetle). But there are many design icons whose renown is based on aesthetic triumphs that bear little relation to their reflection of ideological currents of society.

2. This section is adapted from Douglas B. Holt, "Brands and Branding," Note 9-503-045 (Boston: Harvard Business School, 2003).

3. Of course, individuals' experiences with brands are more complicated. People routinely overlay the public construal of the brand with their own personalized stories, images, and other associations. These many stray stories that individuals weave into their consumption can occasionally add to and alter the conventions of the brand, but this is rare. This personalization process has been a central preoccupation of interpretive consumer research. In line with the dominant methodological individualism in American marketing departments, most studies of consumers and brands glorify the individual act of consumption while ignoring how the brand operates as a conventional symbol in public culture. However, since marketers are interested in aggregations of customers, these idiosyncratic meanings have little managerial relevance unless they aggregate to transform conventions.

4. See, for example, Michael Denning, *Mechanic Accents: Dime Novels and Working-Class Culture in America* (New York: Verso, 1987); Janice Radway, *Reading the Romance: Women, Patriarchy, and Popular Literature* (Chapel Hill: University of North Carolina Press, 1984); and Lary May, *The Big Tomorrow: Hollywood and the Politics of the American Way* (Chicago: University of Chicago Press, 2000).

5. All of the management books on branding that I reference in chapter 2 present one-size-fits-all models.

6. The pioneering academic version of this argument can be found in Scott Lash and John Urry, *Economies of Signs and Space* (London: Sage, 1994).

7. An axiom is a self-evident principle, or a principle accepted as true without proof as the basis for argument. Because conventional branding models are so ubiquitous, managers use these models without questioning their underlying axioms. The purpose of chapters 1 and 2 is to surface these assumptions and specify when they are applicable and when they are not.

8. The foundational premise of the cultural branding model—that iconic brands perform national identity myths that resolve cultural contradictions—is informed by a variety of scholars who have studied the role of myth in modern societies, such as those listed in the "Selected Bibliography." Especially helpful were Roland Barthes, *Mythologies* (New York: Noonday Press, 1973); and Richard Slotkin, *Gunfighter Nation: The Myth of the Frontier in Twentieth-Century America* (Norman, OK: University of Oklahoma Press, 1998).

CHAPTER TWO

1. Al Ries and Jack Trout, *Positioning: The Battle for Your Mind* (New York: McGraw-Hill, 1980).

2. Books by leading academics that advocate versions of mind share include: David A. Aaker, *Managing Brand Equity* (New York: Free Press, 1991); David A. Aaker, *Building Strong Brands* (New York: Free Press 1996); David A. Aaker and Eric Joachimsthaler, *Brand Leadership* (New York: Free Press, 2000); Kevin Lane Keller, *Strategic Brand Management* (New York: Prentice Hall, 1998); and Gerald Zaltman, *How Customers Think: Essential Insights into the Mind of the Market* (Cambridge, MA: Harvard Business School Press, 2003).

3. Former Coca-Cola guru Sergio Zyman is the most zealous advocate of mind share among consultants today (*The End of Marketing As We Know It* [New York: HarperBusiness, 2000]).

4. Rohit Deshpande, Kirsten J. O'Neil-Massaro, and Gustavo A. Herrero, "Corona Beer (A)," Case 9-502-023 (Boston: Harvard Business School, 2001). Anheuser-Busch now owns 50 percent of Cervaseria Modelo, the brewer of Corona.

5. Viral processes were clearly central in Corona's initial success. But noting that people talked about the brand is not an explanation. Many beer brands were circulating many different stories at this time. The question that viral models ignore is this: Why do certain cultural contents become so desirable (and thus tellable) at a particular historical moment? In this case we need to ask, Why was Corona's myth circulated so promiscuously? The answer must reside in the resonance of the story in American society.

6. Mind-share models attempt to address how brands contribute to consumer identities. But extending mind-share assumptions to explain how identity

value works leads to models that are incoherent and unconvincing. They treat consumers' aspirational identities as yet other associations that a brand should try to own. "BMW conveys high status" and "Harley expresses masculinity" are common examples. The problem is that these descriptions of identity are so vague and historical that they don't explain anything. For a more detailed critique of mindshare branding in academic theories, see Douglas B. Holt, "How Societies Desire Brands," in *Inside Consumption: Frontiers of Research on Consumer Motives, Goals, and Desires*, eds. S. Ratneshwar and David Glen Mick (New York: Routledge, forthcoming).

7. Scott Bedbury with Stephen Fenichell, *A New Brand World* (New York: Viking Penguin, 2002) and Marc Gobe, *Emotional Branding: The New Paradigm for Connecting Brands to People* (New York: Allworth Press, 2001); also see Berndt Schmitt, *Experiential Marketing* (New York: Free Press, 1999) for a related argument. In the academic literature, a variant of this idea has been advocated by Susan Fournier, "Consumers and Their Brands: Developing Relationship Theory in Consumer Research" *Journal of Consumer Research* 24, no. 4, 343–374, 1998.

8. Some experts have expanded the idea of relationships to look at communities that form around brands. Every branding expert loves Harley's H.O.G. riders club and encourages managers to emulate it. Observing the active brand communities that have formed around brands like Apple and Harley, and given the Internet's advantages in forming communities across space, experts now routinely advocate that managers should seed these communities through sponsorships and Web sites. Some of the more bombastic gurus have even compared powerful brands to cults in terms of their effectiveness in bringing people together in groups around a set of values. The same cause-versus-effect critique that I apply to emotional branding applies equally to the idea of brand communities. People form communities around a brand when the brand contains a powerful myth that is amplified by group activities. I develop the point later in this chapter in the Snapple genealogy, and in chapter 7 when I analyze Harley-Davidson.

9. Robert Scott, God is My Co-Pilot, quoted in Mark Pendergrast, *For God, Country and Coca-Cola* (New York: Basic Books, 2000), 206.

10. Pendergrast, *For God, Country and Coca-Cola*, 287–288.

11. My description of the making of this ad comes from Bill Backer, *The Care and Feeding of Ideas* (New York: Times Books, 1993). Backer was the legendary adman and lead partner in Backer Spielvogel Bates Worldwide who came up with the creative idea.

12. The Library of Congress publicizes its Coca-Cola advertising collection on-line in a feature entitled "Fifty Years of Coca-Cola Television Advertisements," <http://memory.loc.gov/ammem/ccmphtml/colahome.html>. Both ads can be viewed at this Web site.

13. Sergio Zyman, *The End of Marketing as We Know It*, claims that neither "Hilltop" nor "Mean Joe Greene" ad helped Coke sales, though he presents no

evidence to support his case. At the time, Pepsi was extremely successful in making inroads into Coke's franchise with youth. Without these ads, it's quite likely that Coke's business would have headed south. Regardless, Coke's key problem in this era was that its managers did not understand how these two ads worked, and so they were unable to build a campaign around the ideals they embodied. Rather these were both one-off ads that were broadcast amid a sea of conventional lifestyle Coke advertising. It is no wonder, then, that Coke did not realize strong sales gains.

14. See Nicholas Lemann, *The Promised Land: The Great Black Migration and How It Changed America* (New York: Vintage, 1992).

15. The nurturing of emotionally charged relationships with customers is central to the success of brands in several important sectors of the economy, especially business-to-business firms, services, retailers, and experiential offerings. These sectors create value in their face-to-face interactions with customers. But iconic brands are built differently. Customers' emotional connections result from the effectiveness of the brand's myth in resolving customers' identity anxieties.

16. Major brands now cut to the chase and tell their audiences directly that the brand and its customers do indeed have an intense emotional connection. Chrysler, for instance, sank tens of millions of dollars into a campaign using the tag line "Drive = Love," the premise of which was to show how much Celine Dion loved driving her Chrysler. Similarly, in 2004, McDonald's launched a new global tag line, "I'm loving it." Even the widely celebrated MINI campaign is not above reproach: A recent ad depicts a MINI owner getting a painful tattoo on his forearm, the design of which is supposed to match the customized MINI sitting in his garage. The mistaken assumption in all of these efforts is that claiming that customers have deep emotional connections with the brand will make it true.

17. I differentiate here between viral branding—viral activities meant to increase the value of the brand—and the larger category of viral marketing. Viral marketing is simply the latest variant of what used to be referred to as word of mouth and the diffusion of innovation. Viral techniques are widely applicable in the diffusion process. They help get the word out on a new product, and socialize new consumption patterns, especially in the technology sectors. Here, however, I'm concerned with how viruses act as vehicles to create fashionability: the idea that the product's user creates its *au courant* desirability. The most influential book has been Malcolm Gladwell, *The Tipping Point: How Little Things Can Make a Big Difference* (New York: Little, Brown & Co., 2000). See also Emmanuel Rosen, *The Anatomy of Buzz* (New York: Doubleday, 2000); and Jonathan Bond and Richard Kirshenbaum, *Under the Radar: Talking to Today's Cynical Consumer* (New York: Wiley, 1998).

18. Malcolm Gladwell broke the term in his article "The Coolhunt," *New Yorker,* 17 May 1997. Trend-spotting consultancies have popped up all over, including Sputnik, whose principals wrote a book: Janine Lopiano-Misdom and Joanne De Luca, *Street Trends* (New York: Harper Business, 1996).

19. I discuss the historical development of branding based on the idea of consumer sovereignty in Douglas B. Holt, "Why Do Brands Cause Trouble?" *Journal of Consumer Research*, June 2002, vol. 29, 70–90.

20. An earlier version of the Snapple genealogy was published by Douglas B. Holt, "How to Build an Iconic Brand" *Market Leader*, June 2003.

21. John Deighton, "How Snapple Got Its Juice Back," *Harvard Business Review*, January 2002, 47–52, makes an organizational culture argument for Snapple's early success and partial recovery, maintaining that Snapple could succeed only when the company (the founders, and then again with Triarc) had a playful entrepreneurial culture. But this argument fails to account for Triarc's inability to reignite Snapple's identity value and why the new owner of Snapple, Cadbury-Schweppes, clearly a large bureaucratic company, has done just as well with Snapple as did Triarc. More generally, Deighton assumes that there is a tight coupling between corporate culture and branding. While this close relationship sometimes holds true (e.g., Harley and ESPN in my analyses) and has become a popular argument today (e.g., in Jesper Kunde, *Corporate Religion* (New York: FT Prentice Hall, 2000)), the empirical evidence suggests that such tight linkages are hardly necessary. Three of the five companies described in this book—PepsiCo (with Mountain Dew), Anheuser-Busch (with Budweiser), and Volkswagen—have built extraordinarily powerful brands worth many billions of dollars with management teams that have little affinity for the myth that the brand projects. As it turns out, the ad agency, rather than the client, usually serves as the primary cultural conduit. In my model, I argue that what is at stake is how brands forge authentic relationships to the populist worlds from which they draw. I distinguish between organizational populism (Harley, ESPN, Patagonia) and staged populism (Mountain Dew, Bud, Volkswagen).

22. Gilles Lipovetsky, *The Empire of Fashion: Dressing Modern Democracy* (Princeton, NJ: Princeton University Press, 1994), traces the breakdown of the classical top-down fashion model and the rise of a more heterogeneous, fragmented, and democratic fashion system.

23. Snapple's newest brand owners, first Triarc and now Cadbury-Schweppes, have done their best to recapture the magic of Snapple's halcyon days by echoing its original communications. Snapple's myth of the company of amateurs, which took aim at the particular populist sentiments that erupted in the United States in the early 1990s, has now been distilled to a transcendental brand identity in the mind-share mode: Snapple is "quirky and alternative." American culture and society have moved on, but Snapple performs a watered-down version of a story whose resonance peaked more than a decade ago. As a result, Snapple has become a conventional lifestyle brand. A strategy that has yanked Snapple out of history continues to dilute Snapple's stature as an icon.

24. The same can be said for Snapple's so-called cult status as the nucleus of a brand community. Although Snapple attracted a core of enthusiasts, the occa-

sional gathering of people who like Snapple does not explain how the brand cultivated this affinity in the first place. Certainly, exaggerated analogies to religious cults do not help. Enjoying a Snapple with your lunch and laughing at the ads with your friends is something quite different from giving up your worldly belongings to live in isolation with fellow believers. Snapple developed a following because the drink made these people feel a little better about themselves and their place in the world. As sociologist Emile Durkheim taught us long ago, people routinely gather around shared sentiments to heighten the intensity of those sentiments. What's strategically important isn't the act of gathering, but the content of the shared sentiments that caused them to do so.

25. In the viral model, the content of the brand is not specified, since the authorship of the brand moves from the firm to the consumers. The rash application of this strategy to identity branding is a serious mistake. Iconic brands are valued because they perform myths that customers value. Of course, consumers adapt these myths and use them in all sorts of creative ways. Nevertheless, the brand owner should not abandon its leadership role in telling branded stories.

26. Marlboro is somewhat of an exception, largely because of the withdrawal of cigarette advertising on television in the early 1970s.

CHAPTER THREE

1. The idea that the middle class uses ideologically charged signs such as *hillbilly* (and later *redneck* and *slacker*) as epithets, which the working class flips upside down into terms of respect, is an example of what the seminal Soviet linguist Valentin Voloshinov termed *multiaccentuality*. See Michael Denning, *Mechanic Accents: Dime Novels and Working-Class Culture in America* (New York: Verso, 1987).

2. Prior books have noted that brands are imbued with myths. But these books lack useful models for building brand myths because they fail to describe the specific characteristics of successful myths versus unsuccessful attempts. Like the mind-share model, these treatments do not examine branding activities in any detail. Further, these models fail to address why particular myths resonate at particular historical moments while others don't. This is because the models conceive of myths as universal archetypes, rather than as stories that address particular social contradictions. See Randell Randozo, *The Myth Makers* (Chicago: Probus, 1995); and Margaret Mark and Carol S. Pearson, *The Hero and the Outlaw* (New York: McGraw-Hill, 2001).

3. The idea that new expressive culture becomes especially valuable as a symbolic anchor during periods of tumultuous socioeconomic change is a common and long-standing idea in sociology and anthropology. In particular, see Clifford Geertz's famous essay "Ideology as a Cultural System" in his book *The Interpretation of Cultures* (New York: Basic Books, 2000).

CHAPTER FOUR

1. Douglas B. Holt, "Mountain Dew: Selecting New Creative," Case 9-502-040 (Boston: Harvard Business School, 2002).

2. This argument implies a very different sort of brand manager from those found in most companies today. I hint at the organizational entailments of this argument in chapter 9.

3. See Loren Baritz, *The Good Life: The Meaning of Success for the American Middle Class* (New York: Knopf, 1989).

4. Volkswagen was the first successful postmodern brand—a brand that offered up the product as a resource for individual creativity and self-fulfillment rather than as a collective badge. See Douglas B. Holt, "Why Do Brands Cause Trouble?" *Journal of Consumer Research*, vol. 29, June 2002, 70–90.

5. Thomas Frank, *The Conquest of Cool: Business Culture, Counterculture, and the Rise of Hip Consumerism* (Chicago: University of Chicago Press, 1997), 62, offers one of the best historical treatments of the DDB campaign.

6. Thomas Frank has done a remarkable job of cataloging this appropriation of the 1960s revolution in *One Market Under God: Extreme Capitalism, Market Populism, and the End of Economic Democracy* (New York: Doubleday, 2000), and in his muckraking cultural journal, *The Baffler*.

7. David Brooks, *Bobos in Paradise: The New Upper Class and How They Got There* (New York: Simon & Schuster, 2000).

8. Two of the most respected acolytes of indie music were Ian Mackay and his band, Fugazi, and Steve Albini, producer and front man for various bands, including Big Black. These two indie celebrities derived enormous respect, at least as much for their strident advocacy of DIY culture as for their potent music. It's no coincidence that, when Nirvana's *Nevermind* became one of the top-grossing albums of the decade, Kurt Cobain sought out Albini to produce the sequel—an implicit pledge vowing his continued allegiance to DIY, especially since Albini would coax a sound from the band that would scare away all but the true believers.

9. Douglas Wolk, "Nick Drake's Post-Posthumous Fame," Salon.com, 19 June 2000. <http://dir.salon.com/ent/music/feature/2000/06/19/drake/index.html>, (accessed 19 February 2003).

10. While this spot shone, Volkswagen aired another ad during the same Super Bowl—a spoof in which a bear chases a VW in the forest—that came off as an insecure effort to win the Super Bowl audience with the formula of the day (animals and cheap laughs).

11. Here's what film critic Jane Dark, "Village Voice Film Poll," 2001, <http://www.villagevoice.com/take/three/title.php?title=1026546>, wrote about "Milky Way":

> That's not a movie, it's a commercial, blah blah blah. Desecration of Nick Drake's grave, blah blah blah. In a year where many of the hypercoolest

directors made car ads, mostly for BMW, it seems reasonable to include such work in the cinema scope. I think whoever sold the rights to the song is an asshole. And I have no interest in being a corporate apologist—don't buy Volkswagens, they suck anyway. But in the meantime, this is a brilliant minuscule flick: from the majestic opening shot (tracking vertically along a nighttime river, all abstracted glimmers in the dark, until the flying camera intersects a car crossing a bridge and suddenly the story turns left along the horizontal), to the German-expressionist way all the riders' faces are lit, to the astounding compression of the narrative (which is, in the end, what commercials are best at; they're like labs where theories of narratology get tested and refined). Most of us, we never got invited to those cool parties in the woods; to drive away without ever walking in seems like self-involved apathy. But it also requires a kind of insight about where the action is, a knowledge no kids that age ever had. It is a story about prodigal, melancholy, and finally impossible knowledge—a romantic fantasy of wisdom, compressed into a minimal, expressionistic space. Which, magic of magics, is exactly what Nick Drake and "Pink Moon" have going for them. What's staggering about this movie isn't how poorly matched the crass commercial and the holy song are, but how perfectly.

CHAPTER FIVE

1. The books by David A. Aaker cited in chapter two and Kevin Lane Keller, *Strategic Brand Management* (New York: Prentice Hall, 1998), argue this point explicitly. It is implicit in most other mind-share books.

2. Aside from Budweiser, the full-calorie, premium-beer segment—once the vast majority of beer consumption—had all but disappeared in the 1990s. Most of this share of stomach shifted to light beers, and a smaller percentage to imports. In response, Anheuser-Busch has gradually repositioned Bud alongside imports like Heineken and Corona as a superpremium beer. In effect, Anheuser-Busch responded to the demise of the old American premium segment by jumping up to the pricier tier. But to sell the same product at a higher price point required that the company enhance Bud's identity value to its customers. The strategy couldn't have worked had the company not revitalized Bud as an icon with the "Lizards" and "Whassup?!" campaigns.

3. In this cultural battle, Miller's myth—and not Bud's—stood out. Miller High Life's name reflects its original positioning as a luxury premium beer for middle-class men. Phillip Morris bought the brand in the early 1970s and assigned Backer Spielvogel to the account. Bill Backer and his team designed a new campaign built around the idea that tough working men deserved a time of their own—Miller Time—to celebrate after the end of a hard day's work. Had the

Phillip Morris management supported this idea appropriately, Miller could well have taken over category leadership. Instead, Phillip Morris stumbled with inconsistent communiqués, allowing Anheuser-Busch to move in, swipe the Backer idea, and improve upon it.

4. David M. Gordon, *Fat and Mean: The Corporate Squeeze of Working Americans and the Myth of Managerial "Downsizing"* (New York: Free Press, 1996), 31. See also Kevin Phillips, *Boiling Point: Democrats, Republicans, and the Decline of Middle-Class Prosperity* (New York: Random House, 1993).

5 David A. Aaker and Eric Joachimsthaler, *Brand Leadership* (New York: Free Press, 2000), also include brand loyalty in their definition of brand assets, but this is a tautology. Loyalty is the desired outcome produced by a strong brand, not a characteristic of it. Companies that manage their brands as assets based on mind-share principles seek to improve performance on these metrics. They invest communications budgets with the goal of increasing the percentage of consumers who remember the brand without prompting and who think of the appropriate associations when they're asked to think about the brand. These measures don't come close to capturing what makes identity brands such valuable assets.

6. Anheuser-Busch routinely borrows ideas and moves them back and forth between Bud and Bud Light. The company took the myth treatment from "Lizards"—centered on mocking the man-of-action ideal—and recrafted it into an enormously successful radio campaign for Bud Light. In each spot, a ridiculous job, such as ripping ticket stubs at theaters, is celebrated with the same epic voice of "This Bud's for You," though now Anheuser-Busch's tongue rests firmly in its cheek. The firm then took this campaign to television, promoting Bud in the United Kingdom. On the heels of great success there, Anheuser-Busch has returned to the United States with a television version.

7. Bud reconnected with working men by developing a different kind of myth. "This Bud's for You" was an *affirmative myth,* a myth that allowed Bud drinkers to perceive themselves as part of the American comeback project in the 1980s. The brand's artisan myth aligned with Reagan's national ideology. In contrast, the laconic brotherhood myth, paved by "Lizards" and then spun in "Whassup?!" was a *myth of resistance.* Like Mountain Dew's, this was a myth that championed ideals that directly challenged the national ideology. Budweiser had followed its constituents and done a political flip-flop by changing the kind of myth it championed.

Populist worlds are the cultural raw materials that a nation uses to reimagine itself. They are the symbolic resources that citizens draw from both to sustain the country's ideals (in affirmative myths) and to challenge those ideals (in myths of resistance). Budweiser demonstrates that a brand can rejuvenate its iconic power by moving from one type of myth to another when the identity politics of its core constituency shifts.

CHAPTER SIX

1. I was hired in 2000 by a major media company (not ESPN) to analyze sports television consumption among American men. I conducted lengthy, unstructured interviews in the Chicago and Los Angeles homes of twenty-three men who were active sports spectators.

2. Douglas B. Holt and J. Craig Thompson, "Man-of-Action Heroes: The Pursuit of Heroic Masculinity in Everyday Consumption," *Journal of Consumer Research* (forthcoming), gives an academic account of this mythology and how it was consumed by American men in everyday life during the 1990s.

3. See, for example, Susan Fournier, "Consumers and Their Brands: Developing Relationship Theory in Consumer Research," *Journal of Consumer Research* 24, no. 4, 343–374, 1998.

4. The particular characteristics of the insider-brand relationship depends on the relative centrality of the brand to the populist world. Some iconic brands emerge out of populist worlds (Nike, Patagonia, Harley), while others are mass market products that seek to borrow from the populist world (Bud, Mountain Dew, VW, ESPN). In the case of ESPN, the channel initiated a leadership position in sports in competition with a long-standing cadre of insiders. Hence, insiders were less willing to grant ESPN an authoritative role. Alternatively, for brands like Harley-Davidson, in which the brand's iconic power was initiated within the populist world, the brand retains extraordinary authority among insiders.

5. R. W. Marriott, "How to Spot a Biker Wannabe," <http://www.saintjohn.nbcc.nb.ca/~marriott/Wannabe.htm> (accessed 17 February 2003).

CHAPTER SEVEN

1. I am synthesizing the Harley success story as told by Robert E. Wayland and Paul M. Cole, *Customer Connections: New Strategies for Growth* (Cambridge, MA: Harvard University Press, 1997); Sam Hill and Glenn Rifkin, *Radical Marketing* (New York: Harper Business, 1999); and David A. Aaker, *Building Strong Brands* (New York: Free Press, 1996).

2. The Harley-Davidson Company commissioned brand research that used mind-share assumptions. This research identified the Harley DNA as consisting of three values: American patriotism, machismo, and personal freedom. See John Schouten and James McAlexander, "Subcultures of Consumption: An Ethnography of the New Bikers," *Journal of Consumer Research* 22 (June 1995); 43–61. Aaker, *Building Strong Brands,* draws on this research in his discussion of Harley.

3. Harley forcibly took over the very successful clubs started by its customers in the 1970s. Vaughn Beals did not start them, as suggested by authors like Jesper Kunde (*Corporate Religion* (New York: FT Prentice Hall, 2000)) and Aaker (*Building Strong Brands*). Further, the timing of the club takeover (1984) does not coincide with Harley's extraordinary rise in desirability (early 1990s). Likewise,

Harley's product improvement also happened in the early 1980s and merely caught up to the Japanese quality standards. So neither explanation holds up to empirical examination.

4. For this reason, as mentioned in the appendix, this chapter has a methodological goal in addition to its analytical focus. To push cultural strategy beyond just advertising, I chose to look at Harley as a negative case. The Harley genealogy provides evidence for the robustness of the cultural branding model, extending the model beyond the television advertisements examined in prior chapters. Many accounts of Harley's success have been published; most of them tell roughly the same story. In no account is advertising an important player. Consequently, Harley, as one of the most potent iconic brands in recent history and with little significant advertising, offers a challenging test of the power of the cultural branding framework.

5. Synthesized from Daniel R. Wolf, *The Rebels: A Brotherhood of Outlaw Bikers* (Toronto: University of Toronto Press, 1991); Hunter S. Thompson, *Hell's Angels: A Strange and Terrible Saga* (New York: Ballantine Books, 1996); and Ralph "Sonny" Barger, *Hell's Angel* (New York: William Morrow, 2000).

6. As reported in Brock Yates, *Outlaw Machine: Harley-Davidson and the Search for the American Soul* (New York: Little, Brown & Co., 1999).

7. Brando's bike was a Triumph. In retrospect, because of Harley's later domination, most people assume Brando must have ridden a Harley.

8. Thompson, *Hell's Angels*, 53.

9. *Easy Rider* (Columbia/Tristar Studios, 1969).

10. Garry Wills, *Reagan's America: Innocents at Home* (New York: Doubleday, 1987).

11. Richard Slotkin has conducted an exhaustive historical investigation to show that the gunfighter has been the pivotal archetype in American ideology since the closing of the American frontier at the end of the nineteenth century. Slotkin has written the definitive analysis of the American frontier myth, discussing how the myth has evolved over four hundred years of American history. See especially Richard Slotkin, *Gunfighter Nation: The Myth of the Frontier in Twentieth-Century America* (Norman, OK: University of Oklahoma Press, 1998).

12. Factiva lists: *New York Times, Wall Street Journal, Newsday, USA Today, Washington Post, Globe and Mail,* AP Newswire, and the *Houston Chronicle.* John A. Conway, "Harley Back in Gear," *Forbes,* 20 April 1987, noted that the Reagan visit was a public relations coup for Harley.

13. Martin Jack Rosenblum, "Praise Our Ladies." See <http://www.members.tripod.com/~holyranger/>, excerpted from *The Holy Ranger: Harley-Davidson Poems,* Milwaukee: Lion Publishing, 1989.

14. It's important to distinguish between the use of brands as symbols of a subculture, which rarely happens, and the hijacking of brands by subcultures as ephemeral subversive fashion items, which happens routinely. In the United

States, the most obvious instances of hijacking have occurred in urban African American neighborhoods, where brands like Adidas, Puma, Nike, North Face, Mercedes, BMW, Hilfiger, Polo, and Timberland have all been grabbed and had their meanings repackaged via their subcultural use.

CHAPTER EIGHT

1. The shift was in part motivated by an actor's guild strike, as well as difficulties in coming to contract terms with the campaign's actors, who had become celebrities due to the campaign's success.

2. Developing these techniques in detail is beyond the scope of this chapter and book; they are familiar to all commercial artists, people who tell stories for a living. The cultural studies literature, such as those works listed in the "Selected Bibliography," provide academic treatments.

3. Interestingly, at roughly the same time Nike, jumping on the same third-wave feminist/riot grrl bandwagon, concocted an even more brilliant ad, following the same creative technique, but with a more politicized choice. For its soundtrack, the ad relied on a punked-up version of Helen Reddy's feminist anthem from the early 1970s: "I Am Woman," performed to sound just like the Breeders (a leading indie punk outfit headed by two sisters).

CHAPTER NINE

1. The slacker and indie populist worlds overlap to some extent in their shared appreciation for do-it-yourself culture. Another way to think about these two populist worlds is that they're two tangents of the same countercultural fabric. Volkswagen selectively culled the more bohemian aspects of the counterculture, whereas Mountain Dew focused on its cynical resistance to middle-class life. Populist worlds are not discrete groups or places (though they always reference "real" social life, either contemporary or historic). Rather, they are categories created in mass culture—*discourses*, in academic terminology.

2. To communicate these ideas, I have described the path to building an iconic brand as a linear process. But in reality such brands are never built in a straight line from blueprint to firmament. Rather, managers iterate between gathering knowledge, composing the strategy, and experimenting with executions.

3. Niall Fitzgerald, speech to Publicity Club, London, *Media Week (UK)*, 27 November 2003 (synopsized by World Advertising Research Center <http://www.warc.com/> in their "World Advertising and Marketing News" feature).

APPENDIX

1. A primary weakness of existing brand strategies is that they are derived from snapshot profiles of brands. For example, consider the widely used branding scheme devised by Young & Rubicam, which it calls Brandvaluator. The agency

has assembled reams of brand metric data from around the world and put the information into an algorithm that derives the factors in common for strong brands: Strong brands tend to be well known, distinctive, and relevant. But what is the strategic advice that flows from this observation? That one should emphasize the brand's memorability, distinctiveness, and relevance? The problem is that metrics are not explanations. We need to know the mechanisms that lead these brands to achieve such glowing report cards.

2. Management books on branding usually trade on the apt anecdote: They either rely on a whirlwind of short, secondhand snippets or else use quick, I-was-there insider briefings to demand that the reader accept their arguments. From an academic viewpoint, what is troubling about these books (some of which have been written by academics) is that the empirical data that the authors summon is so thin that they cannot possibly develop an explanatory model. The recommendations that flow out of these models are so vague that it is impossible to distinguish between the activities of the best brands and the most mediocre. Further, much of the "data" that drive the findings in these books are actually assembled from predistilled stories reported in the trade press. So rather than careful primary research, most authors are simply repeating stories that the protagonists (the client and agency) want to tell about their brands. The average analysis of a brand in most of these books extends all of two or three pages, satisfactory for cocktail conversation and not much else.

3. The primary intellectual influences informing the brand genealogy are listed in the "Selected Bibliography."

4. This selection process is extremely challenging, given that each ad is a complex combination of signs and communication codes plucked from public culture. Because the ad's authors learn through trial and error, their choices lead them down blind alleys quite often. But, for the most successful iconic brands, the brand teams eventually triangulate on the right combination of signs and codes and then extend this combination over time.

Selected Bibliography

MARKETING MANAGEMENT

Aaker, David A. *Managing Brand Equity.* New York: Free Press, 1991.

————. *Building Strong Brands.* New York: Free Press, 1996.

Aaker, David A., and Erich Joachimsthaler. *Brand Leadership.* New York: Free Press, 2000.

Bedbury, Scott. *A New Brand World.* New York: Viking, 2002.

Bond, Jonathan, and Richard Kirshenbaum. *Under the Radar: Talking to Today's Cynical Consumer.* New York: Wiley, 1998.

Fournier, Susan. "Consumers and Their Brands: Developing Relationship Theory in Consumer Research." *Journal of Consumer Research* 24 (March 1998): 343–374.

Gladwell, Malcolm. "The Coolhunt." *The New Yorker,* 17 May 1997.

————. *The Tipping Point: How Little Things Can Make a Big Difference.* New York: Little, Brown & Co., 2000.

Gobe, Marc. *Emotional Branding: The New Paradigm for Connecting Brands to People.* New York: Allworth Press, 2001.

Hill, Sam, and Glenn Rifkin. *Radical Marketing.* New York: Harper Business, 1999.

Holt, Douglas B. "How to Build an Iconic Brand." *Market Leader,* June 2003.

————. "What Becomes an Icon Most?" *Harvard Business Review,* March 2003: 43.

Kapferer, Jean-Noel. *Strategic Brand Management.* Dover, NH: Kogan Page, 1997.

Keller, Kevin L. *Strategic Brand Management.* New York: Prentice Hall, 1998.

Klein, Naomi. *No Logo: Taking Aim at the Brand Bullies.* New York: Picador, 1999.

Kunde, Jesper. *Corporate Religion.* New York: FT Prentice Hall, 2000.

Lopiano-Misdom, Janine, and Joanne De Luca. *Street Trends.* New York: Harper Business, 1996.

Rosen, Emanuel. *The Anatomy of Buzz.* New York: Doubleday, 2000.

Schmitt, Bernd H. *Experiential Marketing.* New York: Free Press, 1999.

Wayland, Robert E., and Paul M. Cole. *Customer Connections: New Strategies for Growth.* Cambridge, MA: Harvard University Press, 1997.

Zyman, Sergio. *The End of Marketing As We Know It.* New York: Harper Business, 2000.

THEORIES OF MASS CULTURE AND CONSUMPTION

Barthes, Roland. "Myth Today." Translated by Annette Laves. In *Mythologies.* New York: Noonday Press, 1973.

Bell, Catherine. *Ritual Theory, Ritual Practice.* New York: Oxford University Press, 1992.

Bradley, Raymond T. *Charisma and Social Structure.* New York: Paragon House, 1987.

Denning, Michael. *Mechanic Accents: Dime Novels and Working-Class Culture in America.* New York: Verso, 1987.

Eagleton, Terry. *Ideology: An Introduction.* New York: Verso, 1991.

Eliade, Mircea. *Myths, Dreams, and Mysteries.* New York: Harvill Press, 1960.

Geertz, Clifford. *The Interpretation of Cultures.* New York: Basic Books, 2000.

Goldman, Robert. *Reading Ads Socially,* New York: Routledge, 1992.

———, and Stephen Papson. *Sign Wars: The Cluttered Landscape of Advertising.* New York: Guilford, 1996.

———. *Nike Culture.* Thousand Oaks, CA: Sage, 1998.

Holt, Douglas B. "Why Do Brands Cause Trouble?" *Journal of Consumer Research,* 29 (June 2002): 70–91.

Holt, Douglas B., and J. Craig Thompson. "Man-of-Action Heroes: The Pursuit of Heroic Masculinity in Everyday Consumption." *Journal of Consumer Research,* forthcoming.

Illouz, Eva. *Consuming the Romantic Utopia: Love and the Cultural Contradictions of Capitalism.* Berkeley: University of California Press, 1997.

Lasch, Christopher. *The Culture of Narcissism.* New York: W. W. Norton, 1990.

Lash, Scott, and John Urry. *Economies of Signs and Space.* Thousand Oaks, CA: Sage, 1994.

Levy, Sidney J. *Brands, Consumers, Symbols, and Research: Sydney J. Levy on Marketing.* Edited by Dennis Rook. Thousand Oaks, CA: Sage, 1999.

Lipovetsky, Gilles. *The Empire of Fashion: Dressing Modern Democracy.* Princeton, NJ: Princeton University Press, 1994.

Marchand, Roland. *Advertising the American Dream.* Berkeley: University of California Press, 1985.

Morgan, Edmund S. *Inventing the People: The Rise of Popular Sovereignty in England and America.* New York: Norton, 1988.

Radway, Janice A. *Reading the Romance: Women, Patriarchy, and Popular Literature.* Chapel Hill, NC: University of North Carolina Press, 1984.

Ricoeur, Paul. *Lectures on Ideology and Utopia.* Edited by George H. Taylor. New York: Columbia, 1986.

Slotkin, Richard. *Gunfighter Nation: The Myth of the Frontier in Twentieth Century America.* Norman, OK: University of Oklahoma Press, 1998.

Susman, Warren I. *Culture As History: The Transformation of American Society in the Twentieth Century.* New York: Pantheon, 1984.

Williamson, Judith. *Decoding Advertisements: Ideology and Meaning in Advertising.* London: Marian Boyars, 1978.

Wright, Will. *Sixguns and Society: A Structural Study of the Western.* Berkeley: University of California Press, 1975.

Zizek, Slavoj, ed. *Mapping Ideology.* New York: Verso, 1995.

AMERICAN CULTURAL AND SOCIAL HISTORY

Baritz, Loren. *City on a Hill: A History of Ideas and Myths in America.* New York: John Wiley & Sons, 1964.

———. *The Good Life: The Meaning of Success for the American Middle Class.* New York: Knopf, 1989.

———. *Backfire: A History of How American Culture Led Us into Vietnam and Made Us Fight the Way We Did.* Baltimore: Johns Hopkins University Press, 1985.

Bell, Daniel. *The End of Ideology.* New York: Free Press, 1960.

Braunstein, Peter, and Michael W. Doyle. *Imagine Nation: The American Counterculture of the 1960's and '70s.* New York: Routledge, 2002.

Brooks, David. *Bobos in Paradise: The New Upper Class and How They Got There.* New York: Simon & Schuster, 2000.

Cawelti, John G. *Apostles of the Self-Made Man: Changing Concepts of Success in America.* Chicago: University of Chicago Press, 1965.

Delbanco, Andrew. *The Real American Dream.* Cambridge, MA: Harvard University Press, 1999.

Dickstein, Morris. *Gates of Eden: American Culture in the Sixties.* Cambridge, MA: Harvard University Press, 1977.

Ehrenreich, Barbara. *The Hearts of Men.* New York: Anchor, 1983.

———. *Fear of Falling: The Inner Life of the Middle Class.* New York: Pantheon, 1989.

Englehart, Tom. *The End of Victory Culture: Cold War America and the Disillusions of a Generation.* Amherst: University of Massachusetts Press, 1998.

Faludi, Susan. *Stiffed: The Betrayal of the American Man.* New York: William Morrow and Company, 1998.

Farber, David. *The Age of Great Dreams: America in the 1960s.* New York: Hill and Wang, 1994.

Farber, David, ed. *The Sixties: From Memory to History.* Chapel Hill: University of North Carolina Press, 1994.

Fitzgerald, Frances. *Cities on a Hill.* New York: Simon & Schuster, 1981.

Frank, Thomas. *The Conquest of Cool: Business Culture, Counterculture, and the Rise of Hip Consumerism.* Chicago: University of Chicago Press, 1997.

———. *One Market Under God: Extreme Capitalism, Market Populism, and the End of Economic Democracy.* New York: Doubleday, 2000.

Gibson, James W. *Warrior Dreams: Violence and Manhood in Post-Vietnam America.* New York: Hill and Wang, 1994.

Harrington, Michael, *The Other America.* New York: MacMillan, 1962.

Jewett, Robert, and John S. Lawrence. *The American Monomyth.* Garden City, NY: Anchor Press, 1977.

Kazin, Michael. *The Populist Persuasion: An American History.* New York: Basic Books, 1995.

Kimmel, Michael. *Manhood in America: A Cultural History.* New York: Free Press, 1996.

Lemann, Nicholas. *The Promised Land.* New York: Alfred A. Knopf, Inc., 1991

Linklater, Richard. *Slacker.* New York: St. Martins Press, 1992.

Marwick, Arthur. *The Sixties.* New York: Oxford University Press, 1998.

McCann, Graham. *Rebel Males: Clift, Brando, and Dean.* New Brunswick, NJ: Rutgers University Press, 1991.

Mills, C. Wright. *White Collar: The American Middle Classes.* Oxford: Oxford University Press, 2002.

Mitchell, Lee C. *Westerns: Making the Man in Fiction and Film.* Chicago: University of Chicago Press, 1996.

Nadel, Alan. *Containment Culture: American Narratives, Postmodernism, and the Atomic Age.* Durham, NC: Duke University Press, 1995.

Newman, Katherine S. *Declining Fortunes: The Withering of the American Dream.* New York: Basic Books, 1993.

Riesman, David. *Lonely Crowd: A Study of the Changing American Character.* New Haven: Yale University Press, 2001.

Rotundo, E. Anthony. *American Manhood: Transformations in Masculinity from the Revolution to the Modern Era.* New York: Basic Books, 1993.

Roszak, Theodore. *The Making of a Counter Culture.* New York, Anchor, 1969.

Ryan, Michael, and Douglas Kellner. *Camera Politica: The Politics and Ideology of Contemporary Hollywood Film.* Bloomington, IN: Indiana University Press, 1988.

Spigal, Lynn. *Make Room for TV: Television and the Family Ideal in Postwar America.* Chicago: University of Chicago Press, 1992.

Whyte, William. *Organization Man.* Philadelphia: University of Pennsylvania Press, 2002.

Wills, Garry. *Reagan's America: Innocents at Home.* New York: Doubleday, 1987.

————. *John Wayne's America.* New York: Touchstone, 1997.

AMERICAN ECONOMIC AND POLITICAL HISTORY

Bluestone, Barry, and Bennett Harrison. *The Deindustrialization of America.* New York: Basic Books, 1982.

Castells, Manuel. *The Rise of Network Society, The Information Age: Economy, Society, and Culture.* New York: Blackwell, 1996.

Gordon, David M. *Fat and Mean: The Corporate Squeeze of Working Americans and the Myth of Managerial "Downsizing."* New York: Free Press, 1996.

Harrison, Bennett. *Lean and Mean: Why Large Corporations Will Continue to Dominate the Global Economy.* New York: Guilford, 1994.

Harrison, Bennett, and Barry Bluestone. *The Great U-Turn: Corporate Restructuring and the Polarizing of America.* New York: Basic Books, 1988.

Palley, Thomas I. *Plenty of Nothing: The Downsizing of the American Dream and the Case for Structural Keynesianism.* Princeton, NJ: Princeton University Press, 1998.

Phillips, Kevin. *Post-Conservative America: People, Politics, and Ideology in a Time of Crisis.* New York: Random House, 1982.

———. *Boiling Point: Democrats, Republicans, and the Decline of Middle-Class Prosperity.* New York: Random House, 1993.

BRAND HISTORY

Allen, Frederick. *Secret Formula.* New York: Harper Business, 1994.

Bond, Jonathan, and Richard Kirshenbaum. *Under the Radar: Talking to Today's Cynical Consumer.* New York: Wiley, 1998.

Deshpande, Rohit, Kirsten J. O'Neil-Massaro, and Gustavo A. Herrero. "Corona Beer (A)." Case 9-502-023. Boston: Harvard Business School, 2001.

Hofstede, David. *The Dukes of Hazzard: The Unofficial Companion.* Los Angeles: Renaissance Books, 1998.

Kiley, David. *Getting the Bugs Out: The Rise, Fall, and Comeback of Volkswagen in America.* New York: Wiley, 2002.

Marlboro Archives. Smithsonian Museum of American History, Washington, D.C.

Nike Archives. Smithsonian Museum of American History, Washington, D.C.

Freeman, Michael. *ESPN: The Uncensored History.* New York: Taylor, 2000.

Rasmussen, Bill. *The Birth of ESPN.* Hartsdale, NY: QV Publishing, 1983.

Sobel, Robert. *They Satisfy: The Cigarette in American Life.* Garden City, NY: Anchor Press, 1978.

Thompson, Hunter S. *Hell's Angels: A Strange and Terrible Saga.* New York: Ballantine Books, 1996.

Yates, Brock. *Outlaw Machine: Harley-Davidson and the Search for the American Soul.* New York: Little, Brown & Co., 1999.

Index

About the Author

Douglas B. Holt holds the L'Oréal Chair of Marketing at the University of Oxford. He earned a Ph.D. in Marketing from Northwestern University's Kellogg School, an M.B.A. from the University of Chicago, and an A.B. from Stanford University. Holt moved to Oxford in 2004, following appointments at Pennsylvania State University, the University of Illinois, and the Harvard Business School. He has published widely on consumption and brands from cultural and sociological perspectives.